Interpersonal Communication in Friend and Mate Relationships

SUNY Series, Human Communication Processes
Edited by Donald P. Cushman and Ted J. Smith, III

INTERPERSONAL COMMUNICATION IN FRIEND AND MATE RELATIONSHIPS

Anne Maydan Nicotera & Associates

STATE UNIVERSITY OF NEW YORK PRESS ◆ ALBANY

Published by
State University of New York Press, Albany

Printed in the United States of America

For information, address State University of New York Press,
State University Plaza, Albany, N.Y., 12246

Production by Cathleen Collins
Marketing by Theresa A. Swierzowski

Library of Congress Cataloging in Publication Data

Nicotera, Anne Maydan, 1963-
Interpersonal communication in friend and mate relationships / Anne Maydan Nicotera & associates.
p. cm. — (SUNY series in human communication processes)
Includes bibliographical references and indexes.
ISBN 0-7914-1351-9 — ISBN 0-7914-1352-7 (pbk.)
1. Interpersonal communication — Cross-cultural studies.
2. Interpersonal relations — Cross-cultural studies. 3. Friendship — Cross-cultural studies. 4. Mate selection — Cross-cultural studies.
5. Cushman, Donald P. I. Title. II. Series.
BF637.C45N46 1993
153.6 — dc20

92-3099
CIP

10 9 8 7 6 5 4 3 2 1

For my friend
Don Cushman
who has profoundly
influenced my thinking

and

For my spouse
Gregory Maydan
who has profoundly
influenced my life

Contents

Preface

The inspiration for this book occurred upon the realization that several scholars had conducted theoretically and methodologically similar investigations, in several cultures, of friendship and mate relationship development. Because descriptions of paradigmatic assumptions, theoretic propositions, and common methodology were similar, such material was edited out of the original works and is more appropriately placed in the introductory chapters. Beyond this, every effort was made to maintain the individual character of each chapter.

This book is organized into four parts. Part I provides an overview of Cushman's general theory in three chapters. Chapter 1, by Anne Maydan Nicotera, is an overview of the conceptual theory. Chapter 2, by Charles J. Korn and Anne Maydan Nicotera, provides a summary of the friendship and mate relationship literature on levels and dimensions of such relationships. It also derives from Cushman's conceptual theory seven empirically confirmable propositions around which the book is organized. Finally, Chapter 2 summarizes the methods for analyzing relationship dimensions and levels and for investigating interpersonal penetration. Chapter 3 presents an edited version of the seminal investigations conducted by Valentinsen, Cushman, and Schroeder (1981) in the development of the general theory; portions of Chapter 3 are excerpted directly from those investigations.

Part II consists of three chapters investigating friendship. Chapter 4, by Charles J. Korn, presents a cross-cultural comparison of friendship formation in the United States and Korea.[1] Chapter 5, by Changmo Bahk, is a comparative study of same- and opposite-sex friendship formation in the United States and Korea. Chapter 6, by Andrew A. Moemeka and Anne Maydan Nicotera, investigates friendship in Nigeria. Chapter 7, by Anne

1. Throughout this book, all data reported from Korea is South Korean.

Maydan Nicotera, summarizes these investigations of friendship and discusses their implications in terms of the seven propositions.

Part III concentrates on studies of mate relationship formation. Chapter 8, by Donald P. Cushman and Dudley D. Cahn, is a study of mate relationship formation in two subcultures in the United States. Chapter 9, by Anne Maydan Nicotera, presents a cross-cultural comparison of mate relationship formation in the United States and Korea. Chapter 10, by Andrew A. Moemeka and Anne Maydan Nicotera, investigates the mate relationship in Nigeria. Finally, Chapter 11, by Anne Maydan Nicotera, summarizes these investigations of the mate relationship and discusses their implications in terms of the seven propositions.

In Part IV, Chapter 12, by Yanan Ju, offers a conceptualization of the mate relationship as cultural choice, argues for a theoretic approach that transcends cultural bias, and presents a data-based study to support the argument. Chapter 13, by Anne Maydan Nicotera, integrates the findings, challenges, and future directions of the studies in this book; it offers a critique of this body of research based on the general theory of Cushman and his associates, and provides recommendations for extension and future work.

Though too numerous to list here, many people provided support that made the integration of this body of work and preparation of the manuscript easier. Thanks to all my friends and colleagues who provided that support. I express my appreciation especially to all of the contributors whose work appears in this book. Their patience and cooperative spirit were invaluable. Thanks go to Christine Marley, a diligent proofreader who acted insightfully as a critical consumer of the manuscript, and to Paula McKenzie for proofreading the final manuscript pages. Finally, I owe a special note of thanks to my friend Don Cushman. At a theoretic level, of course, this book could not exist without him. Beyond that, his encouragement and keen critical eye provided me with unwavering support.

Anne Maydan Nicotera

Part I

Background and Overview of the General Theory

1

The Importance of Communication in Interpersonal Relationships

Anne Maydan Nicotera

Communication and Interpersonal Relationships

Interpersonal relationships are a driving force in our lives. Most Americans report that the quality of their lives is determined by the number and quality of their interpersonal relationships (Campbell, 1980). Individuals with good relationships live longer and report less physical and psychological illness and greater satisfaction with life (Duck, 1981). The failure of interpersonal relationships has been associated with suicide (Stech, 1980), psychiatric problems (Bloom, Asher, and White, 1978), social stress (Chiriboga, 1979), and family instability (Albrecht, 1980). Effective communication is a crucial variable in determining the success of interpersonal relationships (Alexander, 1973; Murstein 1972). Communication is requisite for the maintenance of satisfying relationships (Alexander, 1973; Cushman and Cahn, 1985; Murstein, 1972, 1977), and the absence of effective communication causes relational failure (Alexander, 1973).

Two of the most important and problematic types of interpersonal relationships are friend and mate. Cushman and Cahn (1985) conclude from the literature three underlying dimensions of the friend relationship: trust, helping behavior, and self-concept support. As these variables increase in their intensity, the friend relationship increases in intimacy. Friends also fulfill two important roles: confidant and companion. However, as Cushman and Cahn also conclude, "while a clear pattern emerges from the research literature regarding underlying dimensions and levels of friendship, the process by which one selects and sustains such relationships is far from clear" (p. 51). The research reported in this volume attempts to explicate that process in a variety of cultural settings.

The mate relationship accounts for the happiness, satisfaction, and meaning found in life (Albrecht, 1980; Alexander, 1973; Bloom et al., 1978; Campbell, 1980; Chiriboga, 1979; Cushman and Cahn, 1985; Duck, 1981; Murstein, 1972, 1977; Stech, 1980). Further, these relationships function as strong integrating forces represented by love and commitment. Cushman and Cahn (1985) conclude from the literature that love is an integrating force, whereas commitment is a focusing force. Specific attributes of mate relationships differ by culture, but recent research has distinguished two classes of mate relationship attributes: those variables that mark *entry* into such relationships, and those variables that lead to *intensity*. As variables in the latter class deepen, the mate relationship increases in intimacy. For example, in the United States intelligence and physical attraction are entry variables, whereas respect, affection, and psychological support are intensity variables (Cushman and Cahn, 1985). When one perceives an opposite-sex other to be intelligent and physically attractive, one is likely to enter into a mate-type relationship with that person. As respect, affection, and psychological support intensify in that relationship, it progresses to deeper levels of intimacy (Cushman and Kovacic, in press; see also Chapter 3).

Communication is central to the development and maintenance of all interpersonal relationships. The late twentieth century has seen an unprecedented preoccupation with communication processes (Cushman and Cahn, 1985). Self-help books, therapies, and advice columns rebound with the messages that ineffective communication is the root of all our social problems and that good communication is the ultimate panacea. "If you want to find a mate, save a marriage, get a job, sell a used car, educate the public, prevent a war . . . then communicate!" (Cushman and Cahn, 1985, p. 5). Problems of communication are not new to our age; this attention to such problems signifies a new way of thinking about and analyzing social relationships (McKeon, 1957).

Communication is a fashionable topic in contemporary social science. The danger here is in the potential for tautology. Social and interpersonal problems are caused by failed communication; their solutions lie in effective communication. Tidily stated, the problem seems simple, but the primary question of communication lies unanswered. What processes, for example, do we go through in developing and maintaining our interpersonal relationships? How does communication contribute to relational development? Why do some relationships develop past the point at which others stop?

Although our obsession with communication has led to formula answers and tautologies, such concentration on communication processes and problems is essential to sorting out fundamental questions about interpersonal relationships. Further, our fixation with communication is an insightful response to several societal trends, all related to the "shrinking" of the world and the seeming development of Marshall McLuhan's global village: increasing tolerance for diversity; interdependence within and between cultures; availability of the means of communication; and, finally, the need to express respect for diversity as a prerequisite for coordinating action (Cushman and Cahn, 1985).

Paradigmatic Assumptions

These trends have led to a modification in our assumptions about the basic mechanisms of communication processes. For our purposes in discussing interpersonal relationships, the most central of these assumptions is the shift from a positivistic view of humans as reactors to a view of humans as actors. The rules perspective, as an alternative for communication theorists, was introduced by Cushman and Whiting (1972). Rooted in symbolic interactionism and speech–act theory, the rules perspective was intended to move the field of communication away from its preoccupation with laws and positivism. The rules perspective conceives of human beings as conscious, teleological actors who choose to enact specific behaviors based on their goals and the structure of social rules that govern and guide the specific situation (Cushman and Pearce, 1977; Cushman and Whiting, 1972).

The primary assumption in the rules perspective is the action principle: Social behavior is structured and organized. Action within and between human beings is not random. Humans govern their actions by implicit and explicit rules. Finally, choice is involved in social action. According to Cushman and Pearce (1977), rules take the form of the practical syllogism:

> *A* intends to bring about C;
> *A* considers that to bring about *C* s/he must do *B*;
> therefore, *A* sets her/himself to do *B*.

The possible range of actions (*B*) is delimited by the social rule structure. The practical syllogism illustrates the perspective's epistemological assumption of a normative order in the regularities of human action (Cushman and Pearce, 1977).

Human behavior is classified into two categories: movement and action (Cushman, Valentinsen, and Dietrich, 1982). *Movement* can be defined as habit and is governed by nomic necessity, which accounts for reactive behavior and depends on a causal relationship. *Action* is evaluative, purposive, and choice-oriented and is governed by practical necessity, which accounts for proactive or teleological behavior. Action is further classified into *information processing*—perception or thought—and *coordination*—consensus among individuals (Cushman, Valentinsen, and Dietrich, 1982).

In coordination situations, the basic unit of analysis is the standardized usage (Cushman, Valentinsen, and Dietrich, 1982). Acting in concert, individuals coordinate a standardized usage for social rules. The rule structure is either created through negotiation or recognized as a previously existing rule structure (Cushman and Whiting, 1972). Regardless of its origin, the standardized usage is of primary interest to the rules theorist because it defines the set of alternative choices for behavior (*B* in the practical syllogism above).

Characteristics of a standardized usage are as follows: first, a shared class of intentions; second, a common set of expectations; and third, sequences of communicative acts that demonstrate the level of commitment to the standardized usage (Cushman, Valentinsen, and Dietrich, 1982). According to Cushman and his associates (Cushman and Cahn, 1985; Cushman and Craig, 1976; Cushman and Florence, 1974; Cushman and Pearce, 1977; Cushman, Valentinsen, and Dietrich, 1982), all human actions necessarily involve rules. Furthermore, all actions requiring coordination with others involve communication and therefore communication rules. Rules theorists identify two types of rules: *constitutive* rules, which specify the action's content; and *procedural* rules, which specify appropriate strategies for carrying out the action (Cushman and Whiting, 1972).

Given such a conception of human action, *interpersonal relationships can be seen as coordination systems* (Cushman, Valentinsen, and Dietrich, 1982). The function of these systems is to develop and maintain consensus on individual self-concepts. Their structures are dyadic relationships, specifically friend and mate relationships. Their processes center around the development, presentation, and validation of individual self-concepts (Cushman, Valentinsen, and Dietrich, 1982). The following is a discussion of a general theory of the role of communication in interpersonal relationships grounded in the rules perspective; it focuses on self-concept and interaction as the generative mechanisms of relationship formation and growth.

General Theory of the Role of Communication in Relationships

Filters

Kerckhoff and Davis (1962) posit that relationship development progresses through a series of filters, usually conceptualized as stages. Several theorists have drawn upon this notion (e.g., Knapp, 1978; Lewis, 1972, 1973; Murstein, 1972, 1977; Nofz, 1984). Cushman and his associates (Cushman and Cahn, 1985; Cushman, Valentinsen, and Dietrich, 1982) formulate a more complex theory of relationship development. They posit a three-step filtering process for both friendship and mate relationship development. First, individuals are faced with a *field of availables*. This field consists of all the others with whom it is possible to form a relationship. Research exploring initial interaction (typified by Berger and Calabrese, 1975; and Duck, 1976) has shown such interaction to be governed by standardized and general communication rules (Cushman, Valentinsen, and Dietrich, 1982). Within the field of availables, there exists the second filter, the *field of approachables* (Cushman and Cahn, 1985). This field consists of all the others whom the individual finds desirable enough to approach for the purpose of initiating a relationship. A particular set of *entry rules* for the mate relationship and friendship guide such relationship initiation. (see pp. 9 and 10) Within the field of approachables there exists the third filter, the *field of reciprocals* (Cushman and Cahn, 1985). This field consists of those who have reciprocated the individual's attempt to initiate a relationship. These are the people with whom the individual has interpersonal relationships. A particular set of *intimacy/intensity rules* guide the growth of these relationships (see pp. 9 and 10). Once relationship pairs have been filtered to the field of reciprocals, they progress through four relationship levels. For friendship, the levels are acquaintance, casual friend, good friend, and best friend. For the mate relationship, they are casual date, steady date, fiancé, and spouse (Cushman and Cahn, 1985).

The Role of Self-Concept Support

Cushman and his associates (Cushman and Cahn, 1985; Cushman and Craig, 1976; Cushman and Florence, 1974; Cushman, Valentinsen, and Dietrich, 1982) identify self-concept as a cybernetic control system for human action in coordination situations:

> Human actions that take place within a standardized communication situation require common intentions, an established set of rules for the cooperative achievement of those intentions, and a procedure for manifesting the variable practical force the actors feel for participating in the coordination task. (Cushman, Valentinsen, and Dietrich, 1982, pp. 96–97)

Self-concept is an empirically verifiable construct that provides a theoretical representation of the conceptual forms through which individual actors understand and cope with the world. The construct *self-concept* thus allows the exploration of the link between thought and action (Cushman, Valentinsen, and Dietrich, 1982).

The nature of self-concept. Self-concept is composed of self-object relationships, which are divided into three classes (Cushman, Valentinsen, and Dietrich, 1982). First, the *identity self* includes self–object relationships which label what an individual is, such as "I am a teacher." Second, the *evaluative self* includes self–object relationships which declare one's feelings about oneself, such as "I am a good teacher." Finally, the *behavioral self* includes self–object relationships which prescribe appropriate behavior for the identity- and evaluative selves, such as "I am a good teacher and therefore I must have my papers graded on time" (Cushman, Valentinsen, and Dietrich, 1982, p. 98).

Self-concept thus aids the individual in coordination situations in three ways (Cushman, Valentinsen, and Dietrich, 1982). First, the individual's encounter with an object provides information that can be generalized to other objects s/he categorizes in the same *class*. Therefore, s/he need not have an encounter with an object in order to define the self in relation to it. Second, such self–object relationships provide the individual with *expectations* for the nature of those objects s/he subsumes under the same rules. Finally, the self-concept, as it develops, provides the individual with *preconceived plans* of action (Cushman, Valentinsen, and Dietrich, 1982).

> A self–object relationship constitutes a ready-made format for processing experience and initiating action. With such a system, a person is prepared to cope with the future and make sense out of the past. Hence, we regard the self–concept as an organized set of structures that defines the relationship of objects to individuals and that is capable of governing and directing human action. Furthermore, the self–concept, as an organized set of structures, provides the rationale for choice in the form of a valenced repertory (*sic*) of alternative plans of action. (Cushman, Valentinsen, and Dietrich, 1982, p. 98)

Self-concept and interaction. A primary coordination task for any individual in a communication situation is the development of intentions (Cushman and Florence, 1974). These are represented by C in the practical syllogism. Likewise, the individual must develop the means for achieving those intentions (Cushman and Florence, 1974). These action alternatives are represented by *B* in the practical syllogism. These intentions and the acts that achieve them are integral to the most basic coordination task—determining the self, who the individual is and how s/he relates to objects (and others) in his/her environment (Cushman and Florence, 1974).

The development, presentation, and validation of self–concepts is the central feature of the process of interpersonal communication (Cushman and Cahn, 1985; Cushman and Craig, 1976; Cushman and Florence, 1974; Cushman, Valentinsen, and Dietrich, 1982). The function of interpersonal communication systems is to regulate consensus with regard to individuals' self-concepts; the structure is provided by "the standardized code and network rules that guide how and when we can obtain consensus in regard to preferred self–object relationships" (Cushman, Valentinsen, and Dietrich, 1982, p. 104). In interaction, individuals propose identities for themselves and others. These identities are negotiated in interaction: an individual learns who s/he is and what s/he can do in the presence of certain others. *Thus the self-concept, as it is developed, presented, and validated in interaction, defines the nature and type of the interpersonal relationship.*

This logic led Cushman and his associates (Cushman, Valentinsen, and Dietrich, 1982) to postulate that "reciprocated self-concept support serves as a necessary basis for establishing any interpersonal relationship" (p. 104). Furthermore, they propose that different types of self-concept support lead to different types of relationships (e.g., friend or mate), and that different degrees of self-concept support lead to different levels of interpersonal relationships (e.g, casual friend or best friend). (Cushman, Valentinsen, and Dietrich (1982) provide a thorough and cogent review of research literature grounding their conceptualization of self-concept.)

The role of self with friends. As discussed earlier, friends are divided into two types. Confidants are theorized to provide support for evaluative self–object relationships, whereas companions are theorized to provide support for behavioral self–object relationships (Cushman and Cahn, 1985). For the development of friendship, Cushman and his associates (Cushman and Cahn, 1985, p. 52; Cushman, Valentinsen, and Dietrich, 1982, p. 107) posit three entry rules, applied to the field of approachables.

1. The greater an individual's perceived relationship between positive attributes of his/her own self-concept and the perceived attributes of another's self-concept, the greater the likelihood s/he will attempt to initiate communication arrived at by supporting those similar attributes.
2. The greater an individual's perceived likelihood that the other will accept an offer of self-concept support, the greater the likelihood that communication will be initiated.
3. The more frequently an individual provides messages that support some positive-identity, evaluative, or behavioral self–object relationships of another's self- concept, the greater the likelihood that the other person will perceive those messages as an attempt to initiate a friend relationship.

For the field of reciprocals, Cushman and his associates (Cushman and Cahn, 1985, p. 52; Cushman, Valentinsen, and Dietrich, 1982, p. 108) posit two intimacy/intensity rules.

1. The greater an individual's perceived accuracy with regard to the similarity between his/her own and another's self-concept, the greater the likelihood that a friend relationship will grow.
2. The greater the reciprocated self-concept support, the greater the likelihood a friend relationship will grow.

The role of self with mates. A mate is defined as an opposite-sex other for whom one clears the field of competitors (Cushman and Cahn, 1985; Karp,

Jackson, and Lester, 1971). For the development of such a relationship, Cushman and his associates (Cushman and Cahn, 1985, pp. 57–58; Cushman, Valentinsen, and Dietrich, 1982, pp. 109–110) posit five entry rules, applied to the field of approachables.

1. The greater an individual's perceptions that an opposite-sex other is physically attractive, the greater the likelihood of initiating communication aimed at establishing a mate relationship.
2. The greater an individual's perceptions that an opposite-sex other's real self relates to one's ideal self for a mate, the greater the likelihood of initiating communication aimed at establishing a mate relationship.
3. The greater an individual's perception that the male's real-ideal self-concept discrepancy is small, the greater the likelihood of initiating communication aimed at establishing a mate relationship.
4. The greater an individual's perception that an opposite-sex other is likely to accept one's offer of a relationship, the greater the likelihood of initiating communication aimed at establishing a mate relationship.
5. The more frequently an individual provides messages that (a) manifest self-concept support for an opposite-sex other's physical attractiveness; (b) characterize that other as relating to the individual's ideal mate; and (c) indicate a perceived lack of discrepancy between the male's real and ideal selves, the greater the likelihood that the other will perceive those messages as an attempt to initiate a mate relationship.

For the field of reciprocals, Cushman and his associates (Cushman and Cahn, 1985, p. 58; Cushman, Valentinsen, and Dietrich, 1982, p. 111) posit two intimacy/intensity rules.

1. The greater the female's perceived lack of discrepancy between her mate's real and ideal self-concept, the greater the likelihood the relationship will grow.
2. The greater the perception that there is reciprocation of self-concept support, the greater the likelihood the relationship will grow.

The Importance of Cultural Comparison

Friend and mate relationships are ubiquitous human phenomena and are vital to human existence. Every culture in the world acknowledges and encourages both types of interpersonal relationship. In short, interpersonal relationship formation is a universal human communication process. Different cultures define the character, function, and form of interpersonal relationships differently. Cultural systems dictate the foundations upon which relationships are based, the particular processes through which relationships develop, and the appropriate means for communicating these things. Although the general process of interpersonal relationship development is universal, the question remains: *Within the universal process of relationship development, what processual elements transcend culture and what processual elements are culture-specific?* To answer this question, it is necessary to examine different cultures individually and specifically from a consistent theoretic stance.

The chapters of this book provide such examinations of several cultures. Some also provide cultural comparisons. Operating under the rules paradigm and the general assumption that interpersonal relationships are coordination systems, each chapter explores the general developmental process of friend or mate relationships in a particular cultural setting. In considering these investigations, we hope to provide insight to answer the question: To what extent are the developmental processes of interpersonal relationships truly universal?

References

Albrecht, S. L. (1980). Reactions and adjustments to divorce: Differences in the experience of males and females. *Family Relations* 29:59–68.

Alexander, J. F. (1973). Defensive and supportive communication in normal and deviant families. *Journal of Consulting and Clinical Psychology*, 40:223–31.

Berger, C., and R. Calabrese (1975). Some explorations in initial interaction and beyond: Toward a developmental theory of interpersonal communication. *Human Communication Research* 1:99–112.

Bloom, B. L., S. J. Asher, and S. W. White (1978). Marital disruption as a stressor: A review and analysis. *Psychological Bulletin* 85:867–94.

Campbell, A. (1980). *The sense of well-being in America: Patterns and trends*. New York: McGraw-Hill.

Chiriboga, D. A. (1979). Marital separation and stress: A life course perspective. *Alternative Life Style* 2:465–70.

Cushman, D. P., and D. D. Cahn (1985). *Communication in interpersonal relationships*. Albany, NY: State University of New York Press.

Cushman, D. P., and R. T. Craig (1976). Communication systems: Interpersonal implications. In G. Miller (ed.), *Explorations in interpersonal communication* (37–58). Beverly Hills, CA: Sage.

Cushman, D. P., and B. T. Florence (1974). The development of interpersonal communication theory. *Today's Speech* 22:11–15.

Cushman, D. P., and B. Kovacic (in press). A rules perspective on communication theory. In F. L. Casmir (ed.), *Communication Theory*. Albany, NY: State University of New York Press.

Cushman, D. P., and W. B. Pearce (1977). Generality and necessity in three types of communication theory, with special attention to rules theory. *Human Communication Research* 3:341–53.

Cushman, D. P., B. Valentinsen, and D. Dietrich (1982). A rules theory of interpersonal relationships. In F. E. X. Dance (ed.), *Human Communication Theory* (90–119). New York: Harper and Row.

Cushman, D. P., and G. Whiting (1972). An approach to communication theory: Towards consensus on rules. *Journal of Communication* 22:217–18.

Duck, S. (1976). Interpersonal communication in developing relationships. In G. Miller (ed.), *Explorations in interpersonal communication* (127–45). Beverly Hills, CA: Sage.

Duck, S. (1981). A topography of relational disengagement and dissolution. In S. A. Duck (ed.), *Personal relationships 4* (1–27). New York: Academic Press.

Karp, E. S., J. Jackson, and D. Lester (1970). Ideal-self fulfillment in mate selection: A corollary to the complementary need theory of mate selection. *Journal of Marriage and the Family* 32:269–72.

Kerckhoff, A. C., and K. E. Davis (1962). Value consensus and need complementarity in mate selection. *American Sociological Review* 27:295–303.

Knapp, M. (1978). *Social intercourse: From greeting to goodbye*. Boston: Allyn and Bacon.

Lewis, R. A. A. (1972). A developmental framework for the analysis of premarital dyadic formation. *Family Process* 11:17–48.

Lewis, R. A. A. (1973). A longitudinal test of a developmental framework for the analysis of premarital dyadic formation. *Journal of Marriage and the Family* 35:16–25.

McKeon, R. (1957). Communication, truth, and society. *Ethics* 67:89–99.

Murstein, B. I. (1972). Person perception and courtship progress among premarital couples. *Journal of Marriage and the Family* 34:621–27.

Murstein, B. I. (1977). The stimulus-value-role (SVR) theory of dyadic relationships. In S. Duck (ed.). *Theory and practice in interpersonal attraction* (105–27). London: Academic Press.

Nofz, M. P. (1984). Fantasy—testing—assessment: A proposed model for the investigation of mate selection. *Journal of Personality and Social Psychology* 50:428–38.

Stech, S. (1980). The effect of marital dissolution on suicide. *Journal of Marriage and the Family* 42:83–92.

Valentinsen, B., D. P. Cushman, and L. E. Schroeder (1981, May). *The friend and mate formation processes: Testing a rules theory*. Paper presented at the annual meeting of the International Communication Association, Minneapolis, MN.

2

Friend and Mate Relationship Literature, Empirical Propositions, and Methodology

Charles J. Korn and Anne Maydan Nicotera

Friendship

This chapter summarizes and critiques the literature on friend and mate relationships.[1] It is not intended to be a comprehensive review of all the research on relationship development, but rather an overview of the dominant conceptualizations and theories of relationship development. The chapter is organized around levels, dimensions, and theories of friendship and the mate relationship. Following this review of the literature, seven empirically confirmable propositions are derived from the general theory described in Chapter 1. Finally, the common methodologies employed in the studies in Parts II and III are described.

Levels of Friendship

Friendship researchers generally agree that friend relationships progress in phases. Parks (1977) and LaGaipa (1977) are commonly cited for their conceptualizations of friendship levels. Parks (1977) discovers that Americans distinguish the following 10 levels of friendship: acquaintance, casual acquaintance, casual friend, just friend, friend, good friend, close friend, very good friend, best

1. Authorship for this chapter is denoted alphabetically, indicating equal contribution.

Table 2.1
Levels in Friendship Research

Parks (1977)	*LaGaipa (1977)*
Acquaintance	Social aquaintance
Casual acquaintance	
Casual friend	
Just friend	
Friend	
Good friend	Good friend
Close friend	Close friend
Very good friend	
Best friend	Best friend
Intimate friend	

friend, and intimate friend. From these 10 level designations, Parks selects acquaintance, friend, and intimate friend as the primary friendship levels. LaGaipa (1977) describes four levels of friendship: best friends, or your very closest friends, perhaps one or two people; close friends, a rather select group of 10 or 12 people with whom you have established close relationships; good friends, a larger group of people whom you seek out and prefer, but with whom you are not particularly close; and social acquaintances, people you interact with at school or work, or during coffee breaks. LaGaipa supports the contention that friendship dimensions become progressively more important as the friend relationship proceeds and develops from social acquaintance to good friend. Helping behaviors and self-disclosure are most important as the friendship progresses from close to best friend. Positive assistance and intimacy were also found to be most important in higher levels of friendship. Table 2.1 provides an overview of the levels of friendship commonly studied in the research literature.

Dimensions of Friendship

A search of empirical literature was conducted to pinpoint dimensions or attributes of the friend relationship, especially those that are definable as communication variables. A communication variable is a dimension or attribute whose existence necessarily depends on communication or interpersonal interaction.

LaGaipa's (1977) research aims at describing the friendship process and its qualities. After conducting 150 open-ended interviews with high school and college students, eight factors emerged that captured the expectations these subjects hold for friendship: 1) self-disclosure, or feeling free to express intimate information; 2) authenticity, or openness and honesty in the relationship, being real, genuine, and spontaneous; 3) helping behavior, or expressing concern for one's well-being and giving help voluntarily, and providing psychological support; 4) acceptance, or acknowledging one's identity, integrity, and individuality; 5) positive regard, or providing ego reinforcement, enhancing one's feelings of self-worth, treating one as deserving of respect and as an important, worthwhile person; 6) strength of character, or striving to achieve and conform to the objective value system of the society; 7) similarity, or possessing similar points of view, expressing agreement on controversial issues, and possessing similar attitudes and interests; and 8) emphatic understanding, or interpreting accurately the feelings of another person, understanding how one really feels, and really listening to what one has to say.

Rose (1985) identifies similar dimensions of acceptance, help, intimacy, and companionship, which she reliably applies to both same- and cross-sex friendship formation and maintenance. Bailey and his associates (Bailey, Finney, and Bailey, 1974; Bailey, Finney, and Helm, 1975) argue that significant differences exist between long- and short-term friends in the amount of perceived self-concept support. More specifically, they suggest that perceived self-concept support is a more reliable predictor of friendship than perceived similarity. Crawford (1977), after asking people what they meant by the concept close friend, reports the following responses in descending order of frequency of occurrence: someone I trust; someone I can call on for help; someone I go out with; someone I see often; someone who comes into my home; someone I've known for a long time; and someone whose company I enjoy.

Gibbs's (1977) literature review on friendship dimensions found gregariousness, compatibility, status, power, intimacy, and assistance to be the primary characteristics of friendship. Teachers and students rated statements based on the dimensions Gibbs found in the literature on a 5-point scale, from agreement to disagreement (Gibbs, 1977). A factor analysis of these responses revealed the following independent dimensions: intimacy-assistatce; status; and power.

Parks (1977) found perceived closeness, breadth of communication, average depth of communication, predictive understanding, and frequency of verbal metacommunication to be important variables at higher levels of friendship. Indvik and Fitzpatrick (1986) review the primary dimensions underlying five types of interpersonal relationships: workers, acquaintances, friends, best friends, and intimates. Indvik and Fitzpatrick identify the components that comprise the inclusion, affiliation, and control dimensions. For best friend, the inclusion dimension consists of similarity, positive evaluation, stimulation, and relational potential. Caring and empathy constitute the affiliation dimension. Finally, legitimacy, exclusivity, and asymmetrical commitment comprise the control dimension.

These studies suggest that the most important elements or dimensions of friendship are perceived unique self-concept support, helping behavior, trust, respect, and authenticity. These characteristics vary according to the degree of friendship. More specifically, the closer the friendship, the more intensely these dimensions will be present. Of these important variables, self-concept support is clearly the most salient communication variable.

Theories of Friendship

We now review the most salient and fruitful theories regarding the friendship-formation process. Our discussion is restricted to those theorists who have posited comprehensive theories that are clearly applicable to, and of most value when considering, the communication variables that affect, influence, or determine our friendship-formation patterns.

Similarity. Steve Duck and his associates posit a theory of friendship formation that suggests that the communication of similarity leads to attraction and friendship formation. These theorists conceptualize the friendship process in terms of personality similarity. They argue that such similarity leads to relational attraction and subsequently to friendship formation, growth, stability, maintenance, and disintegration. Similarity is operationalized with self-report attitude profiles—such as the Bogus Stranger procedure, the CPI (a traditional personality test), the AVSV (which measures individual values in-depth), and Kelly's Reptest.

Research resulting from this conceptualization of friendship formation is contradictory. Some studies indicate that similarity is an antecedent of attraction; whereas others conclude that similarity is not a contributing factor. Duck (1973) finds that the mean similarity scores of friendship pairs were different from that of nominal pairs. Yet, in this same study, subjects overestimated the similarities between themselves and their friends. Results are discrepant with the posited theory. Duck and Craig (1978) discover that in initial interaction individuals feel more attraction to a person with similar attitudes. At the next stage of friendship development, however, individuals prefer those who possess dissimilar attitudes. For the third stage, established friendships, Duck and his associates again find a positive relationship between attitudinal similarity and attraction.

Such contradictory results lead Duck to pose the vexing question, "Why do some studies show that similarity of needs causes attraction and some not?" (Duck, 1976, p. 146). To solve the varied discrepancies between the similarity and complementarity paradigms (as colloquialized in "birds of a feather flock together" and "opposites attract"), many of these researchers (e.g., Byrne, 1971; Duck, 1973; Duck and Craig, 1978) adjust their theories to match their research findings. Duck (1973), for example, posits a three-stage analysis using similarity as a conceptual foundation for friendship determination. He argues that individuals early and late in life are most likely to prefer others who are most similar to themselves. During middle age, however, Duck suggests that individuals have a proclivity to like others who are different or in some way complementary in nature.

Byrne (1961) and Byrne and Griffitt (1969) use consensual validation as an attempt to explain the tenuous relationship between attraction and attitude similarity. They argue that individuals seek as friends those people who manifest attitudes similar to their own, thereby providing a validation and confirmation of their viewpoint. Following Byrne's work on friendship, Duck (1973) presents a model of friendship development consisting of three processes: systematic gathering of information about a partner's personality; construction, modification, and reconstruction of a model of a partner's likely personality; and assessment of degree of support for one's own personality based upon similarity between one's own personality and that of the partner. An individual's personal processing will determine whether the other provides consensual personality support (i.e., similarity).

The relationship between friendship and similarity is tenuous at best. The major limitation of Duck's research is that he fails to explain friendship in terms of similarity; he does not support his theory. Four additional problems cast further doubt on this theoretical approach. First, Duck (1973) discovers that individuals commonly overestimate their similarity to others. Second, individuals who are unhappy with their real self-concept commonly seek out friends who are radically different. Third, individuals who gain satisfaction by maintaining a unique identity preserve their uniqueness by actively seeking out others who are dissimilar. Finally, Duck's developmental approach to friendship formation fails to predict the dynamic changes that characterize friendship.

The major strength of Duck's research program is that it highlights the need to track changes in the importance of similarity to friendship. His research reveals that perceived similarity in friend relationships is often inaccurate. The disparity between perceived and actual similarity may lead to relational deterioration.

Cost-benefit. Social psychologist Paul Wright (1969, 1978) utilizes a cost-benefit analysis in his conception of the friendship-formation process. Wright develops a three-part model for same-sex friendship-formation. First, friendships are based on voluntary interdependence (VID). Second, partners experience difficulty in maintaining a relationship. Third, partners enjoy certain rewards from the relationship. VID, the single criterion for friendship, is defined as the degree to which plans, decisions, and activities of one partner are contingent upon those of the other in a context where partners may exercise free choice (Wright, 1969). Wright (1978) argues that friends "make it a point to spend time together in the absence of external pressures or constraints" (p. 199). His conceptualization is rich in logical, intuitive, and surface appeal; we commonly consider friends as two individuals who enjoy spending time together and offer each other mutual assistance. VID is a barometer of friendship attraction. An increase indicates a developing relationship; a decrease suggests a deteriorating relationship.

Recognizing a weakness in VID, Wright includes the variable, "difficult to maintain" (DTM), which accounts for misunderstandings, arguments, disagreements, and hurt feelings. By including DTM—as the cost in his cost-benefit analysis—Wright eliminates the implicit assumption that friendships run smoothly. He thus accounts for the dynamic nature of relationships. Finally, Wright proposes friendship rewards: stimulation value (SV), utility value (UV), and ego support value (ESV). SV is realized when one person is interesting, exciting, and imaginative in a way that allows the other person to achieve an innovative outlook. UV is realized when one partner sees the other as cooperative and helpful. ESV is realized when one feels validated by the other as a worthwhile and generally decent person. ESV is synonymous with self-concept support; ego support makes one feel secure, comfortable, and self-assured.

Wright (1978) argues that friendship interactions are voluntary in nature and personalistic in focus. Friendships are intentional, not driven by external constraints. Further, friends relate as whole people, not as occupants of basic roles. As Wright states, "In friendship, each person reacts to the other as a person-qua-person (PQP) or, more specifically, with respect to his or her genuineness, uniqueness, and irreplaceability in the relationship" (p. 199). Wright (1982) reconceptualizes friendship using a mathematical analogy in which VID, DTM, SV, UV, ESV, and PQP sum to total friendship strength (TF). To operationalize his variables, Wright uses a friendship scale known as the Acquaintance Description Form (ADF).

Wright's cost-benefit conceptualization of friendship focuses on the behavioral outcomes of the friendship-formation process. The greater the anticipated reward, the more likely an individual will feel inclined to pursue friendship, regardless of the difficulty to maintain it. More specifically, his work focuses on the direct rewards of friendship—that is, its ability to confirm an individual's outlook, to lead in new directions, and to offer help. The major limitation of the theory lies in its lack of empirical support. Though the theory is intuitively appealing, rich in logical appeal, and readily appears to have surface validity, it is severely lacking in empirical rigor. The theory fails to set forth operational procedures for making data-based predictions; it has not generated an empirical base. Wright provides us with only a retrodictive and descriptive explanation of friendship. As such his theory is an ex post facto description of the way in which a limited number of friendships operate. Wright has, however, accurately described the voluntary nature and quality of friendship. He has argued that friend relationships can be distinguished by their voluntary nature and personalistic focus, and as such has provided the theoretical groundwork upon which to base a program of research.

Uncertainty. Charles Berger and Richard Calabrese's (1975) seminal contribution to the study of initial interaction utilizes uncertainty reduction to conceptualize friendship formation. The friendship-formation process is thus viewed from an information-gathering perspective. At initial stages of interaction, an individual has relatively little information about the other person and thus makes assumptions based on newly garnered information. "Central to the present theory," they argue, "is the assumption that when strangers meet, their primary concern is one of uncertainty reduction or increasing predictability about the behavior of both themselves and others in the interaction" (1975, p. 100). The reduction of uncertainty increases the amount of communication and the amount of interpersonal attraction. It also allows one more accurately to predict the other's behavior and the outcomes of interaction. Berger and Calabrese (1975) argue that uncertainty must be reduced in initial interaction if the relationship is to progress. The reduction of uncertainty is achieved by eliciting information through several strategies. First, passive strategies for uncertainty reduction include reactivity search, social comparison, and disinhibition search. Second, active strategies include asking others about the person and environmental structuring. Finally, interactive strategies include engaging in interrogatory behavior, self-description, self-disclosure, deception detection, and deviation testing (Berger, 1979).

The major limitation of this theory, which Berger and Calabrese (1975) posit as the basis for a developmental theory of interpersonal relations, lies in its focus on initial interaction to the exclusion of later stages of interaction. As such the theory is limited to initial interactions between strangers. As Berger and Calabrese (1975) concede, "A full blown theory of interaction development would have to stipulate broader boundary conditions than the present one" (p. 110). Berger and Calabrese fail to address whether the reduction of uncertainty is a driving need throughout the duration of a relationship. Furthermore, as Bochner (1978) argues,

> it is impossible to predict on the basis of this theory how to measure the amount of certainty or uncertainty in a relationship and when to predict that there will be too much certainty leading to boredom, when there will be just enough certainty leading to satisfaction, and

> when there will be too little certainty leading to termination or relational strain. (p. 187)

Moreover, the concept of uncertainty reduction is unfalsifiable. It is an inevitable function and as such is not particular to friendship. Berger and Calabrese have not posited a theory that clearly distinguishes and demarcates friendship from other phenomena in communication. Finally, they fail to specify the dimensions along which individuals seek the reduction of uncertainty and the types of relationships to which these processes may lead.

Clearly, this research program prompts some vexing concerns that need to be addressed. The major strength of Berger and Calabrese's (1975) theory, however, is that these researchers have clearly defined the important role that uncertainty reduction plays in the initial stage of the friendship-formation process. Moreover, they have substantiated their conception with a strong empirical base.

Summary

This review of the friendship literature reveals a common set of levels and dimensions used to describe friendship. Self-concept support and need gratification are common themes for researchers and theorists. The dynamic and developmental nature of the friend relationship is well established. However, though theories of friendship are abundant, the particular processes of friendship formation remain untapped. As we turn to the mate relationship literature, we find that the same holds true for this area.

The Mate Relationship

Levels of the Mate Relationship

A search of the empirical literature for level designations of the mate relationship reveals that although some researchers use as many as six levels, four both unique and necessary levels are widely agreed upon. In general, researchers recognize an early, casual stage of dating, followed by a steady or exclusive stage, then a stage that implies an intent for permanence, and finally an agreement on actual permanence. Table 2.2 provides an overview of the levels of the mate relationship studied in the research literature.

Many researchers use three levels, not pursuing investigation beyond a level of intent for permanence. Though the terminology differs, the meanings are clearly the same: occasional, steady, and engaged (Bailey and Helm, 1974; Helm, Bailey, and Vance, 1977); random dating, steady dating, and

Table 2.2
Levels in Mate Selection Research

				Researchers
Occasional	Steady	Engaged		(Bailey & Helm, 1974)
Occasional	Steady	Engaged		(Helm et al., 1977)
Random dating	Steady	Engaged		(McDaniel, 1969)
Early	Steady	Engaged		(Bailey & Kelly, 1984)
Dating	Courting	Engaged		(Heiss, 1962)
Casual	Serious	Marriage-bound		(Krain, 1975)
Casual date	Steady date	Fiancé	Spouse	(Chapter 3, this volume)
Casual dating	Exclusive dating	Engaged	Married	(Dion & Dion, 1976)
Casually dating	Seriously dating	Engaged	Marriage	(Lloyd et al., 1984)
Casually dating	Seriously dating or exclusively involved	Engaged	Married	(Lund, 1985)
New dating or dating frequently	Steady	Engaged	Married	(Brim & Wood, 1956)
Dating several or seeing others	Going steady	Engaged	Married	(Newcomb et al., 1986)
Casually dating	Seriously dating or exclusively dating	Engaged	Married	(Indvik & Fitzpatrick, 1986)

engaged (McDaniel, 1969); early, steady, and engaged (Bailey and Kelly, 1984); dating, courting, and engaged (Heiss, 1962). In an effort to identify transitional phases, Krain (1975) uses as his levels casual, early mixed, serious, late mixed, and marriage-bound. The mixed levels, however, are neither necessary nor unique. For all of these researchers, a level of actual permanence is implicit, although not investigated.

Others have investigated the level of actual permanence, using four levels: casual date, steady date, fiancé, and spouse (Chapter 3, this is tested with multidimensional scaling, which not only establishes levels, but also the distances between them); casual dating, exclusive dating, engaged, and married (Dion and Dion, 1976); casually dating, seriously dating, engaged, and marriage, cohabitation, or separation (Lloyd, Cate, and Henton, 1984). Separation denotes a terminated relationship, not a level designation; cohabitation is neither unique nor necessary.

Still other researchers delineate five levels: casually dating, seriously dating, exclusively involved, engaged, and married (Lund, 1985); new dating, dating frequently, steady, engaged, and married (Brim and Wood, 1956). The levels "seriously dating" and "exclusively involved" in the former and "new dating and "dating frequently" in the latter are not unique, creating gray areas that can be eliminated by combining levels.

Some researchers include cohabitation as a relationship level. Though cohabitation undoubtedly introduces numerous variables into a relationship, physical living conditions are not an indication of relational level, merely of residence and/or sexual practice. Cohabitation as a relational level is neither necessary nor unique. Using cohabitation, one can delineate six levels of relationship formation: dating several people, dating one person regularly but also dating others, going steady, engaged, living with boy/girlfriend, and married (Newcomb, Huba, and Bentler, 1986); or casually dating, seriously dating, exclusively dating, engaged, living together, and married (Indvik and Fitzpatrick, 1986). Eliminating cohabitation and the nonunique levels leaves four necessary and unique levels. Newcomb, et al.'s (1986) levels "dating several . . ." and "dating one person regularly but . . ." create yet another blurring of level delineation, as do Indvik and Fitzpatrick's (1986) "seriously dating" and "exclusive dating." Again, condensing these into one level eliminates gray areas.

Dimensions of the Mate Relationship

A search of empirical literature was conducted to pinpoint dimensions or attributes of the mate relationship, especially those that are definable as communication variables. Mate selection research encompasses a vast array of concepts and attributes, but very few dimensions have been extensively examined. Though one can gain a broad view of the topic, the literature is fragmented and of little depth. Without replication of findings, one must be cautious in application of research to theory.

Dimensions or attributes studied comprise a seemingly exhaustive list: physical attraction, sexuality, or physical characteristics (Bailey and Kelly, 1984; Green, Buchanan, and Heuer, 1984; Pam, Plutchik, and Conte, 1973; Pennock-Roman, 1984; White, Speisman, Jackson, Bartis, and Costos, 1986); attachment, commitment, or companionship (Buss and Barnes, 1986; Lund, 1985; Pam et al., 1973; Rusbolt, Johnson, and Morrow, 1986; White et al., 1986); trust (Dion and Dion, 1976; Pam et al., 1973; Rempel, Holmes, and Zanna, 1985); congenial, warm, affectionate, or kind (Buss and Barnes, 1986; Green et al., 1984; Pam et al., 1973); actual/ideal mate congruence (Bailey and Helm, 1974; Kerckhoff and Davis, 1962; Strauss, 1946); social or organizational factors (Green et al., 1984; Dillard and Witteman, 1985; DiMaggio and Mohr, 1985); investment or cost/benefit (Lund, 1985; Rusbolt et al., 1986; Snell and Belk, 1985); similarity or complementarity (Karp, Jackson, and Lester, 1970; Farley and Mueller, 1978; Udry, 1963); respect (Pam et al., 1973); self-concept support or understanding (Buss and Barnes, 1986; Helm, et al., 1977); intelligence (Bailey and Helm, 1974; Buss and Barnes, 1986); involvement or intimacy (Lloyd, et al., 1984; White et al., 1986); love, liking, or affection (Dion and Dion, 1976; Pam et al., 1973); satisfaction (Grover, Russell, Schumm, and Paff-Bergen, 1984; Rusbolt et al., 1986);

altruism (Pam et al., 1973); attitudes and communication (Krain, 1975); age and humor (Green et al., 1984); honest, dependable, loyal, and interesting (Buss and Barnes, 1986); caring/concern and communication (White et al., 1986); and, finally, psychological support (Valentinsen, Cushman, and Schroeder, 1981; see Chapter 3, this volume).

Researchers find several interesting distinctions and associations. Pam et al. (1973) find a clear distinction between a love relationship and one of friendship or dating, with physical attraction and attachment most important in the love relationship. Regarding the relationship between love and trust, Dion and Dion (1976) conclude that these variables are more strongly related for married than for unmarried couples. Similarly, Rempel, et al. (1985) discover love and happiness to be closely tied to feelings of faith and the attribution of intrinsic motivation.

The characteristics of an ideal or desirable mate have been examined for their predictive power in actual dating. Buss and Barnes (1986) show 10 characteristics to be most desired in a mate: good companion, considerate, honest, affectionate, dependable, intelligent, kind, understanding, interesting to talk to, and loyal. In linking the ideal to the real, Strauss (1946) discovers resemblance between the personality traits of ideal and actual mate.

Addressing the initiation of dating relationships, Green, Buchanan, and Heuer (1984) conclude that the important factors are age (men being older, women younger) and physical attractiveness. DiMaggio and Mohr (1985) find that cultural capital has significant effects on marital selection. Finally, Dillard and Witteman (1985) discover the likelihood of romantic involvement at work to be negatively related to formalization and curvilinearly related to organizational size.

Partner similarity has been a commonly studied variable for the prediction of mate relationships. Researchers have explored various dimensions of similarity and mate perceptions. Pennock-Roman (1984) finds spouse correlations for physical dimensions essentially equal regardless of length of marriage. Karp, et al. (1970) conclude that homoganous trait-matching occurs and that where the actual self differs from the ideal self, the ideal self will be matched. Farley and Mueller (1978) find significant assortative (nonrandom) mating for the sensation-seeking motivation.

Self-concept support is also a common variable. Bailey and Kelly (1984) find perceived self-concept support of physical attractiveness to be a predictor of initiation and maintenance of a dating relationship. Helm, et al. (1977) show a positive relationship between interpersonal commitment and perceptions of self-concept support for intelligence. Bailey and Helm (1974) find that commitment predicts a positive relationship between ratings of intelligence for "Date" and "Ideal Date."

Yet another area of study involves predicting relationship maintenance through the investments, rewards, and costs of mate relationships. Lund (1985) determines that a barrier model of investment and commitment is the best discriminator of relationship continuity, and Rusbolt et al. (1986) find support for the investment model of intimate relationships. Snell and Belk (1985) conclude that women involved in relationships with mutual high benefits report more liking for their partners than women in equitable relationships low in net gains. White et al. (1986) find distinct gender differences in relationship maturity, with adjustment for both sexes dependent on the husband's intimacy maturity. Lloyd et al. (1984) determine that involvement, reward level, and chance of marriage are all significant predictors of relationship stability. Grover et al. (1984) find a strong correlation between marital satisfaction and the length of time spent dating spouse; Krain (1975) demonstrated a linear process of communicative development in which communication in later stages of dating is more negentropic.

From the literature cited, numerous communication variables can be identified: attachment, commitment, trust, investment, self-concept support, understanding, involvement, intimacy, love, liking, affection, and psychological support. By exploring such variables we can gain insight into the role of communication in mate relationship development. As with friendship, self-concept support appears to be the most salient communication variable.

Theories of the Mate Relationship

In the following review of theories regarding the mate-formation process, the goal is to extract those variables for communication that are clearly applicable and of value. As is shown, few theories of mate selection pursue communication variables.

Psychoanalytic theory. The psychoanalytic theory of mate selection stems from the work of Freud and Jung, postulating resemblance between the spouse and the opposite-sex parent. Jedlicka (1980) tests the theory with respect to ethnicity. The ethnicity of a first spouse corresponds to the father's ethnicity 61.4% for brides and to the mother's ethnicity 58.6% for grooms. For second marriages, the correspondence is 63.5% for brides and 39.8% for grooms. In drawing his sample, however, Jedlicka chooses from a twice-married Hawaiian population of 9,270 only 980 individuals of ethnically mixed parentage who were married into either their fathers' or mothers' ethnic cohort. This sample represents only 10% of the already limited population. A twice-married population limits generalizability. Furthermore, ruling out those ethnically mixed individuals who did not marry into either parent's ethnicity may skew the findings.

This psychoanalytic theory is limited in the number of variables considered. Though the consideration of parent images in mate selection is important, its only relevance to communication is that we may communicate like our same-sex parent. Therefore, such a limited theory is not useful for exploring the role of communication in relational development.

Turning points. A turning point is any event or occurrence associated with relationship change. Turning points are central to a process view of relationships. Baxter and Bullis's (1986) data reveal a wide array of events associated with relationship change. The researchers identify 759 turning points, then group them into 14 supratypes, some of which have subtypes (Baxter and Bullis, 1986). The supratypes are as follows: get-to-know-time (three subtypes); quality time (three subtypes); physical separation; external competition (three subtypes); reunion; passion (four subtypes); disengagement; positive psychic change; exclusivity; negative psychic change; making up; serious commitment; sacrifice; and other. Baxter and Bullis (1986) report the percentage of relationship talk devoted to each (ranges from 19.8% to 90.9%), the percentage of partner agreement on each as a turning point (ranges from 30.4% to 75%), and the means and standard deviations of relationship change for each.

A strength of this study is that relationships are allowed full freedom for individual differences. However, nearly half of the dyads' perceptions of these important events are incongruent (Baxter and Bullis, 1986). This may be due to self-report or the extreme narrowing of types into supratypes. Meaning may be obscured when the field is reduced from 759 to 14 types, the last of which is simply "other." Such a wide array may be an indication that there is no set of universal turning points that applies to every couple in existence, or even to two individuals in the same relationship. The amount of disagreement between partners may indicate that turning points are an individual occurrence. Furthermore, guidelines for grouping types are unclear; the researchers simply report that they were talked about in similar ways. There is also no explanation for the high standard deviations for commitment change—some are greater than the mean change.

Viewing commitment as the result of a series of relational turning points, rather than as a process of sequential development, is an interesting idea, however, the theory of relational turning points lacks an examination of communication variables and is thus not useful for our purpose.

Relational types. As discussed above for friendship, Indvik and Fitzpatrick (1986) deal with perceptions of inclusion, affiliation, and control in different types of interpersonal relationships. The resulting comparison of relational types allows assessment of relationships as communication contexts. The relationships compared are workers, acquaintances, friends, best friends, and intimates. Intimates scored significantly higher than other relational types on inclusion and affiliation factors. For control factors, intimates differed significantly on legitimacy but not on exclusivity. In general, all three dimensions are definitive of intimate relationships.

The intimate relationship is defined by comparison to other relationship types. A view of relationships as communication contexts sophisticates our classifying system. Fitzpatrick's earlier work uses a typological approach and accuracy to explain communication in relationships (Fitzpatrick, 1977; Fitzpatrick and Indvik, 1982; Fitzpatrick and Winke, 1979). This research focuses on a typological analysis of marital types and communication patterns leading to longevity. At various levels of relationships, messages are communicated differently (Fitzpatrick, 1977). Fitzpatrick (1977) uses her relational typology to examine communication accuracy, isolating four discrete relational types: Independent, Traditional, Separate, and Separate/Traditional. For a significant number, "his" relationship differed from "hers." The husbands classified themselves as Separate, the wives as Traditional. This Separate/Traditional relational type occurred as frequently as Traditional. In this earlier work of Fitzpatrick's (1977) there is little room for change, but she offers important concepts. Specific communication variables, however, are not pursued.

Assortative mating. Assortative mating is any systematic departure from random mating. Studies examine a wide range of variables including social (Dressel, 1980; Elder, 1969), personality (Buss, 1984; Farley and Davis, 1977; Farley and Mueller, 1978), and physical (Pennock-Roman, 1984; Spuhler, 1966) characteristics. Vandenberg (1972) cites numerous sources that support positive assortative mating for age, previous marital status, religion, propinquity, socioeconomic status, education, ethnic background, race, physical traits, and psychological traits.

Numerous contradictory research findings seem to indicate the need for methodological refinement. In an effort to reduce the inaccuracy of self-report, many studies include a partner-rating as well as a self-rating, yet this does not assure accuracy of either. In addition, assortment is investigated only in early relationship establishment. The strength of assortment theory lies in its power to explain initial selection of approachables, but not relationship formation. Demographic, social, environmental, and personality variables do not depend on communication to exist in a relationship. Therefore, theories of assortative mating are not useful to the examination of communication in relational development.

Complementarity. Udry (1963), following Winch, attempts to verify personality complementarity as a variable in mate selection. Mate selection is made from the field of eligibles based on maximum anticipated need gratification. It is assumed that certain traits are more gratifying than others, and that people react to others based on perception. Udry (1963) attempts to determine which personality needs are relevant to mate selection and whether sex differences exist. Results indicate that mates' perceptions of each other exaggerate sex differences in personality. There is a substantial projection of one's own traits, especially for engaged individuals and females. However, accuracy of perceptions is greater for married individuals and for females.

Udry (1963) comments that models of complementarity (including his own) are too simplistic to explain reality adequately and that his instrument determines the relationship found. The pattern that emerges is too complex to be explained by his theory. Thus, difficulty in personality measurement presents a major limitation. Udry's assumptions form a reality-based theoretic foundation, but since complementarity research is lacking in relevant communication variables, it cannot shed light on the examination of the role of communication in relationship development.

Marital quality. Cahn (1987) views empirical study of the mate-selection process as fragmented in several directions: quality, alternative, investments, and system constraints. He proposes a comprehensive model based on the interrelations among the aforementioned approaches. The quality model focuses on personal growth, relationship satisfaction, and perceived understanding. Self-concept support is seen to produce perceived understanding, which in turn positively influences feelings of self-worth and relationship satisfaction. The extent of commitment to a relationship depends on investment size, system constraints, and available alternatives in terms of personal and relationship growth, perceived self-concept support, and mutual perceived understanding.

Research findings (Cahn, 1986) support the quality model in general and pinpoint perceived understanding as most important in relationship development. At the casual stage of dating, socioemotional expression is the best predictor of perceived understanding; at the steady stage, cooperation; and at the engaged or married level, acceptance–appreciation (Cahn, 1986). Results that show such differences between levels seem to illustrate that variables in assortative mating research lack explanatory value in later relationship stages.

Cahn's strength undoubtedly lies in this combination of models, bringing into focus an otherwise fragmented body of theory. Cahn posits that self-concept support leads to perceived understanding, which in turn determines the length of the relationship. This is highly important to understanding the role of communication in relationship development. This work lends support to the general theory of Cushman and his associates (Cushman and Cahn, 1985; Cushman, Valentinsen, and Dietrich, 1982).

Filter and stage theories. Phasic theories represent the most common approach to theories of mate relationship formation. In their seminal work on relationship phases, Kerckhoff and Davis (1962) conceptualize relationship development as the operation of a series of filters. They argue that value consensus and need complementarity will lead to different types of mate-formation processes. Consensus was found to be significant only for short-term couples (less than 18 months); whereas for long-term couples complementarity was significant. Kerckhoff and Davis (1962) interpreted these data as a series of filtering factors. Social-status variables are seen to operate early, value consensus somewhat later, and still later need complementarity.

Others have since drawn upon this filter idea (Cushman and Cahn, 1985; Cushman et al., 1982; Knapp, 1978; Lewis, 1972, 1973; Murstein, 1970, 1972, 1974, 1976, 1977; Nofz, 1984). Although value consensus is a communication variable, because Kerckhoff and Davis (1962) found significance only for short-term couples, it is not considered to represent a continuing developmental process.

Knapp (1978) sees interpersonal relationships as going through 10 distinct stages: initiating, experimenting, intensifying, integrating, bonding, differentiating, circumscribing, stagnating, avoiding, and terminating. The first five are analogous to the mate-selection process. Movement through the stages is a process inherent in social exchange theory, with choices guided by costs and rewards. Alberts (1986) examines the role of couples' conversations in relationship development, using Knapp's (1978) first four stages as the relational development sequence. The study (Alberts, 1986) is a content analysis of conversations from Harlequin romance novels of characters involved in romantic-relationship development. Three specific features recurred: meta-talk, face-threatening acts, and mitigation. Alberts (1986) defends using fiction as a database, citing others who have done so, but makes no attempt to verify the degree of realism in fictional conversations.

Nofz (1984) notes that mate-selection theory rarely, if ever, draws attention to the possibility of differences among relationships. His response is Fantasy-Testing-Assessment (FTA). This is not a sequential process of stages, but rather three modes in which relational partners may interact. Any mode can become the ongoing foundation in a permanent relationship. Nofz contends that individuals' assessments are based not on perceptions, but on rewards and costs for which the individual possesses tangible evidence (Nofz, 1984). However, after initial observation everything is based on perception. An individual cannot possess tangible evidence that is not based on perception. In addition, although Nofz emphasizes that his three modes are not sequential steps of development, they are presented in sequence with a distinct set of levels, each a higher step than the last. The central idea that every relationship is different is an improvement over other theories. This model exhibits flexibility allowing for differences among people and their relationships, while still offering sound description of relational processes. As with most theories of relational development, the role of communication is not specifically addressed.

Lewis's (1972, 1973) Premarital Dyadic Formation (PDF) is a time-order interrelation of six pair processes. Some support was found for the salience of five of the processes (Lewis, 1972, 1973). However, according to Rubin and Levinger (1974), Lewis's sample (1972, 1973) is poorly suited to illumination of early phases. Lewis does not demonstrate any particular sequential relationship (Rubin and Levinger, 1974). On the other hand, PDF integrates a wide range of theoretical resources into a single sequentially ordered framework. Communication variables, however, are not pursued.

Murstein (1970, 1972, 1974, 1976, 1977) proposes the SVR model: Relationships pass through three stages that make up courtship—Stimulus, Value Comparison, and Role. As a couple progresses successfully through these levels, the chance for marriage increases. Consistency with existing data is sufficient only to prove SVR tenable, according to Murstein (1974). In addition, no explicit testing of the sequence has been done (Murstein, 1976), and although SVR is a temporally successive filter theory, the Value component can be seen to act as a filter before the dyad reaches the Stimulus stage, breaking the proposed pattern. Murstein (1976) himself states that the filter is incomplete. No evidence gives significant support to the crucial chronological sequence (Rubin and Levinger, 1974). SVR may be useful in the prediction and explanation of initial attraction and solid premarital relationships, but not in marriage prediction. SVR does not consider communication variables.

Summary

This literature review reveals a common set of levels and dimensions used to describe the mate relationship. Self-concept support and physical attraction are common themes for researchers and theorists. As for friendship, the dynamic and developmental nature of the mate relationship is well established. However, though theories of the mate relationship are abundant, the particular processes of its formation remain untapped.

Propositions

The rules for friendship and mate relationships posited by Cushman's general theory (Cushman and Cahn, 1985; Cushman, Valentinsen, and Dietrich, 1982 [see Chapter 1 for a description]) are not explicitly confirmable or deniable. However, from the conceptual theory (see Chapter 1) and the literature reviewed in this chapter, several basic propositions can be derived. The conceptual origin of all these propositions can be traced directly to the theoretic work presented in Cushman and Cahn (1985, especially pp. 5–100). As such, these propositions are *not* to be considered original theory; rather, *they represent specific empirical statements of the general conceptual theory developed by Cushman and his associates* (Cushman and Cahn, 1985; Cushman, Valentinsen, and Dietrich, 1982). The following propositions are easily operationalized and supported by the literature and by the studies in this volume.

Proposition 1

Perceived self-concept support is the basis of interpersonal attraction.

This proposition is the most basic, and reflects the underlying foundation for the general theory (Cushman and Cahn, 1985). Several decades of research provide support for this proposition (as reviewed above). Two bodies of theory and research that may contest this proposition are the similarity hypothesis (e.g., for friendship: Byrne, 1961, 1971; Byrne and Griffitt, 1969; Duck, 1973; Duck and Craig, 1978; Indvik and Fitzpatrick, 1986; for the mate relationship: Farley and Mueller, 1978; Karp et al., 1970; Pennock-Roman, 1984) and the complementarity hypothesis (e.g., for friendship: Duck, 1973; Wright, 1969, 1978; for the mate relationship: Udry, 1963).

The problems that plague theorists who attempt to reconcile the similarity and complementarity hypotheses (e.g., Duck, 1973) can be resolved when considered in light of the wide body of research supporting the proposition that self-concept support is the basis of interpersonal relationships (e.g., Bailey and Helm, 1974; Bailey and Kelly, 1984; Bailey et al., 1974; Bailey et al., 1975; Buss and Barnes, 1986; Cahn, 1986; Crawford, 1977; Gibbs, 1977; Helm et al., 1977; LaGaipa, 1977; Parks, 1977; Rose, 1985). This proposition allows for both the similarity and complementarity explanations. Proposition 1 can reconcile seemingly disparate theories. By positing perceived self-concept support as the basis for interpersonal attraction, processes that seem incompatible can coexist (e.g., similarity and complementarity).

Proposition 2

Different types of perceived self-concept support are the basis for different types of interpersonal relationships.

This proposition is also a basic foundation for the theory (Cushman and Cahn, 1985). Such self-concept support can be directly or indirectly communicated (see Cushman and Kovacic, in press; also Chapters 7 and 11). The most compelling support for this proposition comes from the studies in this book. The seminal investigations presented in Chapter 3 show that self-concept support provided on different variables and at different intensities leads to the formation and growth of different types of relationships.

Although friendships and mate relationships are both based on perceived self-concept support, that support must be provided on different attributes for each relational type. For example, according to the literature reviewed above, trust, respect, and authenticity are essential areas for friendship, whereas attachment, love, and affection are essential for the mate relationship. Though there may be some contradiction as to the specific attributes for each relationship type, the proposition that different relationship types are predicted by different types of self-concept support is secure.

Proposition 3

Different types of self-concept support are the basis for entry into and increasing intensity of interpersonal relationships.

Self-concept support on a particular set of attributes must be present for initiation or entry into a friend or mate relationship (Cushman and Cahn, 1985; Cushman, Valentinsen, and Dietrich, 1982). Subsequently, increasing self-concept support on another set of attributes leads to increasing intensity of the relationship (Cushman and Cahn, 1985; Cushman, Valentinsen, and Dietrich, 1982). Again, the most compelling support comes from the studies to follow. Like Proposition 2, this proposition is secure; this will be shown in Parts II and III. The specific characters of the attributes are arguable and in need of more research.

Proposition 4

The type and form of self-concept support is homogeneous by culture.

The studies to follow provide evidence for entry and intensity variables for both friendship and the mate relationship in several cultures. Within the cultures tested, the attributes discovered are shown to be homogeneous (see also Cushman and Kovacic, in press). This proposition thus seems secure. However, further testing is required in other cultures.

Proposition 5

Conflict that threatens self-concept support on crucial relationship variables—the lack of it or attacks on it—is the most potentially dangerous type of conflict in interpersonal relationships.

Conflict that threatens to destroy self-concept support on the basis for the relationship and/or its growth can damage the individual and the relationship (Cushman, 1989; Cushman and Cahn, 1985; Cushman and Kovacic, in press; Genshaft, 1980; Levinger, 1980; Rands, Levinger, and Mellinger, 1981; Ritter, 1985; Ting-Toomey, 1983). The evidence for this proposition, discussed thoroughly in Chapters 7 and 11, is indirect. Direct evidence is unattainable because the direct scientific manipulation of conflict based on self-concept support in interpersonal relationships is unethical, if not morally reprehensible. This proposition, directly derivable from the general theory, needs to be tested. Such testing can be achieved only with after-the-fact accounts of relational conflict.

Proposition 6

Negotiation of differences in perceptions of self-concept support on crucial relationship variables cements interpersonal relationships.

This proposition follows from Proposition 5 and must be tested in the same way. When self-concept support is threatened on the basis for the relationship and/or its growth, successful negotiation of the partners' perceptions of this support strengthens the relationship (Billingham and Sack, 1987; Birchler, Weiss, and Vincent, 1975; Cushman, 1989; Cushman and Cahn, 1985; Cushman and Kovacic, in press; Genshaft, 1980; Gottman, Markman, and Notarius, 1977; Noller, 1981; Rands, et al., 1981; Ting-Toomey, 1983). The converse of this proposition implies that when partners' differing perceptions of self-concept support cannot be successfully negotiated, the relationship will be weakened and eventually destroyed. Chapters 7 and 11 provide discussions of this proposition.

Proposition 7

Quality interpersonal relationships consist of intimacy, personal growth, and effective communication on the crucial relationship variables.

Again following from Proposition 5—basically stating the converse—this proposition holds that high-quality relationships are marked by effective communication of self-concept support on crucial relationship variables, leading to intimacy and personal growth on those variables (Aguirre and Kirwan, 1986; Crawford, 1977; Cushman, 1979; Cushman, 1989; Cushman and Cahn, 1985; Fincham and Bradbury, 1989; Gibbs, 1977; Hays, 1984; LaGaipa, 1977; Montgomery, 1981; Rettig and Bubolz, 1983; Spanier and Lewis, 1980). Chapters 7 and 11 provide discussions of this proposition.

Summary

These seven basic propositions, derived from the general conceptual theory (Cushman and Cahn, 1985; Cushman, Valentinsen, and Dietrich, 1982) and the literature reviewed above, comprise the organizing focus for this book. Each proposition is empirically confirmable. Propositions 1–4 find direct support from the studies in this book, whereas 5–7 find indirect support through implications discussed in Chapters 7 and 11.

Chapter 3 describes the seminal investigations of the general theory, which provide support for Propositions 1–3. The studies in Part II (Chapters 4–6) and in Part III (Chapters 8–10) provide direct support for Propositions 1–4. The summary chapters for Parts II and III (Chapters 7 and 11) discuss implications that provide indirect support for Propositions 5–7. Before turning to the actual investigations, we must provide a description of the common methodologies employed.

Common Methodologies Employed in the Studies

Levels and Dimensions

Background. Cushman's concept of a developmental process in relational development is not unique. There is a wide consensus among researchers from a variety of perspectives that interpersonal relationships are developmental (Bailey and Helm, 1974; Bailey and Kelly, 1984; Brim and Wood, 1956; Dion and Dion, 1976; Heiss, 1962; Indvik and Fitzpatrick, 1986; Krain, 1975; LaGaipa, 1977; Lloyd, et al., 1984; Lund, 1985; Murstein, 1972, 1977; McDaniel, 1969; Parks, 1977). Few attempts have been made, however, to develop a measuring instrument that identifies stages in various cultures differentially or that allows for cross-cultural comparison without distortion. One approach that offers this potential and that has been used in the United States and Japan is the method developed by Cushman and his associates (Cushman and Cahn, 1985; Cushman and Nishida, 1984, unpublished study described in Cushman and Cahn, 1985). Authors in this volume follow this method or a variation.

On the basis of interviews and a thorough review of the literature, Cushman and Nishida (1984, unpublished study described in Cushman and Cahn, 1985) developed a measurement instrument that focuses on stages of development and attributes of friendship or mate relationship development. The attributes for the seminal investigation of mate relationship were Intelligent, Physically Attractive, Sexually Appealing, Respect, Psychological Support, Affection, Supportiveness, and Social Support. For friendship, the attributes were Social Support, Psychological Support, Trust, Respect, and

Authenticity. The instruments were validated in the United States in a previously unpublished study, which appears in Chapter 3 of this book.

Cushman and Nishida (1984, unpublished study described in Cushman and Cahn, 1985) then pursued a similar strategy for examining a developmental theory in Japan. Instruments for other cultures are developed and validated throughout the chapters in this book. Such research represents a promising approach to development of a cross-cultural instrument.

Technique. For most of the studies reported in this book, relationships among hypothesized relationship levels and attributes were operationalized using paired comparisons, following the Galileo method of multidimensional scaling (Woelfel and Fink, 1980). Galileo analysis allows measurement of multidimensional separation of concepts in cognitive space. The concepts are arrayed in a questionnaire in all possible paired comparisons, and subjects are directed to quantify the distances between each pair of concepts. The aggregate configuration of concepts is factor-analyzed, quantified, and verified. The Galileo computer program determines the uniqueness of dimensions and perceived social distance relative to a specific point of reference (Woelfel and Fink, 1980). Consistent with the theoretical structure, the relevant points of reference are Real Self and Ideal Self.

The particular rationale for using the paired comparison technique (that is, the Galileo questionnaires) is threefold (Valentinsen, Cushman, and Schroeder, 1981, see Chapter 3). First, the Galileo measurement system (Woelfel and Fink, 1980) models interrelationships among a set of concepts using spatial analysis. The subjects' quantifications of dissimilarity estimates between the concepts are aggregated to produce a mean-distance matrix. This matrix is orthogonally decomposed to produce a factor matrix representing the coordinate locations of the concepts on a set of "independent" dimensions (Valentinsen et al., 1981). The mean-distance and coordinate matrices are then examined for theoretically justifiable configurations of concepts. A spatial analysis allows conventional meanings to be precisely quantified (Valentinsen et al., 1981). Relational development and maintenance are governed and guided by rules corresponding to standardized ways in which actual and would-be partners communicate (Valentinsen et al., 1981). Second, Galileo has been documented as providing a relatively stable measure of the configuration of self–object and object–object relationships (Danes and Woelfel, 1975; Gordon, 1976; Gordon and DeLeo, 1976; Gillham and Woelfel, 1977; Valentinsen et al., 1981). Conventional meanings regarding relationships appear in a theoretically justifiable configuration of concepts. Different types of rules can thus be operationalized (Valentinsen et al., 1981). Third, Galileo can measure changes in shared meanings brought about through communication (Valentinsen et al., 1981). Such experimental applications have been applied in other domains (Valentinsen et al., 1981), such as attitude change (Barnett,

Serota, and Taylor, 1976; Woelfel, Cody, Gillham, and Holmes, 1980) and cross-cultural processes (Woelfel and Fink, 1980).

Because of the limited availability of the Galileo computer program, some of the chapters use other measures of difference (e.g., dependent t-tests) between the paired comparisons. The importance of the application of Galileo is the use of paired comparisons—estimating cognitive distances among a set of concepts. These analyses lack the orthogonal decomposition of the data matrices: they cannot provide a multidimensional "cognitive map" of concepts on a set of coordinates. However, the use of aggregate scores of paired comparison distances does provide a relative measure of the similarities and differences among a set of concepts. The use of paired comparisons in a Galileo-type questionnaire can provide basic information about the relationships among those concepts, even if the Galileo computer program is not applied.

Interpersonal Penetration

Several studies in this volume seek to test and extend the theories of Cushman and his associates. The extension takes the form of an interpersonal penetration analysis, based on the work of Gudykunst (Gudykunst, 1985; Gudykunst and Nishida, 1983). To measure interpersonal penetration, Gudykunst used a scale developed by Taylor and Altman (1966). The items in this social-penetration measurement instrument focus on the degree, breadth, and depth of interpersonal social penetration on specific topics of interaction. In Gudykunst's work, 63 items were randomly selected from a pool of 671 items such that there would be no fewer than three items on any one dimension. Penetration scores were achieved by multiplying the frequency times the intimacy scores and dividing by the number of possible items. In most chapters of this volume, authors have explored this data further with t-tests among topics and between cultures. (For a full discussion of the theory of social penetration, see Bahk, Chapter 5, this volume.)

Since these studies were conducted independently, they do not follow one standard set of procedures. Generally, the studies use some version of Galileo questionnaires. The studies that explore interpersonal penetration use a version of Gudykunst's (1985) instrument. Beyond these similarities, the specific details of each chapter's procedures and analyses are described in the chapters.

References

Aguirre, B., and P. Kirwan (1986). Marriage order and the quality and stability of marital relationships: A test of Lewis and Spanier's theory. *Journal of Comparative Family Studies* 17:247–76.

Alberts, J. K. (1986). The role of couples' conversations in relational development: A content analysis of courtship talk in Harlequin romance novels. *Communication Quarterly* 34:127–42.

Bailey, R. C., P. Finney, and K. G. Bailey (1974). Level of self-acceptance and perceived intelligence in self and friend. *Journal of Genetic Psychology* 124:61–67.

Bailey, R. C., P. Finney, and B. Helm (1975). Self-concept support and friendship. *Journal of Social Psychology* 96:237–43.

Bailey, R., and B. Helm (1974). Matrimonial commitment and date/ideal date perception. *Perceptual and Motor Skills* 39:1356–57.

Bailey, R. C., and M. Kelly (1984). Perceived physical attractiveness in early, steady, and engaged daters. *Journal of Psychology* 116:39–43.

Barnett, G., K. Serota, and J. Taylor (1976). Campaign communication and attitude change: A multidimensional analysis. *Human Communication Research* 2:227–44.

Baxter, L. A., and C. Bullis (1986). Turning points in developing romantic relationships. *Human Communication Research* 12:469–93.

Berger, C. R. (1979). Beyond initial interactions. In H. Giles and R. St. Clair (eds.), *Language and social psychology* (122–44) Oxford: Basil Blackwell.

Berger, C. R., and R. Calabrese (1975). Some explorations in initial interaction and beyond: Toward a developmental theory of interpersonal communication. *Human Communication Research* 1:99–112.

Billingham, R. E., and A. R. Sack (1987). Conflict tactics and the level of emotional commitment among unmarrieds. *Human Relations* 40:59–74.

Birchler, G. R., R. L. Weiss, and J. P. Vincent (1975). Multimethod analysis of social reinforcement exchange between maritally distressed and nondistressed spouse and stranger dyads. *Journal of Personality and Social Psychology* 31:349–60.

Bochner, A. (1978). On taking ourselves seriously: An analysis of some persistent problems and promising directions in interpersonal research. *Human Communication Research* 4:179–90.

Brim, O. G., and N. Wood (1956). Self and other conceptions in courtship and marriage pairs. *Marriage and Family Living* 18:243–48.

Buss, D. M. (1984). Marital assortment for three personality dispositions: Assessment with three different data sources. *Behavior Genetics* 14:111–23.

Buss, D. M. and M. Barnes (1986). Preferences in human mate selection. *Journal of Personality and Social Psychology* 50:559–70.

Byrne, D. (1961). Interpersonal attraction and attitude similarity. *Journal of Abnormal and Social Psychology* 62:713–15.

Byrne, D. (1971). *The attraction paradigm*. New York: Academic Press.

Byrne, D., and W. Griffitt (1969). Attitude evoked anticipatory responses and attraction. *Psychonomic Science* 14:153–55.

Cahn, D. D. (1986). *Male-female communication and relationship development: Communication characteristics of mateship stages*. Unpublished paper, State University of New York at New Paltz.

Cahn, D. D. (1987). *Letting go*. Albany, NY: State University of New York Press.

Crawford, M. (1977). What is a friend? *New Society* 42:116–17.

Cushman, D. P. (1979). Communication in establishing, maintaining, and terminating interpersonal relationships. *Journal of Youth and Adolescence* 8:443–52.

Cushman, D. P. (1989). Communication in establishing, maintaining, and terminating interpersonal relationships: A study of mateship. In S. S. King(ed.), *Human communication as a field of study: Selected contemporary views* (87–104). Albany, NY: State University of New York Press.

Cushman, D. P., and D. D. Cahn (1985). *Communication in interpersonal relationships*. Albany, NY: State University of New York Press.

Cushman D. P., and B. Kovacic, (in press). A rules perspective on communication theory. In F. L. Casmir (ed.), *Communication theory*. Albany, NY: State Univeristy of New York Press.

Cushman, D. P., and T. Nishida (1984). *Mate selection in the United States and Japan*. Unpublished manuscript, State University of New York at Albany.

Cushman, D. P., B. Valentinsen, and D. Dietrich (1982). A rules theory of interpersonal relationships. In F. E. X. Dance (ed.), *Human Communication Theory* (90–119). New York: Harper and Row.

Danes, J., and J. Woelfel (1975, May). *An alternative to the "traditional" scaling paradigm in mass communication research: Multidimensional reduction of ratio judgments of separation*. Paper presented at the annual conference of the International Communication Association, Chicago.

Dillard, J. P., and H. Witteman (1985). Romantic relationships at work: Organizational and personal influences. *Human Communication Research* 12:99–116.

DiMaggio, P., and J. Mohr (1985). Cultural capital, educational attainment, and marital selection. *American Journal of Sociology* 91:1231–61.

Dion, K. L., and K. K. Dion (1976). Love, liking, and trust in heterosexual relationships. *Personality and Social Psychology Bulletin* 2:187–90.

Dressel, P. (1980). Assortive mating in later life. *Journal of Family Issues* 1:379–96.

Duck, S. (1973). Similarity and perceived similarity of personal constructs as influencers of friendship choice. *British Journal of Social and Clinical Psychology* 12:1–6.

Duck, S. (1976). Interpersonal communication in developing relationships. In G. R. Miller (ed.), *Explorations in interpersonal communication* (127–145). Beverly Hills, CA: Sage.

Duck, S., and G. Craig (1978). Personality similarity and the development of friendship. *British Journal of Sociology and Clinical Psychology* 17:237–42.

Elder, G. H. (1969). Appearance and education in marriage mobility. *American Sociological Review* 34:519–33.

Farley, F. H., and S. A. Davis (1977). Arousal, personality, and assortative mating in marriage. *Journal of Sex and Marital Therapy* 3:122–27.

Farley, F. H., and C. B. Mueller (1978). Arousal, personality, and assortative mating in marriage. Generalizability and cross-cultural factors. *Journal of Sex and Marital Therapy* 4:50–52.

Fincham, F., and T. Bradbury (1989). Perceived responsibility for marital events: Egocentric or partner-centric bias? *Journal of Marriage and the Family* 51:27–35.

Fitzpatrick, M. A. (1977). A typological approach to communication in relationships. In B. D. Ruben (ed.), *Communication yearbook 1* (263–75). New Brunswick, NJ: Transaction Books.

Fitzpatrick, M. A., and J. Indvik (1982). The instrumental and expressive domains of marital communication. *Human Communication Research* 8:195–213.

Fitzpatrick, M. A., and J. Winke (1979). You always hurt the one you love: Strategies and tactics in interpersonal conflict. *Communication Quarterly* 27:3–11.

Genshaft, J. L. (1980). Perceptual and defensive style variables in marital discord. *Social Behavior and Personality* 8:81–84.

Gibbs, S. (1977). *A comparative analysis of friendship functions in six age groups of men and women.* Unpublished dissertation, Wayne State University, Detroit, MI.

Gillham, J., and J. Woelfel (1977). The Galileo system of measurement: Preliminary evidence for precision, stability, and equivalence to traditional measures. *Human Communication Research* 3:222–34.

Gordon, T. (1976). *Subject abilities to use MDS: Effects of varying the criterion pair.* Unpublished manuscript, Temple University, Philadelphia.

Gordon, T., and H. C. DeLeo (1976, May). *Structural variation in "Galileo" space: Effects of varying the criterion pair in multidimensional scaling.* Paper presented at the annual conference of the International Communication Association, Portland, OR.

Gottman, J., H. Markman, and C. Notarius (1977). The topography of marital conflict: A sequential analysis of verbal and nonverbal behavior. *Journal of Marriage and the Family* 39:461–77.

Green, S., D. R. Buchanan, and S. K. Heuer (1984). Winners, losers, and choosers: A field investigation of dating initiation. *Personality and Social Psychology Bulletin* 10:502–11.

Grover, K. J., C. S. Russell, W. R. Schumm, and L. A. Paff-Bergen, (1984). Mate selection processes and marital satisfaction. *Family Relations* 34:383–86.

Gudykunst, W. B. (1985). An exploratory comparison of close intracultural and intercultural friendships. *Communication Quarterly* 31:49–55.

Gudykunst, W. B. and T. Nishida (1983). Social penetration in Japanese and American close friendships. In R. N. Bostrom (ed.), *Communication yearbook* 7 (592–610). Beverly Hills, CA: Sage.

Hays, R. B. (1984). The development and maintenance of friendship. *Journal of Social and Personal Relationships* 1:75–98.

Heiss, J. S. (1962). Degree of intimacy and male-female interaction. *Sociometry*, 25:197–208.

Helm, B., R. Bailey, and B. K. Vance (1977). Interpersonal commitment and self-concept support. *Journal of Social Psychology* 102:319–20.

Indvik, J., and M. A. Fitzpatrick (1986). Perceptions of inclusion, affiliation, and control in five interpersonal relationships. *Communication Quarterly* 34:1–13.

Jedlicka, D. (1980). A test of the psychoanalytic theory of mate selection. *Journal of Social Psychology* 112:295–99.

Karp, E. S., J. H. Jackson, and D. Lester (1970). Ideal-self fulfillment in mate selection: A corollary to the complementary need theory of mate selection. *Journal of Marriage and the Family* 32:269–72.

Kerckhoff, A. C., and K. E. Davis (1962). Value consensus and need complementarity in mate selection. *American Sociological Review* 27:295–303.

Knapp, M. (1978). *Social intercourse: From greeting to goodbye.* Boston: Allyn and Bacon.

Krain, M. (1975). Communication among premarital couples at three stages of dating. *Journal of Marriage and the Family* 37:609–18.

LaGaipa, J. J. (1977). Testing a multidimensional approach to friendship. In S. Duck (ed.), *Theory and practice in interpersonal attraction* (249–70). London: Academic Press.

Levinger, G. (1980). Toward the analysis of close relationships. *Journal of Experimental Social Psychology* 16:510–44.

Lewis, R. A. A. (1972). A developmental framework for the analysis of premarital dyadic formation. *Family Process* 11:17–48.

Lewis, R. A. A. (1973). A longitudinal test of a developmental framework for the analysis of premarital dyadic formation. *Journal of Marriage and the Family* 35:16–25.

Lloyd, S., R. M. Cate, and J. M. Henton (1984). Predicting premarital stability: A methodological refinement. *Journal of Marriage and the Family* 46:71–75.

Lund, M. (1985). The development of investment and commitment scales for predicting continuity of personal relationships. *Journal of Social and Personal Relationships* 2:3–23.

McDaniel, C. O. (1969). Dating roles and reasons for dating. *Journal of Marriage and the Family* 31:97–107.

Montgomery, B. M. (1981). The form and function of quality communication in marriage. *Family Relations* 30:21–29.

Murstein, B. I. (1970). Stimulus-value-role: A theory of marital choice. *Journal of Marriage and the Family* 37:265–81.

Murstein, B. I. (1972). Person perception and courtship progress among premarital couples. *Journal of Marriage and the Family* 34:621–27.

Murstein, B. I. (1974). Clarification of obfuscation on computation: A reply to criticism of the SVR theory of marital choice. *Journal of Marriage and the Family* 36:231–34.

Murstein, B. I. (1976). *Who will marry whom?* New York: Springer.

Murstein, B. I. (1977). The stimulus-value-role (SVR) theory of dyadic relationships. In S. W. Duck (ed.), *Theory and practice in interpersonal attraction* (105–27) London: Academic Press.

Newcomb, M. D., G. J. Huba, and P. M. Bentler (1986). Determinants of sexual and dating behaviors among adolescents. *Journal of Personality and Social Psychology* 50:428–38.

Nofz, M. P. (1984). Fantasy-testing-assessment: A proposed model for the investigation of mate selection. *Family Relations* 33:273–81.

Noller, P. (1981). Gender and marital adjustment level differences in decoding messages from spouses and strangers. *Journal of Personality and Social Psychology* 41:272–78.

Pam, A., R. Plutchik, and H. Conte (1973) Love: A psychometric approach. *Proceedings of the 81st annual convention of the APA*, 159–60.

Parks, M. R. (1977, December). *Communication correlates of perceived friendship development.* Paper presented at the annual conference of the Speech Communication Association, Washington, DC.

Pennock-Roman, M. (1984). Assortative marriage for physical characteristics in newlyweds. *American Journal of Physical Anthropology* 64:185–90.

Rands, M., G. Levinger, and G. D. Mellinger (1981). Patterns of conflict resolution and marital satisfaction. *Journal of Family Issues* 2:297–321.

Rempel, J. K., J. G. Holmes, and M. P. Zanna (1985). Trust in close relationships. *Journal of Personality and Social Psychology* 49:95–112.

Rettig, K., and M. Bubolz (1983). Interpersonal resource exchanges as indicators of quality marriages. *Journal of Marriage and the Family* 45:497–509.

Ritter, K. Y. (1985). The cognitive therapies. *Journal of Counseling and Development* 64:42–44.

Rose, S. M. (1985). Same- and cross-sex friendships and the psychology of homosociality. *Sex Roles* 12:63–74.

Rubin, Z., and G. Levinger, (1974). Theory and data badly mated: A critique of Murstein's SVR and Lewis's PDF models of mate selection. *Journal of Marriage and the Family* 36:226–30.

Rusbolt, C. E., D. J. Johnson, and G. D. Morrow (1986). Predicting satisfaction and commitment in adult romantic involvements: An assessment of the generalizability of the investment model. *Social Psychology Quarterly* 49:81–89.

Snell, W. E., and S. S. Belk (1985). On assessing "equity" in relationships. *Representative Research in Social Psychology* 15:16–24.

Spanier, G. B., and R. A. Lewis (1980). Marital quality: A review of the seventies. *Marriage and Family Living* 42:825–39.

Spuhler, J. N. (1966). Assortative mating with respect to physical characteristics. *Eugenics Quarterly* 15:128–40.

Strauss, A. (1946). The ideal and chosen mate. *American Journal of Sociology* 52:204–8.

Taylor, D., and I. Altman (1966). Intimacy-scaled stimuli for use in studies of interpersonal relations. *Psychological Reports* 19:729–30.

Ting-Toomey, S. (1983). An analysis of verbal communication patterns in high and low marital adjustment groups. *Human Communication Research* 9:306–19.

Udry, J. R. (1963). Complementarity in mate selection: A perceptual approach. *Marriage and Family Living* 25:281–89.

Valentinsen, B., D. P. Cushman, and L. E. Schroeder (1981, May). *The friend and mate formation processes: Testing a rules theory.* Paper presented at the annual meeting of the International Communication Association, Minneapolis, MN.

Vandenberg, S. G. (1972). Assortative mating, or who marries whom? *Behavior Genetics* 2:127–57.

White, K. M., J. C. Speisman, D. Jackson, S. Bartis, and D. Costos (1986). Intimacy maturity and its correlates in young married couples. *Journal of Personality and Social Psychology* 50:152–62.

Woelfel, J., M. Cody, J. Gillham, and R. Holmes (1980). Basic premises of attitude change theory. *Human Communication Research* 6:153–68.

Woelfel, J., and E. L. Fink (1980). *The measurement of communication processes: Galileo theory and method.* New York: Academic Press.

Wright, P. H. (1969). A model and a technique for studies of friendship. *Journal of Experimental Social Psychology* 5:295–308.
Wright, P. H. (1978). Toward a theory of friendship based on a conception of sclf. *Human Communication Research* 4:196–207.
Wright, P. H. (1982). Men's friendships, women's friendships, and the alleged inferiority of the latter. *Sex Roles* 8:1–20.

3

The Original Investigations

Edited by Anne Maydan Nicotera

An overview of the general theory of the role of communication in interpersonal relationships was provided in Chapters 1 and 2. This chapter summarizes the findings of a set of unpublished seminal investigations that had originally tested and developed the general theory. These investigations appeared publicly in a paper, from which portions of this chapter are excerpted, entitled *The Friend and Mate Formation Processes: Testing a Rules Theory*, by Barry Valentinsen, Donald P. Cushman, and Laura E. Schroeder, presented at the May 1981 meeting of the International Communication Association (ICA) in Minneapolis, Minnesota.

The Seminal Work

Valentinsen, Cushman, and Schroeder base their paper on a critique of the theory posited by Cushman, Valentinsen, and Dietrich (which did not appear in print until 1982, in F. X. Dance, *Human communication theory*, New York: Harper & Row). Though Valentinsen, Cushman, and Schroeder deem the theoretic analysis conceptually rich, they argue that the validity of the claims is suspect, resting primarily on a literature review of empirical research on friendship, marriage and mate selection, the self-concept, information processing, and communication competency. Consequently, they say, before the explanation of friendship and mate formation can be applied with confidence, it must undergo rigorous empirical testing using procedures deduced from their own theoretical framework. They assert that their study is the first stage of an ongoing program of research designed to validate the theoretic work. Their immediate goal is to develop valid and reliable dependent and independent measures of the key constructs. In-depth interviews were conducted with 50 students. On the basis of these interviews, a careful review of the literature, and the general theory, lists of attributes for friendship formation and mate selection were generated. The hypotheses and research questions reflect these attributes. The instruments for the investigations were generated from these lists.

Valentinsen, Cushman, and Schroeder provide a summary of the theory, followed by a rationale for using the Galileo system of analysis (Woelfel & Fink, 1980). They then provide the hypotheses and design for their study, discuss results, and offer conclusions. Given that the theory has been explicated in previous chapters of this volume, it will not be repeated here; nor will the literature review of friendship and mate relationship levels and dimensions. (The reader may wish to refer to Chapter 1 of this volume for the specific rules as stated in the general theory, and to Chapter 2 for a list of empirical propositions generated from the general theory and the literature.) However, because it is the seminal investigation, part of the rationale for methodology is included in this chapter. Finally, the entire study and their discussion of it is provided here. *The following passages are excerpted from the Valentinsen, Cushman, and Schroeder 1981 ICA conference paper. These passages were edited for clarity and parsimony.*

Hypotheses

Friendship. Five hypotheses and one research question are posed for the friendship-formation process:

H1: Best Friend is the level of friendship most closely associated with the attributes of Psychological Support, Trust, Respect, and Authenticity, followed by Good Friend, Casual Friend, and Acquaintance, respectively.

H2: The friendship level of Good Friend is more closely associated with the level of Best Friend than are the levels of Casual Friend and Acquaintance; and the level Casual Friend is more closely associated with the level Good Friend than is the level Acquaintance.

H3: Psychological Support is more closely associated with a Confidant than with a Companion, and Social Support is more closely associated with a Companion than with a Confidant.

H4: *Best Friend is the level of friendship most closely associated with the Real- and Ideal-Self Concepts, followed by the levels Good Friend, Casual Friend, and Acquaintance, respectively.*

H5: *Best Friend is the level of friendship most closely associated with the concepts Companion and Confidant. Followed by Good Friend, Casual Friend and Acquaintance, respectively.*

In developing friendships, individuals perceive a correspondence between certain behavioral and evaluative qualities. If they are matching qualities (or *entry variables*), then such qualities as psychological support and social support will share about the same amount of association with all levels of friendship. If these are developmental qualities (or *intensity variables*), they will be more closely associated with the more intimate levels of friendship than with the less intimate ones.

RQ1: *Are rules for friendship formation qualitative and matching in nature or quantitative and developmental in nature?*

Mate formation. Two hypotheses and one research question are posed for the mate formation process:

H6: *The level Spouse is the level of mates most closely associated with the concept Ideal Mate, followed by the levels Fiancé, Steady Date, and Casual Date, respectively.*

H7: *The level Spouse is the level of mates most closely associated with the concepts Physical Attractiveness, Intelligence, and Sexual Appeal, followed by the levels Fiancé, Steady Date, and Casual Date.*

These hypotheses test the rules that suggest that if an individual perceives another as conforming to his/her ideal for a mate, physically attractive, sexually appealing, and intelligent, that person will initiate communication seen as an attempt to start a mate relationship.

RQ2: *Are these characteristics developmental or categorical in nature?*

The hypotheses connote a developmental relationship. That is, the people we marry will be smarter, prettier, sexier, and more closely correspond to our ideal for a mate than the people we date. If they are categorical, we do not differentiate among levels of mates, at least along these attributes; these concepts would be roughly the same distance from all of the levels (i.e., entry variables as opposed to intensity variables).

The Galileo System as a Measure of Friendship and Mate Formation

The Galileo measurement system (Woelfel & Fink, 1980) is selected to operationalize the concepts discussed thus far for three main reasons. (Because these arguments are summarized in Chapter 2, they are only briefly presented here). The first reason is that Galileo uses spatial analysis to model interrelationships among a set of concepts. A spatial analysis is particularly useful because it allows conventional meanings to be precisely quantified. It has been argued that developing and maintaining relationships is governed and guided by rules, corresponding to standardized ways in which actual and would-be friends communicate. Second, Galileo provides a relatively stable measure of configuration of self–object and object–object relationships. Generally, several studies (Danes & Woelfel, 1975; Gordon, 1976; Gordon & DeLeo, 1976; Gillham & Woelfel, 1977) show that with a sufficiently large sample size, the reliability for the aggregate improves. If there are conventional meanings regarding friendship, they will show up in a theoretically justifiable configuration of concepts. In other words, it is possible to operationalize different types of rules. The third reason is that the Galileo system can measure changes in conventional meanings brought about through communication.

From this discussion, one final research question concerning the stability of the rules is cast. If there are stable rules, the relevant self–object and object–object relations should have low error terms associated with them. This raises the following question:

RQ3: How large can the error terms associated with the object–object and self–object relations be before the conventionality of the rules should be called into question?

No hypotheses or research questions are framed regarding the third reason for selecting Galileo. However, the conclusion suggests future research directions involving the manipulation and measurement of changes in the concepts.

Method

The study is not a complete testing of Cushman and his associates' theory of friendship and mate formation. Because it employs a cross-sectional design, uses only self-report measures, and does not control or manipulate any part of these processes, the results will apply most directly to the theoretical propositions pertaining to establishing one's field of approachables (i.e., perceived self-concept support and the impetus to engage in communication to initiate a friendship or a mate relationship).

Subjects. Eighty-seven subjects were selected from undergraduate classes in communication at the State University of New York at Albany. The students received no class credit or compensation, and their participation was voluntary.

Instrumentation

Friendship. Two versions of the questionnaire were used. The first was administered to 29 subjects and contained the following concepts: Companion, Confidant, Real Self, Ideal Self, Respect, Psychological Support, Best Friend, Good Friend, Acquaintance, Ideal Friend, Intelligent, Trust, Authenticity, Casual Friend, Affection, and Supportiveness. The second version was administered to 58 subjects and contained the following concepts: Best Friend, Steady Date, Relative, Neighbor, Respect, Psychological Support, Financial Support, Social Support, Real Self, Ideal Self, Ideal Date, Real Date, Ideal Friend, Physical Attractiveness, Companion, Confidant, and Actual (real) Friend.

Initial pretest comparisons across independent groups found the instruments to be stable. These are the correlations of the position vectors for the friendship concepts between the two groups: Respect, 0.93; Psychological Support, 0.67; Social Support, 1.22; Real Self, 1.00; Ideal Self, 0.87; Companion, 0.71; Confidant, 0.93. Some of the correlations are greater than 1 because differences between the concepts are calculated across both real and imaginary dimensions of the multidimensional space. The correlations for the dimensions for each matrix ranged between 0.58 and 0.97 for the real dimensions and between 0.12 and 0.86 for the imaginary dimensions.

Mate formation. Thirty-one male and female undergraduate students received a questionnaire containing the following concepts: Real Self, Ideal Self, Companion, Intelligent, Physically Attractive, Sexually Appealing, Steady Date, Fiancé, Spouse, Casual Date, Ideal Mate, Confidant, Respect, Best Friend, Good Friend, Psychological Support, Affection, Supportiveness, and Social Support.

Data Analysis

The data are analyzed using version 5.2 of the Galileo program of metric multidimensional scaling. Mean distance (separation) matrices and coordinate matrices are generated. The configuration of the concepts is examined according to the hypotheses delineated earlier. The data from the first questionnaire version are used to test hypotheses 1, 2, 4, and 5. Hypothesis

Table 3.1
Comparison of Mean Distances Between Friendship Levels

	Acquaintance	*Casual Friend*	*Good Friend*
Best Friend			
Mean	76.310	63.750	35.862
Std. Err.	5.329	6.255	4.694
Good Friend			
Mean	56.724	42.393	
Std. Err.	4.996	5.240	

3 is tested using data collected with the second questionnaire version. The data from the mates questionnaire are used to test hypotheses 6, 7, and 8.

Results: Friendship Formation

Hypothesis 1. The first hypothesis suggests that levels of friendship can be arrayed ordinally with Good Friend perceived to be closer to Best Friend than are Casual Friend and Acquaintance, and Casual Friend perceived to be closer to Good Friend than is the concept Acquaintance. The results shown in Table 3.1 support the hypothesis. The concept Good Friend is closer to the concept Best Friend followed by Casual Friend and Acquaintance. Likewise, the concept Casual Friend is closer to the concept Good Friend than is the concept Acquaintance.

Hypothesis 2. The second hypothesis suggests that Best Friend should be the level of friendship most closely associated with the attributes of Psychological Support, Trust, Respect, and Authenticity, followed by Good Friend, Casual Friend, and Acquaintance, respectively. The results shown in Table 3.2 provide evidence that generally supports the hypothesis.

The evidence is strongest for the concepts Authenticity and Psychological Support. Though the mean distance separating Acquaintance and Psychological Support is not significantly different from the mean distance between Casual Friend and Psychological Support, the trend does hold for the other levels and Psychological Support—that is, distances get progressively smaller. This becomes clear when the difference between any two mean distances is compared to the standard errors for each distance. For example, the difference between Acquaintance and Casual Friend with respect to Psychological Support is 1.793. However, the standard error for both is roughly 5.8.

Table 3.2
Comparisons of Mean Distances Between Friendship Levels and Attributes

	Psychological Support	*Trust*	*Respect*	*Authenticity*
Best Friend				
Mean	8.414	10.483	15.759	11.646
Std. Err.	3.570	5.229	6.079	4.470
Good Friend				
Mean	20.793	18.241	14.300	20.370
Std. Err.	3.879	3.963	4.516	3.566
Casual Friend				
Mean	49.000	57.852	45.600	49.462
Std. Err.	5.804	6.454	6.301	6.909
Acquaintance				
Mean	51.793	69.714	40.100	72.731
Std. Err.	5.793	6.745	5.752	6.803

For the concepts Trust and Respect, evidence for the trend is not as clear-cut as it is for Psychological Support. Again it appears that the difference between Acquaintance and Casual Friend is not significant with respect to Trust and Respect. Likewise, some doubt exists as to whether the difference between Best Friend and Good Friend, with respect to these attributes, is significant. In sum, the results do support the hypothesis that these attributes are more closely associated with higher levels of friendship than with lower levels.

Hypothesis 3. By postulating that the concept Psychological Support is closer to the concept Confidant than to the concept Companion, and that the concept Social Support is closer to the concept Companion than to Confidant, the third hypothesis tests the proposition that providing Psychological Support and Social Support validates the evaluative and behavioral self concepts.

The results presented in Table 3.3 indicate that the hypothesis is supported for Psychological Support and Confidant but not for Social Support and Companion. The concept closest to Psychological Support is Confidant, and Confidant is closer to Psychological Support than to Social Support. However, Companion is not closer to Social Support than is Confidant, and Companion is closer to Psychological Support than to Social Support. Again,

Table 3.3
Comparison of Mean Distances Between Psychological Support, Confidant, Social Support, and Companion

	Psychological Support	*Social Support*
Companion		
Mean	27.672	30.397
Std. Err.	4.212	4.676
Confidant		
Mean	21.193	27.983
Std. Err.	4.758	5.997

it should be mentioned that the relationships among these concepts need to be tempered with the standard errors for each distance. One cannot distinguish among these concepts with much confidence.

Hypothesis 4. This hypothesis claims that the concept Best Friend will be closest to Real and Ideal Self concept, followed by the concepts Good Friend, Casual Friend, and Acquaintance. At issue is the self-concept rule, which holds that one will attempt to initiate a friendship if a positive relationship is perceived between some aspect of one's own real or ideal self-concept and some aspect of another's real self-concept.

Table 3.4 shows that the order of the friendship levels' closeness to Real Self is as hypothesized. For Ideal Self, the ordering is generally in the hypothesized order. Though Casual Friend and Acquaintance are both farther away from Real and Ideal Self than are Good and Best Friend, there is virtually no difference (0.357) between Casual Friend and Acquaintance with respect to their mean distances from the Ideal Self.

Also of interest is the observation that Ideal Self appears to be more closely associated with Acquaintance and Casual Friend than is Real Self. However, both Real and Ideal Self are roughly the same distance from Good and Best Friend. This suggests that in the early stages of the friendship-formation process perceiving a relationship between one's ideal self-concept and the real self-concept of another may be more important in accounting for relational growth than a relationship between one's real self and the real self of another.

The results in Table 3.4 also provide support for the self-concept rule which states that a friendship will grow in relation to the amount of perceived self-concept support. There is a general trend that suggests that the higher the level of friendship the more closely that level is associated with Real or Ideal Self. The strength of this inference rests on the extent to which the distance between a friendship level and Real or Ideal Self reflects perceived self-concept support.

Table 3.4
Comparison of Mean Distances Between Friendship Levels and Real and Ideal Self-Concepts

	Real Self	*Ideal Self*
Best Friend		
Mean	24.700	25.517
Std. Err.	5.788	6.151
% Err.	23.400	24.100
Good Friend		
Mean	38.133	38.069
Std. Err.	5.888	5.717
% Err.	15.400	15.000
Casual Friend		
Mean	61.429	55.536
Std. Err.	6.019	6.011
% Err.	29.200	10.800
Acquaintance		
Mean	73.793	55.893
Std. Err.	6.296	6.780
% Err.	8.500	12.100

Hypothesis 5. This hypothesis posits that the concept Best Friend is the level of friendship closest to the concepts Companion and Confidant, followed by Good Friend, Casual Friend, and Acquaintance, respectively. In essence, this tests the proposition that when initiating or maintaining a friendship one provides messages that are perceived, or interpreted, as supporting another's evaluative or behavioral self-concept.

Table 3.5 clearly shows that the hypothesized relations hold between Confidant and the friendship levels. However, for Companion, the relationship did not hold. It appears that the importance of being a companion levels off once a friendship has been established. Companion is closer to Casual Friend than it is to Acquaintance. However, this relationship does not change when compared to Good Friend, and the distance increases at the Best Friend level. The resulting difference between Good Friend and Best Friend (10.355) is considered unstable because of the errors around each mean distance. Also of interest is that being a companion, or providing support for the behavioral self-concept, appears to be more important at the later stages of friendship.

Research Question 1. Here we are concerned with whether the rules are qualitative and of a matching nature or quantitative and of a developmental nature (i.e., entry or intensity variables). This issue requires more research

Table 3.5
Comparison of Mean Distances Between Friendship Levels and Confidant and Companion

	Confidant	*Companion*
Best Friend		
Mean	10.839	48.355
Std. Err.	3.853	6.937
% Err.	35.500	14.300
Good Friend		
Mean	23.129	38.000
Std. Err.	4.732	6.039
% Err.	6.200	15.200
Casual Friend		
Mean	76.581	38.645
Std. Err.	4.749	5.869
% Err.	6.200	15.200
Acquaintance		
Mean	84.167	59.355
Std. Err.	5.275	6.041
% Err.	6.300	10.200

because a quick look at tables 3.4 and 3.5 reveals that they exhibit both characteristics. For example, from the data in Table 3.5, one could conclude that being a companion is based on an either/or condition. Regardless of the level of friendship, a person either is or is not a companion. With the errors folded in, Companion is roughly equidistant from all friendship levels. On the other hand, Confidant exhibits developmental characteristics. That is, Confidant is closer to the more intimate friendship level concepts than it is to the less intimate ones.

Discussion: Friendship Formation

Two main conclusions can be drawn from this phase of the study. First, the reported findings are consistent with previous research on friendship (e.g., LaGaipa, 1972; Gibbs, 1977; Crawford, 1977). Second, the study supports the theoretical stance assumed by Cushman and his associates. The results confirm the first two hypotheses, which indicate that friends are perceived along dimensions of trust, respect, authenticity, and providing psychological support, and that different levels of friendship are perceived according to varying levels of intimacy. Further, the higher the level of friendship, the greater the amount of intimacy. For example, it is shown that the attributes of trust, respect, authenticity, and psychological support are more closely associated with a best friend than with an acquaintance (i.e, they are intensity variables).

Though the study does support the friendship theory posited by Cushman, Valentinsen, and Dietrich (1982), two refinements in their position appear necessary. First, the data suggest a modification in the self-concept rule specifying that a friendship is likely to be initiated and maintained if one perceives a positive association between some aspect of his/her real or ideal self-concept and the real self-concept of another. At the early stages of friendship—acquaintance and casual friend—the ideal self is more closely associated with friends than is the real self. However, at the levels of good and best friend ideal and real self-concept seem to be about equally associated.

The second aspect of the theory in need of refinement is the rule specifying the nature of the self-concept support one should provide. The theory postulates that support for the evaluative and behavioral self-concept should be conveyed, and that such support is manifested through the roles of a confidant and companion, respectively. Though the data (see Table 3.3) suggest that a confidant is associated with providing psychological support, it is unclear if one can differentiate between a companion and a confidant with respect to social support. Hence, some doubt is cast on the roles of confidant and companion as the means through which evaluative and behavioral self-concept support are manifested. At this point in the development of the theory, the overlap of providing evaluative and behavioral self-concept support is unclear. Future research should be conducted to ascertain their unique qualities. This overlap notwithstanding, Table 3.5 suggests that being a companion is more important than being a confidant at the levels of acquaintance and casual friend, whereas being a confidant is more important than being a companion at the levels of good and best friend.

Results: Mate Formation

Hypothesis 6. It was asserted that an individual will initiate communication toward the formation of a mate relationship if that individual perceives the other's real self to correspond to his/her ideal for a mate. If this is correct, we would expect to find the distances between Ideal Mate and the different levels of mate relationships to be distributed in ascending order from the most intimate to the least intimate. We can see from Table 3.6 that Ideal Mate is closest to the level Spouse followed by Fiancé, Steady Date, and Casual Date. Though the difference between the Fiancé/Ideal Mate mean distances and the Spouse/Ideal Mate distances as well as the difference between the Fiancé/Ideal

Table 3.6
Mean Distances Between Levels of Mates and Ideal Mate, Physical Attractiveness, Sexual Appeal, and Intelligence

	Ideal Mate	*Physical Attractiveness*	*Sexual Appeal*	*Intelligence*
Spouse				
Mean	24.484	24.633	23.387	25.667
Std. Err.	6.505	7.358	9.124	7.161
% Err.	26.500	29.800	39.000	27.800
Fiancé				
Mean	32.767	26.300	21.700	22.267
Std. Err.	9.264	6.639	7.193	7.691
% Err.	29.800	25.200	33.400	28.200
Steady Date				
Mean	42.419	24.677	19.774	28.065
Std. Err.	6.059	5.262	5.018	6.445
% Err.	14.100	24.600	25.300	22.900
Casual Date				
Mean	74.355	30.839	23.871	32.419
Std. Err.	6.374	6.068	5.417	5.588
% Err.	8.500	19.800	22.600	17.200

Mate and the Steady Date/Ideal Mate distances are not significant, the data overall show a trend that supports the hypothesis.

Hypothesis 7. Here we are testing the perceptual rule that, if an individual perceives another as physically attractive, sexually appealing, and intelligent, that person will initiate communication seen as an attempt to start a mate relationship. We would expect a pattern similar to the one for hypothesis 5. That is, these attributes are closer to the more intimate levels than to the less intimate ones.

The data show that one of the attributes varies more than six units over the four mate levels. This implies that, though these attributes are important, we do not expect the occupants of the role to manifest any more of the attributes at one level of intimacy than at another. The research literature suggests that a type of "matching" phenomena may regulate perceptions. That is, the people with whom we find ourselves most likely to engage in a mate relationship are those who are about as physically attractive, sexually appealing, and intelligent as ourselves.

Research question 2. This question queries the nature of the attributes Ideal Mate, Physical Attractiveness, Sexual Appeal, and Intelligence. Table 3.6

reveals that Ideal Mate is developmental and that the others are categorical. As the mate-formation process progresses, then, we are more likely to view the other as more closely conforming to our ideal for a mate. However, for the other attributes it is only necessary that at some point in the initial interaction we recognize that the other person is roughly similar to ourselves with respect to physical attractiveness, sexual appeal, and intelligence.

Discussion: Mate Formation

The results reported in this section are important for two reasons. First, the findings are consistent with other research that documents the importance of being an ideal mate, physically attractive, sexually appealing, and intelligent. Also, the findings generally support Cushman and his associates' perceptual rules regarding the importance of these attributes.

These results do, however, suggest a change in their theory— the idea that physical attractiveness, sex appeal, and intelligence are matching variables for all degrees of intimate relationships (i.e, they are entry variables). In other words, in order to form a mate relationship with either a fiancé or casual date—no matter the degrees of differences in terms of the relationships—intimacy, physical attractiveness, sex appeal, and intelligence have equal amounts of importance in their formation.

Future Directions

The results from the study generally conform to expectations. Inconsistencies that occur provide valuable insights into problems facing the theory. Specifically, Valentinsen, Cushman, and Schroeder's investigations found that friends are perceived along dimensions of trust, respect, authenticity and providers of psychological support, and that different levels of friendship are perceived according to different levels of intimacy. Further, the higher the level of friendship, the greater the amount of intimacy. The data support the theory, but with two recommended changes: (1) support for the ideal self-concept is more important in the earlier stages of friendship; and (2) being a companion is more important than being a confidant in the early stages of friendship, whereas being a confidant is more important than being a companion in the more intimate stages of friendship.

For mates, they found the results inconsistent with the perceptual rules, in that it is important for one to perceive an opposite-sex other as being physically attractive, sexually appealing, intelligent, and as resembling one's ideal for a mate. Likewise, the data suggest changes in the theory, namely that the attributes physical attractiveness, sexual appeal, and intelligence are of a matching (entry) quality, whereas ideal mate is of a developmental nature. Though these findings do not represent a comprehensive testing of the theory, they and the results pertinent to the final research question (concerning the conventionality of the rules) demonstrate the validity of key constructs.

Research question 3. Calculating the percent of error for the object–object and the self–object distances yields an estimate of the relative stability of these relationships. This estimate allows for a rough idea of the degree of conventionality the rules possess. For our purposes, relationships exceeding 20% are problematic. This figure is arbitrary and may be considered too high. However, given the relatively small sample size and the stage of instrument development, it suits current needs. It will serve as a useful reference point for assessing the relative merit of future research options.

Tables 3.4 and 3.5 show that most of the relationships fall within this range. The exceptions are the Best Friend/Real Self, Best Friend/Ideal Self, Best Friend/Confidant, and Casual Friend/Real Self distances. These figures suggest some refinements in the theory but generally support the position taken by Cushman and his associates. One possible explanation for the relative instability of the relationships involving Best Friend is that the perceptual rules operating at the best friend level are more person-specific or creative in nature, whereas for the other levels a wider range of individuals can meet the expectations established by the rules. We would expect this error to drop when specific best friends are used. For mates, nearly all of the distances have errors greater than 20%. However, all errors are less than 30%. Consequently, with larger sample and person-specific measures we would expect these values to drop.

This study clearly provides a useful starting point. However, two methodological changes should be made to allow better prediction and control of the social actions of *particular people* toward actual and would-be friends and mates. First, we need to shift our focus away from treating the role of friend or mate as the primary dependent measure to using the type of social actions particular people display as the dependent measure. After all, we do not enter into relationships with people in general; we develop relationships with specific individuals. Second, we need to show that the rules can be manipulated. If they can, then it would be possible to teach the proper set of cuing and listening skills that would enable people to construct and convey as well as interpret accurate messages initiating a friendship or a mate relationship. Finally, the theory should be tested across time. Cushman and his associates posit a developmental framework; consequently, the factors having an impact on relational development should be placed in proper temporal order.

Summary of Contributions

The seminal investigations conducted by Valentinsen, Cushman, and Schroeder, excerpted above, contribute to the development of the theory in five broad areas. First, their investigations generally validate the theorized friendship and mate relationship levels as distinct with regard to real and ideal self- concepts. Further, they establish the importance of the two self-concept types for the different levels—ideal self being more important in the early stages. Second, they begin to clarify the roles of ideal self, real self, and self-concept support in relationship growth for two different types of interpersonal relationships. *They provide support for Propositions 1 and* 2 (see Chapter 2).

Third, this set of investigations first establishes variables that in later works (e.g., Cushman and Cahn, 1985) are referred to as entry variables—those attributes that mark entry into a mate relationship, but do not vary with relationship growth. These entry variables are Physically Attractive, Sexually Appealing, and Intelligent. *They provide support for Proposition 3* (see Chapter 2).

Fourth, they begin to clarify the roles of confidant and companion. These roles seem to be less clear-cut than was theorized. The amount of statistical error in the data for confidant and companion precludes conclusiveness. Clearly, however, the role of companion is seen as less intimate than the role of confidant. This finding validates our cherished belief that communication (seen here as confiding in a friend) defines intimacy.

Finally, and perhaps most crucial for the subsequent works appearing in this volume, they establish and validate a measuring system for testing the theory. Their careful consideration of error terms and rule stability serves as an example for other scholars. Perhaps more important, the standards for interpretation established in these investigations equip us with a guide by which we may understand, interpret, and critically assess work presented in the subsequent chapters of this book.

References

Crawford, M. (1977). What is a friend? *New Society* 42:116–17.

Cushman, D. P., and D. D. Cahn (1985). *Communication in interpersonal relationships*. Albany: State University of New York Press.

Cushman, D. P., B. Valentinsen, and D. Dietrich, (1982). A rules theory of interpersonal relationships. In F. E. X. Dance (ed.), *Human communication theory* (90–119). New York: Harper and Row.

Dance, F. X. (ed.). (1982). *Human communication theory*. New York: Harper and Row.

Danes, J., and J. Woelfel (1975, May). *An alternative to the "traditional" scaling paradigm in mass communication research: Multidimensional reduction of ratio judgments of separation.* Paper presented at the annual conference of the International Communication Association, Chicago.

Gibbs, S. (1977). *A comparative analysis of friendship functions in six age groups of men and women.* Unpublished doctoral dissertation, Wayne State University, Detroit, MI.

Gillham, J., and J. Woelfel (1977). The Galileo system of measurement: Preliminary evidence for precision, stability, and equivalence to traditional measures. *Human Communication Research* 3:222–34.

Gordon, T. (1976). *Subject abilities to use MDS: Effects of varying the criterion pair.* Unpublished manuscript, Temple University, Philadelphia.

Gordon, T., and H. C. DeLeo (1976, May). *Structural variation in "Galileo" space: Effects of varying the criterion pair in multidimensional scaling.* Paper presented at the annual conference of the International Communication Association, Portland, OR.

LaGaipa, J. J. (1977). Testing a multidimensional approach to friendship. In S. Duck (ed.), *Theory and practice in interpersonal attraction* (249–70). London: Academic Press.

Woelfel J., and E. L. Fink (1980). *The measurement of communication processes: Galileo theory and method.* New York: Academic Press.

Part II

Investigations of Friendship

4

Friendship Formation and Development in Two Cultures: Universal Constructs in the United States and Korea

Charles J. Korn

Introduction

Few interpersonal relationships are more important to most people than their friendships (Campbell, Converse, and Rogers, 1976). Friendship provides much of the substance, continuity, and quality of our lives. Friends bolster and support an individual's most salient attitudes and beliefs (Duck, 1973). They provide reassurance as to one's value as a unique and important individual.

Given the universal importance accorded friendship, recent research suggests friendship is an interpersonal relationship of paramount importance for quality of life and physical health, irrespective of cultural diversity (e.g., Duck, 1983; Lynch, 1977, 1985; Shattuck, 1980). Although interpersonal relationships among individuals vary across cultures, there appear to be readily classifiable dimensions of interpersonal relationships that subsume cultural variability (Fitzpatrick and Indvik, 1986; Indvik and Fitzpatrick, 1986). In short, theoretical structures of interpersonal relationships may exist in all cultures (Gudykunst, 1989). Despite cultural dissimilarities regarding interpersonal relationships, all cultures may have identifiable universals that can be consistently tested in research programs.

Friendship, one type of relational pattern, is a central construct in cross-cultural research on communication in interpersonal relationships.

Despite the universal importance of friendship, research has shown that friendship patterns emerge as culturally specific (e.g., Fitzpatrick and Indvik, 1986; Indvik and Fitzpatrick, 1986). Cultural norms regulate and govern such a relationship (Cushman and Cahn, 1985; Gudykunst, 1983, 1985). The friend relationship is characterized by each culture's own unique set of values and dimensions. Because friendship is culturally specific, researchers have studied the nature of this interpersonal relationship across cultures (Atsumi, 1980; Barnlund, 1975; Gudykunst, 1983, 1985, 1989; Gudykunst and Nishida, 1983; Mochizuki, 1981; Yum, 1983).

According to the literature reviewed in Chapter 2 of this volume, one can clearly discern and delineate the underlying dimensions and levels unique to the friend relationship. Self-concept support, helping behavior, psychological support, trust, respect, and authenticity are important variables necessary for the initiation and maintenance of the friend relationship. For levels of friendship, the following distinctions can be made: Acquaintance, Casual Friend, Good Friend, Best Friend (Valentinsen, Cushman, and Schroeder, 1981; see Chapter 3).

Relational Development and Cross-Cultural Study

The study of friendship is most fruitfully conducted within the context of a developmental model of interpersonal relationships. Over the years a growing number of researchers have adopted such a paradigm (Altman and Taylor, 1973; Bochner, 1978; Knapp, 1978; Knapp and Miller, 1985; Miller, 1978). However, developmental models have been limited in cross-cultural application. Indeed, there has been a relative dearth of studies that examine relational development within the contexts of differing cultures. One such research program has been developed and used in both Eastern and Western cultures (Cushman and Cahn, 1985; Cushman and Nishida, 1984, unpublished study described in Cushman and Cahn, 1985; also Chapter 3, this volume).

Purpose

Independent verification of the friendship levels and dimensions in the United States is a main goal of this research. The primary purpose is to validate the efficacy of Cushman's theoretical structure (Cushman and Cahn, 1985; Cushman, Valentinsen, and Dietrich, 1982) and its accompanying operationalization across cultures (Cushman and Nishida, 1984, unpublished study described in Cushman and Cahn, 1985). Korea was selected as the second culture; the reasons for this selection are addressed below.

Hypotheses and Research Questions

Of the many studies that proffer specific levels and characteristics of friendship development, a good number are culturally specific; they have demonstrated that friendship patterns vary across cultures. However, initial evidence suggests that universal dimensions of interpersonal relations may exist (Gudykunst, 1989). Thus, an instrument that can function in both intra- and intercultural contexts is needed. The use of such an instrument would provide a means of finding such universals. In addition, usage of such an instrument is further warranted for its ability to articulate more specific and richer aspects of the friend relationship within a given culture. In sum, the study of friendship can be advanced both intra- and interculturally.

The United States

The primary goal of conducting this study within the United States is to replicate the findings of Cushman's preliminary research program (summarized in Chapter 3) by posing parallel research questions and stating related hypotheses.

Several studies have delineated the underlying fundamental levels, dimensions, and processual character of friendship (Bailey, Finney, and Bailey, 1974; Crawford, 1977; Gibbs, 1977; Indvik and Fitzpatrick, 1986; LaGaipa, 1977; Parks, 1977; Rose, 1985; also Chapter 3, this volume; for a full discussion of such literature, refer to Chapter 2 of this volume). Based upon the empirical research conducted in the field and consistent with Cushman's program of study (see Chapter 3), a list of dimensions characteristic of the friend relationship in the United States was generated: psychological support, trust, respect, and authenticity. These characteristics are expected to increase in intensity as the relationship develops.

Based upon the common friendship designations gleaned from theory and research, the following hypothesis is offered:

H1: ***Acquaintance, Casual Friend, Good Friend,*** *and* ***Best Friend*** *represent stable and significantly different semantic markers for increasing degrees or levels of friendship among the American sample.*

As we have stated regarding the dimensions of friendship and the relationship of these characteristics to the degrees of friendship previously delineated, the following hypothesis is offered:

H2: ***Psychological Support, Trust, Respect,*** *and* ***Authenticity*** *are intensity variables of the friend relationship in the U.S. that* *increase in intensity with increasing degrees of intimacy as the relationship develops.*

Korea

A Korean sample provides a rich cross-cultural comparison yielding both practical and theoretical implications. Three reasons motivated the selection of Korea as a divergent culture as compared to the U.S. First, Korean friendship has received preliminary specification and investigation (e.g., Gudykunst, Yang, and Nishida, 1985, 1986; Samovar, Porter, and Jain, 1981), thereby allowing a basis for building strong measures of comparison. Second, Korea offers significant variance in respondents' attributes and differs along most major dimensions of cultural variability (Hall, 1976; Hofstede, 1980). Korean culture is radically divergent from American culture. Hall's (1976) high/low context continuum offers a particularly useful means of illustrating the differences between these two diametrically opposed cultures. Korean culture is high-context; American culture is low-context. Third, Korea has maintained its rich Eastern heritage and traditions; it has not become as Westernized as other Eastern cultures such as Japan (Samovar et al., 1981). A comparison between an Occidental culture and an Asian culture allows for a rich perspective from which to discern and assert theoretical universals. (See Chapter 5 for a full discussion of differences between the United States and Korea).

Following the procedure of Cushman and Nishida (1984, unpublished study described in Cushman and Cahn, 1985), 40 students were interviewed in Korea in their native language. Based upon these interviews, a questionnaire was developed that included four friendship levels and seven dimensions. All concepts and items from the Korean questionnaire appearing hereafter are back-translations into English. In the interviews, the following level designations were most commonly made: Acquaintance, Ordinary Friend, Close Friend, and Best Friend. Based upon the theoretical and empirical base, the following hypothesis is offered:

H3: ***Acquaintance, Ordinary Friend, Close Friend,*** *and* ***Best Friend*** *represent stable and significantly different semantic markers for increasing levels of friendship among the Korean sample.*

In the interviews, the following dimensions of friendship were most common: Congeniality, Sympathy, Unselfishness, Responsibility, Honesty, Generosity, and Intelligence. Based upon the operation of friendship dimensions in the United States, the following parallel hypothesis is offered:

H4: ***Congeniality, Sympathy, Unselfishness, Responsibility, Honesty, Generosity,*** *and* ***Intelligence*** *are intensity variables of the friend* *relationship in Korea that increase in intensity with increasing degrees of intimacy as the relationship develops.*

Social Penetration

Social penetration theory is one of the most promising of many theories to address the role of communication in the development of interpersonal relationships. (See Chapter 5 for a full discussion of the theory.) In an attempt to extend the theory into the exploration of the role of communication in the friend relationship, the following exploratory research question is examined. Penetration is defined as the degree, depth, and breadth of intimacy in a given relationship (following Altman and Taylor, 1973; and Taylor and Altman, 1966).

RQ: *Do the American and Korean samples discuss specific, identifiable, and stable topics at differing levels of penetration in the friend relationship?*

Method

Sample

United States. The United States sample was drawn from undergraduate students at a moderate-sized northeastern university. The sample included 53 respondents (20 males and 33 females), with an average age of 20.8 years. Among the American respondents, 88.5% had completed at least one year of college. The average length of time respondents had known their best friend was 7.7 years. Participation was voluntary, with no compensation provided.

Korea. The Korean sample was drawn from undergraduate students studying at Yonsei University in Seoul. The sample included 40 subjects (14 males, 23 females, and 3 individuals who did not specify their sex), with an average age of 21.3 years. Among the Korean respondents, 97.4% had completed at least one year of college. The average length of time respondents had known their best friend was 4.6 years. The subjects were students in the social sciences who volunteered to participate in the research project.

A comparison of the two samples reveals no statistically significant differences regarding age, sex, year in school, and other demographic variables. Despite the use of nonrandom samples of convenience, the samples are relatively comparable and equivalent (Brislin and Baumgardner, 1971).

Measurement of Variables

Levels and dimensions. All subjects completed a survey packet containing measures of friendship levels, dimensions, penetration analysis, and demographic variables. The Korean subjects completed a questionnaire in their native language that was specifically developed to ascertain the levels, characteristics, and topics particular to the friendship relationship in Korea. Each subject independently responded to the questionnaire using his or her own best friend, at the time of administration of the survey, as a reference person. Subjects were asked to keep this individual in mind while answering the questions.

This study utilizes the measures of friendship developed by Cushman and his associates (see Chapter 3). Such a measure enables one to discern and identify the levels and attributes particular to each culture. The friendship levels identified earlier were paired with friendship dimensions in a Galileo format such that respondents answered 120 paired comparisons. The American subjects were administered the following concepts: Real Self, Ideal Self, Respect, Psychological Support, Trust, Authenticity, Acquaintance, Casual Friend, Good Friend, Best Friend, and Ideal Friend. The Korean subjects were administered the following concepts: Real Self, Ideal Self, Congeniality, Sympathy, Unselfishness, Responsibility, Honesty, Generosity, Intelligence, Acquaintance, Ordinary Friend, Good Friend, Best Friend, and Ideal Friend. The data were analyzed using version 5.2 of the Galileo Program of Metric-Multi-Dimensional Scaling.

Interpersonal penetration. Measurement of intracultural interpersonal penetration is based upon the work of Altman and Taylor (1973), Taylor and Altman (1966), Gudykunst (1985), and Gudykunst and Nishida (1983). For this study, 30 items were randomly selected from an original pool of 63 items (Altman and Taylor, 1973). Subjects rated both the frequency and the intimacy with which they discussed each item in their relationship with a close friend. The respondents were instructed to rate each topic on a 6-point scale, where 0 = not at all and 6 = all the time. Regarding intimacy, subjects rated each item on another 6-point scale, where 0 = superficial depth and 6 = very intimate depth.

Topical categories. The scale includes 10 dimensions, each composed of 3 items. The following dimensions of interpersonal penetration are used in this study: (1) Relationships with Others, or the views and opinions as to dealing with others, being with others, being with friends, and being in social situations; (2) Parental Family, or the respondents' parental family, including their beliefs, opinions, and practices; (3) Love, Dating, Sex, or the attitudes toward, opinions of, and actual experiences in love, dating, and sex; (4) Physical Condition and Attractiveness, or what the respondent likes and dislikes about his/her appearance, attitudes about his/her physical state, and facts about physical characteristics; (5) School–Work, or past and present school and work experiences, including facts, feelings, and relationships in these settings; (6) Money and Property, or attitudes, opinions, practices concerning money and financial matters; (7) Own Marriage and Family, or the type of person the respondent wants to marry, type of relationship with spouse, and how children should be raised; (8) Emotions and Feelings, (e.g., the respondents' embarrassment, fears); (9) Personal Attitudes, Values, and Self-Evaluation, or the general attitudes and beliefs respondents hold about life, living, and a code of ethics; and (10) Interests, Hobbies, and Habits. Because the investigation of social penetration is exploratory, each item within the 10 dimensions is analyzed separately to achieve the maximum possible amount of information. For both samples, the overall social penetration index for each item was computed following Altman and Taylor's (1973) procedure.

Data Analysis

Friendship levels and dimensions. Differences between the friendship levels in hypotheses 1 and 3 are operationalized as differences in their mean distances from Real Self and Ideal Self, consistent with the theoretical structure. The levels are considered to be different from one another for a given reference point (Real or Ideal Self) if their mean distances in terms of those reference points plus or minus the standard error differ.

The intensities of friendship dimensions in hypotheses 2 and 4 are operationalized by examining their closeness to the friendship levels, comparing mean distances of levels using each dimension in turn as point of reference. The same procedure for the levels in each culture is used to assess whether the dimensions mark different levels of friendship and become more intense as the relationship increases in intimacy.

Penetration. For the social penetration analysis, t-tests were used to assess the differences between the American and Korean samples on each of the penetration items. The number of t-tests increases the chance of Type I error. However, because the question is exploratory in nature, an alpha level of 0.05 was maintained for the significance of each test. This allows the gain of maximum information for future testing.

Table 4.1
American Sample: Comparison of Mean Distances Between Friendship Level and Real and Ideal Self

	Acquaintance	*Casual Friend*	*Good Friend*	*Best Friend*	*Ideal Friend*
Real Self					
Mean	86.058	75.792	42.827	32.226	42.226
Std. Err.	9.350	11.076	6.348	9.896	8.574
Std. Dev.	67.427	80.636	45.773	72.043	62.416
Ideal Self					
Mean	73.113	69.151	36.491	27.849	18.887
Std. Err.	9.235	13.003	6.428	6.814	3.861
Std. Dev.	67.234	94.664	46.798	49.609	28.110

Results

Hypothesis 1

Acquaintance, Casual Friend, Good Friend, and Best Friend represent stable and significantly different semantic markers for increasing degrees or levels of friendship among the American sample.

Table 4.1 contains the means, standard deviations, and standard errors of four semantic levels of friendship (and the concept Ideal Friend) in their distance from the concepts Real Self and Ideal Self. The results shown in Table 4.1 provide strong support for the hypothesis. The friendship level Best Friend was closest to the concepts Real Self and Ideal Self, followed by Good Friend, Casual Friend, and Acquaintance. Moreover, the relatively small standard error around the mean distance of these semantic markers from the Real Self demonstrates a fairly uniform or standard interpretation of these relationships within the American sample. The standard error of the mean distance between Casual Friend and Real Self, 11.076, is fairly large and may be attributed to extreme values of 490, 300, and 150. The distance between Casual Friend and Ideal Self also has a large standard error, which may be attributed to extreme values of 500, 200, and 150—each reported twice. Also, the relatively small sample (N = 53) may have contributed to the fairly large standard deviation in the sample distribution. Casual Friend and Acquaintance do not differentiate from each other as much as they do from more intimate levels of friendship.

Table 4.2
American Sample: Comparison of Mean Distances Between Friendship Levels and Attributes

	Acquaintance	*Casual Friend*	*Good Friend*	*Best Friend*
Psychological Support				
Mean	77.075	57.519	38.226	12.509
Std. Err.	18.824	5.382	13.156	2.341
Std. Dev.	137.041	38.808	95.774	17.046
Trust				
Mean	79.170	57.698	23.491	9.547
Std. Err.	7.810	6.068	3.954	3.277
Std. Dev.	56.855	44.179	28.787	23.857
Respect				
Mean	51.472	53.642	18.981	14.943
Std. Err.	5.344	6.100	3.347	2.983
Std. Dev.	38.908	44.411	24.369	21.716
Authenticity				
Mean	82.717	59.415	32.075	15.314
Std. Err.	11.238	6.195	4.361	4.453
Std. Dev.	81.816	45.102	31.751	31.804

Hypothesis 2

Psychological Support, Trust, Respect, and Authenticity are defining characteristics of the friend relationship in the United States that increase in intensity with increasing degrees of intimacy as the relationship develops.

Table 4.2 contains the means, standard deviations, and standard errors of the distances between the friendship levels and dimensions. These results support the hypothesis. The friendship attributes were more closely associated with higher levels of friendship. Best Friend is closest to these concepts, followed by Good Friend, Close Friend, and Acquaintance, respectively. The standard errors are also relatively small, showing stability in the data.

Exceptions to this stability can be noted for the standard error for Psychological Support and Good Friend, due to an extreme value of 700. The distribution is also skewed for the distance between Psychological Support and Acquaintance; for this distance, extreme values of 1,000, 200, and 120 occurred in the data. Finally, the distribution is skewed for the distance between Authenticity and Acquaintance, due to extreme values of 500, 300, 210, and 200.

Table 4.3
Korean Sample: Comparison of Mean Distances Between Friendship Level and Real and Ideal Self

	Acquaintance	*Ordinary Friend*	*Good Friend*	*Best Friend*	*Ideal Friend*
Real Self					
Mean	86.625	64.250	45.550	32.450	36.538
Std. Err.	3.370	3.809	6.308	10.120	6.800
Std. Dev.	21.104	24.087	39.897	64.002	42.469
Ideal Self					
Mean	64.625	50.513	39.250	26.450	24.825
Std. Err.	3.770	3.370	5.260	6.950	5.160
Std. Dev.	23.896	21.082	32.273	43.954	32.664

Hypothesis 3

Acquaintance, Ordinary Friend, Close Friend, and Best Friend represent stable and significantly different semantic markers for increasing levels of friendship among the Korean sample.

Table 4.3 contains the means, standard deviations, and standard errors of the four semantic levels of friendship (and the concept Ideal Friend) in their distance from the concepts Real Self and Ideal Self. The results provide support for the hypothesis. The distances decrease as the levels increase in intimacy. Close Friend and Best Friend overlap slightly for Real Self; there is a greater degree of instability for Best Friend/Real Self. However, both Real and Ideal Self distances reveal a theoretically uniform progression of these friendship levels for the Korean sample. Given the relatively small sample ($N = 40$), the overall stability in the data is notable.

Hypothesis 4

Congeniality, Sympathy, Unselfishness, Responsibility, Honesty, Generosity, and Intelligence are defining characteristics of the friend relationship in Korea that increase in intensity with increasing degrees of intimacy as the relationship develops.

Table 4.4 contains the mean distances, standard deviations, and standard errors for the levels and attributes of friendship for the Korean sample. These results generally support the hypothesis. Best Friend is closest to the

Table 4.4
Korean Sample: Comparison of Mean Distances Between Friendship Levels and Attributes

	Acquaintance	*Ordinary Friend*	*Close Friend*	*Best Friend*
Congenial				
Mean	62.600	48.450	33.625	27.700
Std. Err.	8.230	5.702	4.380	5.012
Std. Dev.	52.049	36.060	27.700	31.698
Sympathy				
Mean	68.375	63.800	40.325	36.425
Std. Err.	12.159	12.305	5.422	5.884
Std. Dev.	76.898	77.823	34.293	37.212
Unselfish				
Mean	61.325	55.700	43.875	34.875
Std. Err.	7.689	7.335	4.312	4.596
Std. Dev.	48.631	46.393	27.272	29.069
Responsible				
Mean	58.525	50.744	47.950	36.775
Std. Err.	5.702	5.153	6.629	6.408
Std. Dev.	36.065	32.181	41.924	40.528
Honesty				
Mean	60.975	50.650	50.325	37.075
Std. Err.	5.656	4.943	7.994	6.388
Std. Dev.	35.772	31.265	50.557	40.401
Generous				
Mean	70.175	53.975	40.225	37.250
Std. Err.	12.338	6.115	4.021	4.952
Std. Dev.	78.098	38.675	25.429	31.319
Intelligent				
Mean	65.675	48.300	52.200	42.000
Std. Err.	9.644	4.086	6.437	4.735
Std. Dev.	60.996	25.844	40.712	29.950

attributes, followed by Close Friend, Ordinary Friend, and Acquaintance, respectively. Again, extreme values in the data can account for some instability: Ordinary Friend/Sympathy, 440, 300, and 120; Acquaintance/Sympathy, 500 and 150; Acquaintance/Generous, 500 and 200.

Table 4.5
United States and Korean Social Penetration Scores and Tests of Significant Differences for Topical Categories

		United States Social Penetration Index	*Korean Social Penetration Index*	*t* =
1.	Whether or not you have discouraged your friend	4.88	4.93	–0.117
2.	Whether or not you like something new or out of the ordinary	9.20	10.00	–0.618
3.	Your feeling in case your parents were separated or divorced	6.10	3.41	1.916*
4.	The importance of money in happiness	7.62	5.42	2.099*
5.	How firmly you defend your opinion against an objection	8.82	6.35	2.344**
6.	How warm and peaceful your home is compared to others	8.00	7.78	0.185
7.	How much you feel yourself free from the family rules	6.65	9.16	–1.824*
8.	Your opinion on asking for a loan from a bank	3.49	1.50	2.204*
9.	What you don't feel like talking about to others	9.31	6.92	1.902*
10.	Your opinion on sexual morality	11.27	8.78	1.817*
11.	Whether or not other people are prerequisite for your happiness	9.08	9.48	–.297
12.	Your opinion on how long it would be better for you to have premarital relations with your going-to-be spouse	7.48	7.41	0
13.	Whether or not you would practice birth control if you get married (or are married)	8.36	4.88	2.258*
14.	Whether or not it would be permissible to tell a lie	6.39	7.76	–1.086
15.	Your strong belief on the importance of education	8.12	11.92	–2.848*
16.	How important it is to take in proper nutrition for your health	8.15	7.24	0.610

(Continued)

Table 4.5 Continued

		United States Social Penetration Index	Korean Social Penetration Index	t =
17.	When you feel self-esteem with your own accomplishment in school, work, or society	10.76	9.64	0.810
18.	When your feel like criticizing your teachers or superiors	8.59	7.30	0.830
19.	Your feeling or thought about your outward appearance	9.65	8.93	0.468
20.	What is the amount in your savings account	5.73	4.09	1.288
21.	When you feel lonely	8.74	9.38	–0.444
22.	Whether or not you want to wander about the nation or to live another place	7.06	7.58	–0.344
23.	Your opinion on the extent of premarital sexual relations	10.24	7.25	2.026*
24.	Ideal type of the opposite sex with whom you would like to have relations before marriage	10.53	9.06	1.065
25.	An event or situation which might perplex you	9.24	7.70	1.199
26.	An episode or a tale of bravery that you had experienced	12.15	6.16	4.257***
27.	Chronic anxiety about the health problems of your own	5.61	4.13	1.206
28.	Whether or not it matters that you get married to non–virgin	5.61	5.78	–0.064
29.	When you had been confronted with a terror	6.58	6.58	0
30.	Your feeling or thought about duty or responsibility	8.70	12.55	–2.827**

*$p < .05$; **$p < .01$; ***$p < .001$

Note: Scale items are back-translated from the Korean survey for the purposes of interpretation.

Research Question

Do the American and Korean samples discuss specific, identifiable, and stable topics at differing levels of penetration in the friend relationship?

Table 4.5 presents the social penetration indices for the American and Korean samples and the t-tests between them. There are significant differences for the following items: feelings regarding separated or divorced parents; the importance of money for happiness; defending one's opinion against objection; requesting a loan from a bank; feelings when talking to others; opinions regarding sexual morality; if one were married, the likelihood of practicing some form of birth control; opinion regarding the extent of premarital sexual relations; the recounting of an episode, tale, or narrative personally experienced; how free one feels from family rules and structure; belief about the importance of education; feelings and thoughts about duty and responsibility.

American respondents achieved greatest interpersonal penetration vis-à-vis the breadth and depth of the following items: opinion regarding sexual morality (11.27); feeling of self-esteem derived from accomplishments in school, work, or society (10.76); opinion regarding the extent of premarital sexual relations (10.24); ideal type of person with whom one would desire to have sexual relations with prior to marriage (10.53); an episode or tale one has experienced (12.15); and feelings or thoughts about one's outward appearance (9.65).

Korean respondents obtained the highest social penetration scores vis-à-vis the following items: one's preference for something new or out of the ordinary (10.0); one's belief regarding the importance of education (11.92); one's feeling of self-esteem gained from school, work, or societal accomplishments (9.64); and one's feelings and thoughts about duty or responsibility (12.55).

Conclusions

All hypotheses were generally supported. These results replicate the results of the seminal study (Chapter 3) in the United States. More importantly, these results provide evidence that the general theory can be applied cross-culturally. The examination of the research question revealed that categories of conversation for friends differ between the cultures. Based on these results, it is suggested that future research attention be devoted to topics shown to differentiate between the two cultures. Such work could help determine specific patterns of interaction regarding these topical categories and the extent to which social penetration is achieved in the friend relationship.

Specifically, the results for the research question revealed that respondents from both Korea and the United States have specific, identifiable, and stable topics that they discuss. T-tests revealed that 12 topical categories were significantly different between the two samples at or beyond the 0.05 level. These results suggest that American respondents achieve higher overall social penetration than Korean respondents on the following topical categories: feelings regarding separated or divorced parents; money; defending one's own opinion; loans; talking to others; sexual morality; practicing birth control; the extent of premarital sexual activities; and episodes of bravery. The Korean respondents achieve higher overall social penetration than American respondents on family rules, the importance of education, and responsibility. Thus, it is suggested that further research attention be devoted to these salient topics. Such work can help determine specific patterns of interaction regarding these topical categories and the extent to which social penetration is achieved vis-à-vis the friend relationship.

Implications

The social penetration profile as conducted within this study offers a unique and substantial contribution to the study of communication in both cross-cultural and intracultural friend relationships. Findings indicate that topics of discussion may be distinguished from one another in the friend relationship between and perhaps within both cultures. Thus, interpersonal penetration indices specific to the friend relationship in Eastern and Western cultures are deemed worthy of future research attention. One possible avenue of study could compare social penetration profiles at differing levels of friendship, using the friendship levels specified herein.

Additionally, the social penetration analysis conducted within this study supports the application of social penetration theory in cross-cultural contexts. Such an analysis may have broader and exceedingly more profound results when applied to the diverse ethnic groups represented within the United States.

Results for both samples lend strong support to the theoretical, conceptual, and methodological structure of Cushman's general theory. Indeed, the American sample yielded further support for the previously validated levels and dimensions. This study also provides support for the initial conceptualization of friendship-formation processes in Korean culture as specified by theory developed and validated in the United States.

This study lends credence and empirical support to Gudykunst's (1989) assertion that universal relational dimensions across cultures are readily discernable. As Gudykunst suggests, the implications of such findings should not be underemphasized. The following reasons suggest the possible importance of such empirical findings. First, such findings imply that the dimensions of social relations are discernible, irrespective of cultural differences.

Second, this study underlines the importance of treating culture as a theoretical variable and the need to conduct further cross-cultural research. Third, many practical implications are manifest that can readily be applied to cross-cultural relationships, at the personal or social level and at the business or governmental level. Knowledge of specific topical categories common to everyday parlance within intra- and intercultural friendships could facilitate the maintenance of such intercultural relationships.

References

Altman, I., and D. Taylor (1973). *Social penetration: The development of interpersonal relationships*. New York: Holt, Rinehart and Winston.

Atsumi, R. (1980). Patterns of personal relationships. *Social Analysis* 5:63–78.

Bailey, R. C., P. Finney, and K. G. Bailey (1974). Level of self-acceptance and perceived intelligence in self and friend. *Journal of Genetic Psychology* 124:61–67.

Barnlund, D. (1975). *Public and private self in Japan and the United States: Communicative styles in two cultures*. Forest Grove, IL: International Scholarly Book Services.

Bochner, A. (1978). On taking ourselves seriously: An analysis of some persistent problems and promising directions in interpersonal research. *Human Communication Research*, 4:179–90.

Brislin, R. W., and S. Baumgardner (1971). Non-random sampling of individuals in cross-cultural research. *Journal of Cross-Cultural Psychology* 2:397–400.

Campbell, A., P. E. Converse, and W. L. Rogers (1976). *The quality of American life*. New York: Russell Sage Foundation.

Crawford, M. (1977). What is a friend? *New Society* 42:116–17.

Cushman, D., and D. Cahn (1985). *Communication in interpersonal relationships*. Albany, NY: State University of New York Press.

Cushman, D. P., and T. Nishida (1984). *Mate selection in the United States and Japan*. Unpublished manuscript, State University of New York at Albany.

Cushman, D. P., B. Valentinsen, and D. Dietrich (1982). A rules theory of interpersonal relationships. In F. E. X. Dance (ed.), *Human communication theory* (90–119). New York: Harper and Row.

Duck, S. (1973). Similarity and perceived similarity of personal constructs as influencers of friendship choice. *British Journal of Social and Clinical Psychology* 12:1–6.

Duck, S. (1983). *Friends for life: The psychology of close relationships*. New York: St. Martin's.

Fitzpatrick. M. A., and J. Indvik (1986). On alternative conceptions of relational communication. *Communication Quarterly* 34:19–23.

Gibbs, S. (1977). *A comparative analysis of friendship functions in six age groups of men and women.* Unpublished dissertation, Wayne State University, Detroit, MI.

Gudykunst, W. B. (1983). Uncertainty reduction and predictability of behavior in low- and high-context cultures: An exploratory study. *Communication Quarterly* 31:49–55.

Gudykunst, W. B. (1985). An exploratory comparison of close intracultural and intercultural friendships. *Communication Quarterly* 33:270–83.

Gudykunst, W. B. (1989). Culture and the development of interpersonal relationships. In J. A. Anderson (ed.), *Communication yearbook 12* (315–54). Newbury Park, CA: Sage.

Gudykunst, W. B., and T. Nishida (1983). Social penetration in Japanese and American close friendships. In R. N. Bostrom (ed.), *Communication yearbook 7* (592–610). Beverly Hills, CA: Sage.

Gudykunst, W. B., S. M. Yang, and T. Nishida (1985). A cross-cultural test of uncertainty reduction theory: Comparisons of acquaintances, friends, and dating relationships in Japan, Korea, and the United States. *Human Communication Research* 11:407–54.

Gudykunst, W. B., S. M. Yang, and T. Nishida (1986, May). *Self-consciousness and self-monitoring in Japan, Korea, and the United States.* Paper presented at the annual meeting of the International Communication Association, Chicago, IL.

Hall, E. (1976). *Beyond culture.* New York: Doubleday.

Hofstede, G. (1980). *Culture's consequences: International differences in work-related values.* Beverly Hills, CA: Sage.

Indvik, J., and M. A. Fitzpatrick (1986). Perceptions of inclusion, affiliation, and control in five interpersonal relationships. *Communication Quarterly* 34:1–13.

Knapp, M. (1978). *Social intercourse: From greeting to goodbye.* Boston: Allyn and Bacon.

Knapp, M., and G. R. Miller (eds.). (1985). *Handbook of interpersonal communication.* Beverly Hills, CA: Sage.

LaGaipa, J. J. (1977). Testing a multidimensional approach to friendship. In S. Duck (ed.), *Theory and practice in interpersonal attraction* (249–70). London: Academic Press.

Lynch, J. J. (1977). *The broken heart: The medical consequences of loneliness.* New York: Basic Books.

Lynch, J. J. (1985). *The language of the heart: The body's response to human dialogue.* New York: Basic Books.

Miller, G. R. (1978). The current status of theory and research in interpersonal communication. *Human Communication Research* 4:164–77.

Mochizuki, T. (1981). Changing patterns of mate selection. *Journal of Comparative Family Studies* 12:318–28.

Parks, M. R. (1977, December). *Communication correlates of perceived friendship development.* Paper presented at the annual conference of the Speech Communication Association, Washington, DC.

Rose, S. (1985). Same- and cross-sex friendships and the psychology of homosociality. *Sex Roles* 12:63–74.

Samovar, L., R. Porter, and N. Jain (1981). *Understanding intercultural communication.* Belmont, CA: Wordsworth.

Shattuck, R. (1980). *The forbidden experiment: The story of the Wild Boy of Aveyron.* New York: Farrar, Straus, and Giroux.

Taylor, D., and I. Altman (1966). Intimacy-scaled stimuli for use in studies of interpersonal relations. *Psychological Reports* 19:729–30.

Valentinsen, B., D. P. Cushman, and L. E. Schroeder (1981, May). *The friend and mate formation processes: Testing a rules theory.* Paper presented at the annual meeting of the International Communication Association, Minneapolis, MN.

Yum, J. O. (1983). Social network patterns of five ethnic groups in Hawaii. In R. N. Bostrom (ed.), *Communication yearbook 7* (574–91). Beverly Hills, CA: Sage.

5

Interpersonal Perceptions of Same-Sex and Opposite-Sex Friendships in the United States and Korea

Changmo Bahk

Introduction and Rationale

The issue of why people establish, maintain, and dissolve friend relationships has been gaining much attention from a number of studies. There are two prominent approaches to the explanation of friendship formation and dissolution: social exchange theory and self-concept support theory. (See also Chapter 2 of this volume.) Social exchange theory, developed by social psychologists (see Blau, 1967; Homans, 1961; Thibaut and Kelley, 1959), explains friendships in terms of costs and rewards. Thibaut and Kelley (1959) assert that experiencing "good" outcomes in initial interactions leads to the expectation of those outcomes in the future and, as a result, motivates further interactions. According to social exchange theory, individuals calculate the ratio of rewards to costs in a friend relationship with another person and decide whether to continue the relationship or not on the basis of this calculation. The greater the "profit," that is, the amount of rewards minus costs, the more likely the development and continuation of the friend relationship. In a similar manner, the greater the costs for the friendship compared to the benefits, the more likely the termination of the relationship. Thus, an important area of research in social exchange theory centers on identifying the rewards and costs individuals take into account in their friend relationships (for example, Wright, 1969). Cushman and his associates explain the rewards of friend relationships in terms of mutual self-concept support.

Cushman and Cahn's (1985) self-concept support theory (see Chapters 1 through 3 of this volume) considers friendship to be a form or pattern of interpersonal communication that provides reciprocal support for the self-concepts of the persons involved in a dyadic relationship. Complementary to the notion of mutual self-concept support, Cushman and Cahn (1985) provide a concept of "perceived understanding," or "feeling understood," for understanding friend relationships. Perceived understanding, or feeling understood, is considered to be necessary for perceiving the support of one's self-concept.

Perceived understanding refers to the degree to which person A perceives, or feels, person B (a friend) accurately perceives person A's feelings, thoughts, values, and behavior. Regarding the relationship of perceived understanding to self-concept, Cahn (1985) states that perceived understanding "alerts" the self-concept to correct an individual's behavior when that behavior leads the self-concept astray from the "preferred" self-concept. Perceived understanding is viewed as playing a more important role in the maintenance than in the initiation of friend relationships.

Cushman and Cahn (1985) emphasize that communication between friendship partners functions to provide consensus about their self-concepts. By means of communication, friends not only validate their self–object relationships in the culture they belong to, but also provide each other with the information of their unique self–object relationships for mutual self-concept support. The development of a friendship is characterized by gradual disclosures of self-concepts of both friendship partners. Forgas (1985) asserts that a friendship is deepened by one's telling a friend about oneself and finding out about the friend. Drawn from Altman and Taylor's (1973) social penetration theory, the concept of "conversational penetration," or "interpersonal penetration," is used to represent the breadth and depth of communication between two friendship partners.

The present study intends to explicate Cushman and his associates' conceptualizations on friendship relations and to test them across same-sex and opposite-sex friendships, across males and females, and across North American and East Asian cultures represented by the United States and Korea. The study presents recapitulations of basic concepts constituting their friendship theory—self-concept similarity and accuracy, perceived understanding and liking, and conversational penetration—and reviews the studies related to friendship variations by friendship type, gender, and culture.

Background Literature

Self-Concept Similarity and Accuracy

The unique way in which persons conceive of themselves can be referred to as "self-concept." Symbolic interactionists Cooley (1902) and Mead (1934) define self-concept as the information an individual has regarding his/her relationship to objects, people, and places. In a broad sense, an individual's self-concept is made up of his/her identity, personality, attitudes and values, and behavioral rules and patterns.

In the field of friendship studies, a handful of research deals with the role of self-concept in the formation and maintenance of friend relationships. It is generally found that people tend to have friend relationships with those who they perceive have self-concepts similar to theirs. McKenna, Hofstaetter, and O'Connor (1955) studied 90 female college students, correlating subjects' "ideal" or preferred self-concepts and their friends' self-concepts. They found that the congruence of the self-concepts of subjects and their friends was relatively high. Kipnis (1961) studied the changes of self-concepts from a sample of 87 male college freshmen living in a dormitory. The results showed that subjects perceived fewer differences between themselves and their best friends than between themselves and "a least liked roommate," and that subjects who perceived the self-concepts of their best friends as different from theirs had changed their self-concepts during a six-week interval so that they perceived smaller differences at the end than at the beginning of the experiment.

Some scholars have distinguished various dimensions of self-concept perception and the role of these in friend relationships (e.g., Bailey, Finney, and Helm, 1975; Thompson and Nishimura, 1952). Bailey, et al. (1975) suggest three viewpoints for studying the development of friend relationships: (a) perceptions of self-concept, (b) perceptions of interpersonal similarity, and (c) perceptions of self-concept support. Based on these distinctions, they examine the effects on friendship duration of perceived and actual similarities between the self-concepts of subjects and their same-sex friends. Confirmed by the results of Bailey, DiGiacomo, and Zinser's (1976) follow-up research, they conclude that "an individual may tend to seek out those whom he perceives as sharing his own self-view, thus providing him with consensual validation as well as cognitive consistency" (Bailey et al., 1975, p. 242).

Cushman and his associates systematize the concept of self-concept in relation to the processes of the formation, maintenance, and deterioration of friend relationships (see Chapters 1 and 2). The perception of similarities in the scope, depth, and configuration of self-concept between two interactants leads to "positive self-concept support" (Cushman and Cahn, 1985). Self-concept support is also viewed as closely related to a person's role-taking ability, which makes possible his/her accurate perception of the other's self-concept—that is, "self-concept accuracy" (Cushman and Cahn, 1985). Mead (1934) states that role-taking is the central mechanism by which one comes to understand one's own self-concept and the characteristics in others enabling him/her to provide self-concept support for similar characteristics in others (Cahn, 1987). Effective self-concept support is most probable when a person accurately perceives the qualities or traits characterizing the other person's self–object relationship (Cahn, 1987). An individual's role-taking ability determines not only the accuracy of his/her perception of other people's self-concepts, but also the effectiveness of his/her support of the self-concepts, which play significant roles in the formation and maintenance of friend relationships.

Perceived Understanding and Liking

The concept of perceived understanding, or feeling understood, is defined as a person's perception or feeling that his/her interaction partner accurately understands his/her self-concept. Cahn (1987) introduces Laing's multilevel model of interpersonal perception (Laing, Phillipson, and Lee, 1966) to illustrate the difference between empathy, or role-taking, and perceived understanding. At the first level of interpersonal perception, persons A and B each have their direct perception of an object or concept. At the second level, they have the perception of the other's direct perception of the object or concept, which is referred to as empathy, role-taking, or "metaperspective." Finally, at the third level, they have "meta-metaperspective" as their perception of the other's empathy, role-taking, or metaperspective. Perceived understanding is derived from the comparison of a person's meta-metaperspective with his/her direct perspective (Cahn, 1987). This perceived understanding provides the basis on which a person constructs, organizes, and reorganizes his/her course of action for establishing "preferred" self-concepts.

Perceived understanding is considered a useful measure of commitment in long-term relationships. Cahn and Frey (1982) report that subjects high in perceived understanding are more attracted to one another than subjects low in the perception of being understood (Cahn, 1985). Based on Cahn's classification of variables related to the development of relationships, perceived understanding is an intensity variable that changes in relative importance at each stage of relational development. In other words, perceived understanding may become a more important factor as a friend relationship progresses than at the beginning stage of the friendship development. When the level of perceived understanding for any party of a friendship pair drops below the point where he/she expects to be for the continuation of his/her relationship commitment, the friendship may deteriorate or be terminated.

Another dimension of interpersonal perception that influences the initiation, maintenance, and disengagement of friend relationships is "perceived liking." Perceived liking is defined as a person's perception of how much his/her interactional partner actually likes, or is attracted to, him/her. Cushman and Cahn (1985) regard liking as one of two important components in initiating and maintaining an interpersonal relationship, which they call the "affective component." According to Cahn's (1985) classification of variables related to the development of relationship, perceived liking is a marker variable that continues to be important at all stages of the relationship development. Forgas (1985) asserts that people like those who like them and dislike those who dislike them. Perceived liking plays an important role in the initiation or formation of a friend relationship through the processes for the selection of a friendship partner in the fields of available, approachable, and reciprocal interactions (Cushman and Cahn, 1985). Perceived liking also influences the acceleration or dissociation of friend relationships. A person's decision to continue the commitment to the relationship or not depends in part on the extent to which he/she perceives his/her friendship partner's liking as a reciprocation of his/her own emotional commitment. When the person perceives his/her friendship partner's liking to decrease, he/she may stop acting committed to the relationship and instead look for an alternative partner.

Conversational Penetration

As a friend relationship progresses through the development of self-concept accuracy, self-concept similarity, perceived understanding, and perceived liking, there is also a change in the communication patterns between two parties of the friendship. The growth of friendship is characterized by an increasing amount of "intrusiveness" and "revelation" in verbal and nonverbal communication (Duck, 1988). Gudykunst and Ting-Toomey (1988) agree that as relationships progress, communication takes on a more personalistic focus, with increasing depth and breadth of communication between the two parties.

The conceptualization of the depth and breadth of communication between two relationship partners has been drawn from Altman and Taylor's (1973) theory of "social penetration," which deals with the breadth and depth dimensions of personality disclosure in interpersonal relationships. Analogous to the notion of social penetration, the concept of "conversational penetration," also called interpersonal penetration, is used to indicate the breadth and depth of interpersonal communication concerning self–object relationships of two relationship participants. The breadth of conversational penetration reflects the scope and frequency in conversation between two people, whereas the depth of conversational penetration indicates how intimately relationship partners deal with various conversational topic areas.

Friendship Type, Gender, and Cultural Differences

Traditionally, friendship research has been more concerned with same-sex friendships than opposite-sex friendships. Therefore, only a handful of studies have been done to compare same-sex and opposite-sex friendships. In general, opposite-sex friendships are often considered to contain "erotic" aspects, which is ostensibly rare in same-sex relationships (see Rawlins, 1982). Davis (1985) suggests that same-sex friends share more with each other (in terms of both personal confidences and practical assistance) and feel more stability about their relationship than do opposite-sex counterparts.

Lipman-Blumen (1976) argues that the sex segregation and the low status of women in occupational settings promote "homosociality." This tendency may, in turn, lead to the preference of same-sex friendships over opposite-sex friendships and the expectancy of less reciprocity and intimacy from opposite-sex friendships. Rose (1985), in a study testing homosocial norms of close friendships, asserts that same-sex friendships are characterized by acceptance, effort, time, communication, common interests, and affection, and that opposite-sex friendships, sometimes initiated by sexual attraction, are considered by friendship partners to offer less help and loyalty than same-sex friendships. As a consequence, it can be inferred that relatively long and deep commitments are found in same-sex relationships rather than in opposite-sex relationships.

Mahoney and Heretick (1979) found self-concept similarity as the cause of the formation of same-sex friendships but not of opposite-sex friendships. As a result of their study of 43 male and 45 female college students, they assert that same-sex relationships with best friends are based on similarity, whereas complementarity characterizes opposite-sex relationships. They specify that through a continuous relationship with same-sex friends, individuals achieve some degree of predictability and experience support of their own self-concept by perceived similarity and that this is not found in opposite-sex relationships.

Argyle and Henderson (1985) assert that women and men perceive friendship differently. Women value emotional closeness with a high level of self-disclosure, especially in same-sex friendships, whereas men prefer doing activities together, but with less intimacy. The studies of sex differences in same-sex friend relationships have often found that compared with men, women have fewer friends (Booth, 1972), establish more intimate and affectively richer relationships (Booth, 1972; Burke and Fuqua, 1987; Mazur and Olver, 1987; Williams, 1985), have higher levels of empathy (Fox, Gibbs, and Auerbach, 1985), and show greater involvement and depth in conversations with their friends, especially about personal and family matters (Aries and Johnson, 1983; Barth and Kinder, 1988; Johnson and Aries, 1983). This tendency may come from the sex-role expectation that males should show "manliness"—traits such as independence, sociability, and assertiveness. However, according to Rawlins (1982), males sharply differentiate between same-sex and opposite-sex friendships (see also Bukowski, Nappi, and Hoza, 1987) and seek to obtain emotional gratification from cross-sex relationships (see also Burke and Fuqua, 1987), whereas females find intimacy from both friendship types.

On the other hand, the initiation and formation of friend relationships are largely determined by culture, which has its unique normative and value orientations as well as social and organizational structures. Cultures have their own systems of rules that direct their members to certain behavioral patterns and that distinguish their members from others. Several studies have attempted to generate indices for comparing different cultures. Individualism/collectivism is one of the most frequently utilized indices for interpreting cultural differences in interpersonal communication (Gudykunst and Ting-Toomey, 1988; Yum, 1988).

In individualistic cultures, as in the United States (see Hofstede, 1980, 1983), individual goals are more emphasized than collective concerns or interests, which may lead to the formation of friendships that contribute most to the achievement of personal interests and welfare "for the time being." In collectivistic cultures, as in Korea (see Hofstede, 1980, 1983), in contrast, individuals are socialized to value harmonious human relationships transcending personal interests, which may lead to deep and long-lasting emotional commitments to each friendship partner, sometimes for a lifetime. From a comparative study of friendships in the United States and Japan, Cushman and King (1986) indicate that friend relationships in collectivistic societies are based on mutual liking, attraction, and common values, especially in same-sex friendships formed early in school days, whereas people in individualistic societies form friendships with those who have some attributes similar to those contained in their self-concepts.

The dimensions of low- and high-context communication and masculinity/femininity are also considered to differentiate cultural variabilities in interpersonal communication. In high-context communication cultures, as in Korea (see Hofstede, 1980, 1983), a small part of the information is coded and transmitted explicitly and a large portion of the information is communicated in an implicit way, resting on the interpretation of the context, whereas, in low-context communication cultures, as in the United States (see Hofstede, 1980, 1983), most of the information is transmitted in explicit and rather fixed codes, emphasizing the avoidance of ambiguity and the efficiency of communication.

On the other hand, masculinity, according to Hofstede (1980), refers to the tendency of people to place high values on things, power, and assertiveness, whereas femininity indicates the inclination to value people, quality of life, and nurturance. In other words, masculinity-oriented cultures are characterized by distinct sex roles, performance, ambition, and independence. Femininity-oriented cultures emphasize flexible sex roles, life quality, service, and interdependence. Gudykunst and Nishida (1986) show that perceptions of communication behavior related to opposite-sex versus same-sex relationships are influenced by different cultural orientations to masculinity/femininity. In societies where sex roles are clearly differentiated because of high masculinity informal relationships between males and females are not encouraged and the content of communication tends to be narrow and shallow.

Gudykunst and Ting-Toomey (1988) report scores on Hall's (1976) and Hofstede's (1980, 1983) dimensions of cultural variability for selected countries, including the United States and Korea. In the dimensions of individualism and masculinity, scores are higher for the United States (91 and 62 respectively) than for Korea (18 and 39). In the dimension of high- and low-context communication, Korea is recognized as a high-context communication culture, whereas the United States is found to be a low-context culture. However, for the masculinity dimension, a doubt arises about the results because the definition of masculinity has two contradictory aspects as it pertains to Korean culture. Hofstede's dimension of masculinity includes both high sex-role differentiation and independence, rather than interdependence (see Yum, 1987). Traditional Korean culture, deeply rooted in Confucianism, has historically denied equality between men and women and distinguished sex roles rather strictly, even as its collectivistic culture simultaneously emphasizes interdependence. Until a few decades ago, social rules "Ahm-Tag-Yi-Wool-Myun-Jib-Ahn-Yi-Mang-Hahn-Dah" (women should not talk or assert much), "Yuh-Pil-Jong-Boo" (women should follow men's decisions), and "Nahm-Nyo-Chil-Se-Boo-Dong-Suk" (a man and a woman should not sit together after the age of seven, unless they are married) were the hallmarks of sex-role differentiation and resulted in the avoidance of opposite-sex relationships in Korea.

In an endeavor to elaborate the friendship model of Cushman and his associates, the present study attempts to unveil dynamic effects of friendship type, gender, and culture on five self-concept support determinants: self-concept similarity, self-concept accuracy, perceived understanding, perceived liking, and conversational penetration.

The present study intends to resolve the following research questions:

RQ1: *Are there differences in the perceptions of friendship levels between the United States and Korea, between same-sex and opposite-sex friendships, and between males and females?*

RQ2: How different are the perceptions of self-concept similarity, self-concept accuracy, perceived understanding, and perceived liking between the United States and Korea, between same-sex and opposite-sex friendships, and between males and females?

RQ3: How do culture, friendship types, and gender create differences in the levels of conversational penetration?

Method

Sample

For the American sample, 75 students enrolled in two communication courses at a northeastern university responded to a self-administered questionnaire. Two versions of the questionnaire with different introductions for same-sex and opposite-sex friendships were randomly distributed among the respondents. Participation was voluntary, with no compulsion and with no interference until the completion of the survey. The sample included 17 male and 18 female respondents to the same-sex friendship questionnaire and 14 male and 21 female respondents to the opposite-sex friendship questionnaire. The remaining five subjects did not specify their sex. Their responses were dropped from relevant analyses.

For the Korean sample, 182 students enrolled in communication courses at Yonsei University in Seoul and at Jeon-Nam University in Kwang-Joo participated in the survey. Participation was voluntary. The sample included 50 male and 44 female respondents to the same-sex friendship questionnaire and 30 male and 51 female respondents to the opposite-sex friendship questionnaire. The remaining seven subjects did not specify their sex. Their responses were dropped from relevant analyses.

Measurement of Variables

Friendship levels. In this study, the levels of friendship were classified and tested across friendship types and cultures by four categories: acquaintance, ordinary friend, close friend, and best friend. For the comparison of friendship levels, psychological distances of each friendship category from self were measured by the Galileo pair-concept question technique. The standard distance of 100 between self and "neighbor" was given as a reference score. The distances between each pair of friendship categories were also measured for the purpose of testing the significance of the difference.

Self-concept similarity. For the measurement of self-concept similarity, subjects were asked to write perceived distances from themselves and from their best friends for self-concept adjectives, such as Honest, Responsible, Congenial, Unselfish, Intelligent, Generous, and Sympathetic. The coefficient of similarity for each self-concept was obtained by calculating a correlation coefficient between the scores of subjects and their best friends regarding the given self-concept item.

Self-concept accuracy. To measure self-concept accuracy, subjects were asked to mark, with a number from 0 to 100, their degree of assurance in predicting the feelings, value judgments, thoughts, and behavior of their best friend. The scores of these four items were then summed and divided by 400 so that the minimum score of self-concept accuracy was 0.00 and the maximum 1.00.

Perceived understanding and perceived liking. For the measurement of perceived understanding, subjects were asked to mark a number from 0 to 100 in response to the question, "How far can you go in believing that your best friend might understand feelings and thoughts which you didn't express either by words or by behaviors?" Perceived liking was measured by the question, "How far can you go in feeling confident that your best friend likes you?" which was also answered by marking a number from 0 to 100. The maximum scores for perceived understanding and perceived liking are 1.00 and the minimum scores are 0.00, the original scores being divided by 100.

Conversational penetration. To get an index of conversational penetration, subjects were given 30 topic statements and asked to check a number from 0 to 6 on two separate 7-point scales for frequency and intimacy, in which 0 indicates "never" and "superficial," and 6 indicates "always" and "intimate" in frequency and intimacy, respectively (Altman and Taylor, 1973). The 30 statements were factor-analyzed and reduced to a smaller number of representative dimensions in conversational topic areas. The index for conversational penetration in each topic dimension was calculated by multiplying the average scores for frequency and intimacy. In addition, an overall conversational penetration index was obtained by totaling the scores in separate conversational dimensions.

Statistical Analysis

T-tests were executed to test the differences in friendship levels by friendship type, gender, and culture. The differences in self-concept similarity, self-concept accuracy, perceived understanding, perceived liking, and conversational penetration were tested using analysis of variance (ANOVA). In addition, factor analysis was executed for 30 communication topic statements in order to classify them into a smaller number of dimensions.

Table 5.1
Distances Between Self and Friendship Levels in the United States and Korea

	Acquaintance	*Ordinary Friend*	*Close Friend*	*Best Friend*
United States				
Mean	61.7	48.4	32.8	26.1
Std. Dev.	23.3	28.2	25.9	27.9
Korea				
Mean	92.6	71.2	52.0	26.0
Std. Dev.	36.8	36.8	49.9	26.5
t =	−7.36***	−5.26***	−3.96***	*n.s.*

*** $p < .001$; *n.s.* = not significant

Results

As for friendship levels, American subjects' perceptions of psychological distances between self and acquaintance, between self and ordinary friend, and between self and close friend were found to be significantly different from Korean subjects, whereas the distances between self and best friend in both samples appeared to be almost the same (see Table 5.1). Because it was supposed that the distance between self and neighbor is 100, the distances at which Korean students perceive acquaintances (92.6), ordinary friends (71.2), and close friends (52.0) are not as far from neighbor (100) as those of American students (61.7, 48.4, and 32.8). However, there is little difference between American and Korean students in the perceptions of best friend (26.1 for American sample and 26.0 for Korean sample).

Considering friendship type and gender, Tables 5.2 and 5.3 show t-test results of the distances between friendship levels in the American and Korean samples. In the American sample, females in same-sex friendships and males in opposite-sex friendships tend to differentiate between all friendship levels, whereas Korean females most clearly distinguish between acquaintance and ordinary friend, between ordinary friend and close friend, and between close friend and best friend in both same-sex and opposite-sex friendships (all $p < .001$).

Perceived similarities between the self-concepts of subjects themselves and their best friends were examined by calculating correlations between the scores in seven adjective descriptions according to subjects' culture, gender, and friendship type (see Table 5.4). In general, American students, except for male same-sex friendships, tend to show higher self-concept similarities than do Korean students. American males and females in same-sex friendships and

Table 5.2
American Sample: *t*-tests of Distance Differences Between Friendship Levels in Same- and Opposite-Sex Friendships

	Same-Sex Friendship		*Opposite-Sex Friendship*	
	male	*female*	*male*	*female*
Acquaintance and Ordinary Friend	*n.s.*	3.50**	3.09**	2.98**
Ordinary Friend and Close Friend	2.41*	2.66*	3.33**	*n.s.*
Close Friend and Best Friend	3.27**	2.65*	2.63*	*n.s.*

* $p < .05$; ** $p < .01$; *n.s.* = not significant

Table 5.3
Korean Sample: *t*-tests of Distance Differences Between Friendship Levels in Same- and Opposite-Sex Friendships

	Same-Sex Friendship		*Opposite-Sex Friendship*	
	male	*female*	*male*	*female*
Acquaintance and Ordinary Friend	2.58*	5.41***	3.59**	6.42***
Ordinary Friend and Close Friend	*n.s.*	5.86***	*n.s.*	4.82***
Close Friend and Best Friend	7.80***	6.12***	2.31*	8.52***

* $p < .05$; ** $p < .01$; *** $p < .001$; *n.s.* = not significant

Korean males in both same- and opposite-sex friendships consider Generous as the self concept item most similar between self and best friend, whereas Honest represents the most similar self-concept in American male opposite-sex and Korean female same-sex friendships, and Sympathetic and Congenial in American and Korean female opposite-sex friendships respectively (see Table 5.5). On the other hand, Unselfish is not found to be as high in the self-concept similarity perceptions of Korean subjects as in those of American subjects.

Self-concept accuracy scores were examined with a 2 (culture) × 2 (friendship type) × 2 (sex of subjects) ANOVA (see Table 5.6). There are main effects for friendship type ($F = 22.65$, $p < .001$) and culture ($F = 6.42$, $p < .05$). The friendship-type main effect indicates that subjects in same-sex friendships are more confident in accurately perceiving their best friends'

Table 5.4
Self-Concept Similarity in Same- and Opposite-Sex Best Friend Relationships: Correlation Coefficients Between Self and Best Friend

	United States		*Korea*	
	Same-Sex Friendship	*Opposite-Sex Friendship*	*Same-Sex Friendship*	*Opposite-Sex Friendship*
Honest				
Male	.24	.77	.28	.40
Female	.88	.73	.90	.71
Responsible				
Male	.40	.65	.45	.40
Female	.85	.73	.45	.64
Congenial				
Male	.49	.51	.49	.37
Female	.83	.73	.69	.77
Unselfish				
Male	.76	.65	.31	.31
Female	.89	.66	.40	.50
Intelligent				
Male	.52	.64	.58	.43
Female	.91	.63	.54	.52
Generous				
Male	.91	.63	.78	.48
Female	.91	.63	.82	.52
Sympathetic				
Male	.31	.74	.73	.45
Female	.87	.75	.22	.63
Total				
Male	.52	.66	.52	.41
Female	.88	.70	.57	.61

self-concepts than are those in opposite-sex friendships. The main effect for culture, on the other hand, implies that American students perceive more self-concept accuracy than do Korean counterparts. There are no interaction effects.

As for perceived understanding, there are statistically significant main effects for friendship type ($F = 4.97, p < .05$) and culture ($F = 4.42, p < .05$) (see Table 5.7). The results indicate that subjects tend to perceive themselves as better understood by same-sex best friends than by opposite-sex best

Table 5.5
Rankings of Similar Self-Concepts by Friendship Type, Sex, and Culture

United States

	Same-Sex Friendship		*Opposite-Sex Friendship*	
	male	*female*	*male*	*female*
1.	GENER*	GENER*	HONES*	SYMPA*
2.	UNSEL*	INTEL*	SYMPA*	HONES*
3.	INTEL*	UNSEL*	UNSEL*	CONGE*
4.	CONGE	HONES*	RESPO*	RESPO*
5.	RESPO	SYMPA*	INTEL*	UNSEL*
6.	SYMPA	RESPO*	GENER*	INTEL*
7.	HONES	CONGE*	CONGE*	GENER*

Korea

	Same-Sex Friendship		*Opposite-Sex Friendship*	
	male	*female*	*male*	*female*
1.	GENER*	HONES*	GENER	CONGE*
2.	SYMPA*	GENER*	SYMPA	HONES*
3.	INTEL*	CONGE*	INTEL	RESPO*
4.	CONGE	INTEL*	HONES	SYMPA*
5.	RESPO	RESPO	RESPO	INTEL*
6.	UNSEL	UNSEL	CONGE	GENER*
7.	HONES	SYMPA	UNSEL	UNSEL

* Similarity (Pearson correlation coefficient) r > .50.

friends, whereas American students report higher perceived understanding than do Korean students. There are no interaction effects.

Perceived liking—that is, the degree of subjects' perception that they are liked by their friends—was also examined with a 2 × 2 × 2 ANOVA. Significant main effects on the perceived liking measure were obtained for culture ($F = 18.98, p < .001$) and friendship type ($F = 4.32, p < .05$) (see Table 5.8). The results indicate that American subjects perceive more than do Korean counterparts that their friends like them, whereas more perceived liking is found in same-sex friendships than in opposite-sex friendships. There are no interaction effects.

The topics for the measurement of conversational penetration were factor-analyzed and classified into eight topic dimensions: Sexual Relations,

Table 5.6
Self-Concept Accuracy Toward Same- and Opposite-Sex Best Friends in the United States and Korea

		United States		*Korea*
Same-Sex Friendship				
Male		.78*		.80
Female		.81		.77
Opposite-Sex Friendship				
Male		.77		.67
Female		.76		.68
ANOVA:				
Main Effects	Culture	$F =$	6.42	$p < .05$
	Friendship type	$F =$	22.65	$p < .001$
	Sex	$F =$	0	*n.s.*
Interaction Effects	Culture × Friendship type	$F =$	2.75	*n.s.*
	Culture × Sex	$F =$	0	*n.s.*
	Friendship type × Sex	$F =$	.29	*n.s.*
	Culture × Friendship type × Sex	$F =$	.78	*n.s.*

* minimum = 0; maximum = 1; *n.s.* = not significant

Table 5.7
Perceived Understanding from Same- and Opposite-Sex Best Friends in the United States and Korea

		United States		*Korea*
Same-Sex Friendship				
Male		.71*		.72
Female		.74		.68
Opposite-Sex Friendship				
Male		.76		.66
Female		.69		.59
ANOVA:				
Main Effects	Culture	$F =$	4.42	$p < .05$
	Friendship type	$F =$	4.97	$p < .05$
	Sex	$F =$	3.01	*n.s.*
Interaction Effects	Culture × Friendship type	$F =$	.91	*n.s.*
	Culture × Sex	$F =$	.09	*n.s.*
	Friendship type × Sex	$F =$	.71	*n.s.*
	Culture × Friendship type × Sex	$F =$	.31	*n.s.*

*minimum = 0; maximum = 1.; *n.s.* = not significant

Table 5.8
Perceived Liking from Same- and Opposite-Sex Best Friends in the United States and Korea

			United States	*Korea*
Same-Sex Friendship				
Male			.93*	.85
Female			.88	.75
Opposite-Sex Friendship				
Male			.91	.71
Female			.87	.73
ANOVA:				
Main Effects	Culture	$F =$	18.98	$p < .001$
	Friendship type	$F =$	4.32	$p < .05$
	Sex	$F =$	2.89	*n.s.*
Interaction Effects	Culture × Friendship type	$F =$	.78	*n.s.*
	Culture × Sex	$F =$	0	*n.s.*
	Friendship type × Sex	$F =$	2.48	*n.s.*
	Culture × Friendship type × Sex	$F =$	.80	*n.s.*

*minimum = 0; maximum = 1.; *n.s.* = not significant

Interpersonal Dealing, Emotional Experiences, Social Concerns, Practical Concerns, Personal Values, Health and Money Matters, and Family Relations (see Table 5.9). The overall score of conversational penetration was examined with a 2 (culture) × 2 (friendship type) × 2 (sex of subjects) ANOVA. As Table 5.10 indicates, a main effect for sex ($F = 4.31, p < .05$) was found. Females show higher conversational penetration in general than do males, except for Korean same-sex friendships, in which males and females have about the same levels of conversational penetration. No other main or interaction effects were found for the overall measurement of conversational penetration.

Separate measurement of conversational penetration in each of eight topic areas was also obtained and tested with a 2 × 2 × 2 ANOVA. First, the topic area of Sexual Relations showed main effects for culture ($F = 4.28, p < .05$) and friendship type ($F = 10.66, p < .01$) (see Table 5.11). The results indicate that same-sex friends, especially in Korea, tend to talk more about their opinions of sexual relations than do opposite-sex friends and that American students converse more about sexual interests and values with their best friends than do Korean students. No significant interaction effects were found.

The second topic dimension, Interpersonal Dealing, includes conversations about respondents' experiences of criticizing or discouraging other

Table 5.9
Factor Loadings and Inter-Item Reliabilities for Eight Dimensions of Conversational Topics

Factor	*Eigen-value*	*Alpha*	*Factor Loading*	*Scale Items*
I. Sexual Relations				
	7.83	.79	.80	1. opinion on the extent of premarital sexual relations
			.73	2. whether or not it matters that you get married to non-virgin
			.73	3. opinion on sexual morality
			.53	4. opinion on how long it would be better for you to have premarital relations with your going-to-be spouse
			.44	5. ideal type of the opposite sex with whom you would like to have relations before marriage
II. Interpersonal Dealing				
	1.89	.69	.66	1. when you feel like criticizing your teachers or superiors
			.58	2. whether or not you have discouraged your friend
			.55	3. whether or not it would be permissible to tell a lie
			.48	4. your feeling or thought about your outward appearance
			.47	5. how firmly you defend your opinion against an objection
III. Emotional Experiences				
	1.86	.73	.67	1. when you had been confronted with a terror
			.66	2. whether or not you want to wander about the nation or to live in another place
			.60	3. when you feel lonely
			.49	4. an event or situation which might perplex you
			.46	5. an episode or a tale of bravery that you had experienced

(Continued)

Table 5.9 Continued

Factor	Eigen-value	Alpha	Factor Loading		Scale Items
IV. Social Concerns					
	1.59	.66	.66	1.	your belief on the importance of education
			.61	2.	when you feel self-esteem with your own accomplishment in school, work, or society
			.60	3.	your feeling or thought about your duty or responsibility
			.45	4.	whether or not other people are prerequisite for your happiness
V. Practical Concerns					
	1.24	.66	.76	1.	your opinion on asking for a loan from the bank
			.70	2.	whether or not you would practice birth control if you get married (or are married)
			.45	3.	how important it is to take in proper nutrition for your health
VI. Personal Values					
	1.21	.66	.62	1.	your feeling in case your parents were separated or divorced
			.60	2.	whether or not you like something new or out of the ordinary
			.53	3.	what you don't feel like talking about to others
VII. Health and Money Matters					
	1.19	.54	.69	1.	chronic anxiety about health problems of your own
			.53	2.	importance of money in happiness
			.49	3.	what is the amount in your savings account
VIII. Family Relations					
	1.06	.47	.78	1.	how much you feel free from family rules
			.54	2.	how warm and peaceful your home is compared to others

Cumulative percent of variance = 59.6.

Note: Scale items are back-translated from the Korean survey for the purposes of interpretation.

Table 5.10
Overall Score (Sum) of Conversational Penetration in Same- and Opposite-Sex Friendships in the United States and Korea

		United States		*Korea*
Same-Sex Friendship				
Male		159.1*		171.5
Female		190.9		172.6
Opposite-Sex Friendship				
Male		156.6		156.7
Female		203.3		171.6
ANOVA:				
Main Effects	Culture	F =	1.58	*n.s.*
	Friendship type	F =	.29	*n.s.*
	Sex	F =	4.31	$p < .05$
Interaction Effects				
	Culture × Friendship type	F =	.56	*n.s.*
	Culture × Sex	F =	3.44	*n.s.*
	Friendship type × Sex	F =	.90	*n.s.*
	Culture × Friendship type × Sex	F =	0	*n.s.*

* minimum = 0; maximum = 384; *n.s.* = not significant

Table 5.11
Conversational Penetration on Sexual Relations

		United States		*Korea*
Same-Sex Friendship				
Male		24.5*		27.3
Female		26.5		22.7
Opposite-Sex Friendship				
Male		24.8		17.8
Female		25.6		19.4
ANOVA:				
Main Effects	Culture	F =	4.28	$p < .05$
	Friendship type	F =	0.66	$p < .01$
	Sex	F =	.57	*n.s.*
Interaction Effects	Culture × Friendship type	F =	2.49	*n.s.*
	Culture × Sex	F =	1.12	*n.s.*
	Friendship type × Sex	F =	.90	*n.s.*
	Culture × Friendship type × Sex	F =	1.33	*n.s.*

* minimum = 0; maximum = 48; *n.s.* = not significant

Table 5.12
Conversational Penetration on Interpersonal Dealing

		United States	Korea
Same-Sex Friendship			
Male		20.3*	19.2
Female		24.5	20.7
Opposite-Sex Friendship			
Male		21.8	19.8
Female		29.2	20.2
ANOVA:			
Main Effects	Culture	$F =$ 13.86	$p < .001$
	Friendship type	$F =$ 0	*n.s.*
	Sex	$F =$ 5.44	$p < .05$
Interaction Effects	Culture × Friendship type	$F =$ .83	*n.s.*
	Culture × Sex	$F =$ 4.97	$p < .05$
	Friendship type × Sex	$F =$ .09	*n.s.*
	Culture × Friendship type × Sex	$F =$ 2.00	*n.s.*

* minimum = 0; maximum = 48; *n.s.* = not significant

Table 5.13
Conversational Penetration on Emotional Experiences

		United States	Korea
Same-Sex Friendship			
Male		17.1*	23.5
Female		24.6	24.9
Opposite-Sex Friendship			
Male		20.1	21.8
Female		27.4	24.6
ANOVA:			
Main Effects	Culture	$F =$ .56	*n.s.*
	Friendship type	$F =$ .24	*n.s.*
	Sex	$F =$ 10.28	$p < .01$
Interaction Effects	Culture × Friendship type	$F =$ 1.19	*n.s.*
	Culture × Sex	$F =$ 4.48	$p < .05$
	Friendship type × Sex	$F =$ 0	*n.s.*
	Culture × Friendship type × Sex	$F =$ .39	*n.s.*

* minimum = 0; maximum = 48; *n.s.* = not significant

Table 5.14
Conversational Penetration on Social Concerns

			United States	Korea
Same-Sex Friendship				
Male			24.8*	28.0
Female			29.0	27.4
Opposite-Sex Friendship				
Male			22.1	26.5
Female			33.2	30.5
ANOVA:				
Main Effects	Culture	$F =$	.50	*n.s.*
	Friendship type	$F =$	.82	*n.s.*
	Sex	$F =$	6.62	$p < .05$
Interaction Effects	Culture × Friendship type	$F =$	.14	*n.s.*
	Culture × Sex	$F =$	4.14	$p < .05$
	Friendship type × Sex	$F =$	3.55	*n.s.*
	Culture × Friendship type × Sex	$F =$	.20	*n.s.*

* minimum = 0; maximum = 48; *n.s.* = not significant

people, telling a lie, and defending their opinion against objections. ANOVA revealed main effects for culture ($F = 13.86, p < .001$) and sex ($F = 5.44, p < .05$) and an interaction effect between culture and sex ($F = 4.97, p < .05$) (see Table 5.12). American subjects, especially females, show higher conversational penetration on Interpersonal Dealing than do Korean subjects. In the Korean sample, however, there was little difference between males and females in the level of conversational penetration on Interpersonal Dealing.

The ANOVA for the third topic dimension, Emotional Experiences, revealed a main effect for sex ($F = 10.28, p < .01$) and an interaction effect between culture and sex ($F = 4.48, p < .01$) (see Table 5.13). The results indicate that in the American sample female subjects tend to talk more about their emotional experiences than do male subjects, whereas little difference between males and females was shown in the Korean sample. In addition, Korean male subjects are found to converse more about Emotional Experiences than do American counterparts.

Social Concerns, the fourth topic dimension, is characterized by topics such as duties or achievements in society and relations with other people. This dimension shows a main effect for sex ($F = 6.62, p < .05$) and an interaction effect between sex and culture ($F = 4.14, p < .05$) (see Table 5.14). In the American sample, females were found to converse more than males with both their same-sex and opposite-sex friends about matters of social

Table 5.15
Conversational Penetration on Practical Concerns

		United States	Korea
Same-Sex Friendship			
Male		18.8*	15.8
Female		19.0	13.7
Opposite-Sex Friendship			
Male		10.6	12.3
Female		16.7	11.4
ANOVA:			
Main Effects	Culture	$F =$ 3.31	*n.s.*
	Friendship type	$F =$ 4.72	$p < .05$
	Sex	$F =$ .03	*n.s.*
Interaction Effects	Culture × Friendship type	$F =$ .34	*n.s.*
	Culture × Sex	$F =$ 3.18	*n.s.*
	Friendship type × Sex	$F =$ .56	*n.s.*
	Culture × Friendship type × Sex	$F =$ .13	*n.s.*

* minimum = 0; maximum = 48; *n.s.* = not significant

concern. However, the Korean sample shows little difference between males and females in conversational penetration on Social Concerns.

The fifth dimension, Practical Concerns, refers to topics such as borrowing money from a bank, practicing birth control, and taking proper nutrition. Only one main effect for friendship type was found ($F = 4.72$, $p < .05$) (see Table 5.15). The result indicates that subjects in both the American and Korean samples are more likely to talk with their same-sex best friends about matters of practical concern than with their opposite-sex friends. There are no significant interaction effects.

The sixth conversational dimension, Personal Values, includes personal feelings and preferences about social practice. There are main effects for culture ($F = 12.34$, $p < .01$) and sex ($F = 7.39$, $p < .01$), but no interaction effects (see Table 5.16). The results indicate that American subjects are more inclined than are Korean subjects to converse about personal values and that females talk more about them than do males.

Finally, the seventh and eighth dimensions, represented by Health and Money Matters and Family Relations, revealed no statistically significant effects from the ANOVA. In other words, there is little difference in the breadth and depth of the conversation about health, money problems, and family matters between the American and Korean subjects, between females and males, and between same-sex and opposite-sex friendships.

Table 5.16
Conversational Penetration on Personal Values

		United States		Korea
Same-Sex Friendship				
Male		21.1*		17.1
Female		24.1		19.3
Opposite-Sex Friendship				
Male		19.2		15.4
Female		27.8		18.8
ANOVA:				
Main Effects	Culture	$F =$	12.34	$p < .01$
	Friendship type	$F =$	.06	*n.s.*
	Sex	$F =$	7.39	$p < .01$
Interaction Effects	Culture × Friendship type	$F =$	.68	*n.s.*
	Culture × Sex	$F =$	.57	*n.s.*
	Friendship type × Sex	$F =$	.99	*n.s.*
	Culture × Friendship type × Sex	$F =$	.66	*n.s.*

* minimum = 0; maximum = 48; *n.s.* = not significant

Discussion

The present study attempted an empirical application of Cushman and his associates' friendship theory to samples of college students representing different cultures (American and Korean), friendship types (same-sex and opposite-sex), and gender. Five self-concept support determinants (self-concept similarity, self-concept accuracy, perceived understanding, perceived liking, and conversational penetration) were individually tested to clarify the effects of culture, friendship type, and gender. As Cushman and his associates' theory posits, the scores of self-concept similarity, self-concept accuracy, perceived understanding, perceived liking, and conversational penetration were generally high in all sample groups. However, culture, friendship type, and sex of subjects were found to have distinct effects on some of these self-concept support components.

In almost all self-concept support components (i.e., self-concept similarity, self-concept accuracy, perceived understanding, perceived liking, and conversational penetration), American students' relationships with their best friends showed higher levels than those of Korean counterparts. These results indicate that Cushman's friendship model fits American friendships more aptly than it does Korean friendships. Cushman and King (1986) suggest that American friendships are strongly based upon reciprocal helping behavior as well as mutual self-concept support. The emphasis on self-concept support and reciprocity in friendships may lead to high levels of self-concept similarity, self-concept accuracy, perceived understanding, perceived liking, and conversational penetration. In other words, it is more probable in America than in Korea that the perceptions of decreasing self-concept similarity, accuracy, understanding, liking, and communication lead to the dissolution of a friendship.

Subjects of same-sex friendships showed higher self-concept accuracy, perceived understanding, perceived liking, and conversational penetration on Sexual Relations and Practical Concerns than opposite-sex friendship counterparts. These results partially support Mahoney and Heretick's (1979) finding that same-sex friends tend to achieve more predictability, (i.e, self-concept accuracy) and experience more support of self-concepts. Furthermore, because of the influence of prevalent homosocial norms of close friendships, as Lipman-Blumen (1976) and Rose (1985) assert, more intimacy and reciprocity are also found in same-sex than in opposite-sex friend relationships. Considering that perceived understanding and perceived liking are the indices of reciprocity in friendships, the result that the same-sex friendship subjects had high scores in both measures is understandable. Also, it is notable that same-sex friends talk more than opposite-sex friends about sexual relations as one of the most intimate conversational topics.

Subjects' gender influenced only self-concept similarity and the overall conversational penetration level with specific effects in the topic areas of Interpersonal Dealing, Emotional Experiences, Social Concerns, and Personal Values, in all of which females scored higher than males. Previous studies of sex difference in friendships revealed that women show more emotional closeness or intimacy and greater involvement and depth in conversations with their friends. This tendency is confirmed to some degree in the present study by the result of females' higher scores in conversational penetration, which measures the breadth and depth of communication between friendship partners.

The self-concept item Generous shows the greatest similarity between subjects and their friends in both American and Korean same-sex friendships, whereas the similarity of the self-concept item Honest appears to be emphasized in opposite-sex friendships. It was also found that the similarity of the self-concept item Unselfish is higher in American friendships than in Korean friendships. This result indicates that unselfishness is more important to friendship formation and maintenance in America than in Korea. The emphasis on reciprocal helping behavior in American friendships may explain high scores in perceiving the similarity of the self-concept item Unselfish.

Korean same-sex friends tend to converse more about their sexual interests and values with each other than do opposite-sex friends. There is little difference in conversational penetration on sexual relations between American same-sex and opposite-sex friends. These results may be explained by the fact that Korean culture, traditionally rooted in Confucianism, has repressed opposite-sex friend relationships. Furthermore, in the past, conversation between a man and a woman on such topics as sexuality was as rare as opposite-sex friend relationships outside of marriage, although the sexual mores in Korean society are now changing gradually toward greater openness and liberalism. However, the traditional taboo still accounts for the different characteristics of opposite-sex friendships in Korea and America.

The perceptions of distances among friendship levels were found to be different between American and Korean students. More specifically, the distances between the perceptions of neighbor and friendship-level categories are much smaller in the Korean sample than in the American sample. In other words, American subjects appear to differentiate more than do Korean subjects acquaintances and friends from neighbors as common people living around them. It may be possible that the individualism prevalent in the United States influences people to narrow the scope of acquaintanceship and to be reluctant in establishing interpersonal relationships with many people. Because the traditional collectivistic culture emphasizes harmonious human relationships transcending personal interests or goals, Koreans are encouraged to accept other people, including their neighbors, as their relationship partners with little reservation or reluctance. The differentiation between friendship levels was shown more clearly in women's same-sex friendships and in men's opposite-sex friendships than in other friendships. Rawlins (1982) asserts that males seek to obtain from opposite-sex friendships the emotional intimacy that they miss in same-sex friendships because of the sex-role expectation that men should show "manliness." Friendships accompanied by emotional commitment may have many distinctions in themselves.

In sum, the results generally support Cushman and his associates' friendship theory based on the assumption that mutual self-concept support underlies the formation and maintenance of friendships. Focusing on interpersonal relationships with best friends, the present study attempted to control the effects of friendship length or strength.

American subjects, same-sex friendships, and females were found to show somewhat higher scores in self-concept support determinants than their counterparts. These variations were attributed to the emphasis on rather strict reciprocity in American friendships, the homosocial intimacy of same-sex friendships, and the emotional closeness and deep conversational involvement of female friendships. Further research is needed to validate and extend the results of the present study. Above all, more research should be conducted with a variation in operationalization of basic constructs of Cushman and his associates' friendship theory.

For the measurement of differentiation among friendship levels, the present study used the Galileo pair-concept question technique. Based on the arbitrary distance of 100 between self and neighbor, the Galileo technique gives only general configuration regarding psychological distances among concepts. The weakness of this measurement, however, is that the results from different groups of people with different perceptions or understandings of the base concept, such as neighbor, can hardly be compared and tested in a strict statistical sense. The operationalization of self-concept similarity using seven self-concept adjectives should also be expanded to include all aspects of self-concept: identity self-concept, evaluative self-concept, and behavioral self-concept at both real and ideal self levels. Further replications of the present research with methodological improvements as well as the inclusion of other factors (for instance, age) varying the role of self-concept support in friend relationships will contribute to the internal and external validation and elaboration of Cushman and his associates' friendship theory.

References

Altman, I., and D. Taylor (1973). *Social penetration: The development of interpersonal relationships*. New York: Holt, Rinehart and Winston.

Argyle, M., and M. Henderson (1985). *The anatomy of relationships*. London: William Heinemann.

Aries, E., and F. Johnson (1983). Close friendship in adulthood: Conversational content between same-sex friends. *Sex Roles* 9:1183–96.

Bailey, R., R. DiGiacomo, and O. Zinser (1976). Length of male and female friendship and perceived intelligence in self and friend. *Journal of Personality Assessment* 40:635–40.

Bailey, R., P. Finney, and B. Helm (1975). Self-concept support and friendship duration. *Journal of Social Psychology* 96:237–43.

Barth, R., and B. Kinder (1988). A theoretical analysis of sex differences in same-sex friendships. *Sex Roles* 19:349–63.

Blau, P. (1967). *Exchange and power in social life*. New York: John Wiley and Sons.

Booth, A. (1972). Sex and social participation. *American Sociological Review* 37:183–92.

Bukowski, W., B. Nappi, and B. Hoza (1987). A test of Aristotle's model of friendship for young adults' same- and opposite-sex relationships. *Journal of Social Psychology* 127:595–603.

Burke, R., and D. Fuqua, (1987). Sex differences in same- and cross-sex supportive relationships. *Sex Roles* 17:339–52.

Cahn, D. (1985). Communication and the feeling of being understood. *Informatologia Yugoslavica* 17:191–99.

Cahn, D. (1987). *Letting go: A practical theory of relationship disengagement and reengagement.* Albany, NY: State University of New York Press.

Cahn, D., and L. Frey, (1982, November). *Interpersonal attraction and trust: The effects of feeling understood/misunderstood on impression formation processes.* Paper presented at the annual convention of the Speech Communication Association, Louisville, KY.

Cooley, C. (1902). *Human nature and the social order.* New York: Scribner's.

Cushman, D., and D. Cahn (1985). *Communication in interpersonal relationships.* Albany, NY: State University of New York Press.

Cushman, D., and S. King (1986). The role of communication rules in explaining intergroup interaction. In W. Gudykunst (ed.), *Intergroup communication* (39–50). London: Edward Arnold.

Davis, K. Near and dear: Friendship and love compared. *Psychology Today*, February 1985, 22–30.

Duck, S. (1988). *Relating to others.* Montery CA: Brooks/Cole.

Forgas, J. (1985). *Interpersonal behavior: The psychology of social interaction.* New York: Pergamon.

Fox, M., S. Gibbs, and D. Auerbach (1985). Age and gender dimensions of friendship. *Psychology of Women Quarterly* 9:489–502.

Gudykunst, W., and T. Nishida (1986). The influence of cultural variability on perceptions of communication behavior associated with relationship terms. *Human Communication Research* 13:147–66.

Gudykunst, W., and S. Ting-Toomey (1988). *Culture and interpersonal communication.* Beverly Hills, CA: Sage.

Hall, E. (1976). *Beyond culture.* New York: Doubleday.

Hofstede, G. (1980). *Culture's consequences: International differences in work-related values.* Beverly Hills, CA: Sage.

Hofstede, G. (1983). Dimensions of national cultures in fifty countries and three regions. In J. Deregowski, S. Dzuirawiec, and R. Annis (eds.), *Explications in cross-cultural psychology* (335–55). Lisse, The Netherlands: Swets and Zeitlinger.

Homans, G. (1961). *Social behavior: Its elementary forms.* New York: Harcourt Brace Jovanovich.

Johnson, F., and E. Aries (1983). Conversational patterns among same-sex pairs of late-adolescent close friends. *Journal of Genetic Psychology* 142:225–38.

Kipnis, D. (1961). Changes in self concepts in relation to perceptions of others. *Journal of Personality* 29:449–65.

Laing, R., H. Phillipson, and A. Lee, (1966). *Interpersonal perception.* New York: Springer.

Lipman-Blumen, J. (1976). Toward a homosocial theory of sex roles: An explanation of the sex segregation of social institutions. In M. Blaxall and B. Reagan (eds.), *Women and the workplace* (15–32). Chicago: University of Chicago Press.

Mahoney, J., and D. Heretick (1979). Factor-specific dimensions in person perception for same- and opposite-sex friendship dyads. *Journal of Social Psychology* 107:219–25.

Mazur, E., and R. Olver (1987). Intimacy and structure: Sex differences in imagery of same-sex relationships. *Sex Roles* 16:539–58.

McKenna, H., P. Hofstaetter, and J. O'Connor (1955). The concepts of the ideal self and of the friend. *Journal of Personality* 24:262–71.

Mead, G. (1934). *Mind, self, and society.* Chicago: University of Chicago Press.

Rawlins, W. (1982). Cross-sex friendship and the communicative management of sex-role expectations. *Communication Quarterly* 30:343–52.

Rose, S. (1985). Same- and cross-sex friendships and the psychology of homosociality. *Sex Roles* 12:63–74.

Thibaut, J., and H. Kelley (1959). *The social psychology of groups.* New York: John Wiley.

Thompson, W., and R. Nishimura (1952). Some determinants of friendship. *Journal of Personality* 20:305–14.

Williams, D. (1985). Gender, masculinity-femininity, and emotional intimacy in same-sex friendship. *Sex Roles* 12:587–600.

Wright, P. (1969). A model and a technique for studies of friendship. *Journal of Experimental Social Psychology* 5:295–309.

Yum, J. (1987). The practice of Uye-Ri in interpersonal relationships in Korea. In D. Kincaid (ed.), *Communication theory from Eastern and Western perspectives* (87–100). New York: Academic Press.

Yum, J. (1988). The impact of Confucianism on interpersonal relationships and communication patterns in East Asia. *Communication Monographs* 55:374–88.

6

The Friendship Formation Process in Nigeria: A Preliminary Study of Cultural Impact, Communication Pattern, and Relationship Variables

Andrew A. Moemeka and
Anne Maydan Nicotera

The English language is replete with colloquial phrases extolling the value of friendship. Indeed, such adages are universal—expressed in different words and ways in different cultures but all a manifestation of the very important place of friendship in the life of human beings. A wise saying of the Igbo of Nigeria—"Ezi oyi ka ego"—loosely translates as "a good friend is more valuable than riches."

However universal the act of friendship (Gudykunst, 1989), its formation, growth, and maintenance appear to differ from culture to culture. Several studies have shown that friendship patterns are culture-specific—that is, are regulated and governed by cultural norms and values (Atsumi, 1980; Cushman and Cahn, 1985; Cushman, Valentinsen, and Dietrich, 1982; Gudykunst, 1985, 1989; Gudykunst and Nishida, 1986; Thompson and Nishimura, 1952; Wright, 1978; Yum, 1983, 1988). For example, in the United States the roles of spouse and best friend are usually performed by one person; a mother and her child could see themselves (and be accepted so by society) as best friends; brothers and sisters proudly refer to themselves as best friends. In Nigeria, such references would be seen as insulting and degrading to levels of blood relationships. Even though an individual might be very fond of a parent and confide in that parent, the individual would not refer to the relationship as a friendship.

Purpose and Rationale

This study is directed at identifying the factors—social, cultural, human, and communication—that influence the formation, development, and maintenance of friendship in Nigeria. There is no existing study of friendship as a relational pattern in that nation. The existing literature on friendship-formation patterns contains no information from the continent of Africa, nor does it adequately account for cultural variability in friendship patterns around the world. This vacuum is conspicuous in light of demands for intercultural communication research, which is fast becoming the cornerstone of international understanding and world peace. Information from different parts of the world on factors or social forces that underlie systems of interpersonal relationships can provide insight for peoples of the world as to why people from other cultures behave the way they do. The present study examines one form of relational pattern in Nigeria toward the goal of greater comprehension among various cultures.

We are concerned with two basic issues. First, we attempt to identify the variables or qualities which Nigerians consider important in the formation and maintenance of friendship. Second, we attempt to determine the importance attached to each variable or quality in the process (see Moemeka, 1983). The findings of this preliminary study may enhance the pursuit of other significant issues—for example, the impact of existing friendship patterns on the social system, the necessity to distinguish between same-sex and opposite-sex friendship patterns (see Bahk, chapter 5), the importance of identifying subcultural (idiosyncratic) variations within the culture, and the significance of the conditions that make for friendship termination.

Cultural Background

Nigeria is the most populous country in Africa with a 1990 population estimation of 110 million. If UNESCO's estimate of the population of Africa as just over 400 million is accurate, every fourth African is a Nigerian. The size of Nigeria's population, its enormous natural resources, and the quantity and quality of its human resources make Nigeria a force to reckon with in Africa. This enviable position, although it seems to have evaporated in recent years because of economic crisis, has acted as a culturally binding force that tends to make Nigerians behave amicably toward one another, providing an enhanced environment for friendship formation.

Nigeria is a multiethnic society. There are about 300 ethnic groups (tribes), each with its own distinct language and easily identifiable subculture. Thus, the country is rich in cultural diversity and has developed a national sensitivity toward the need for "unity in diversity." Political leaders, since before independence from the United Kingdom in 1960, have stressed the need for interethnic understanding that could lead to friendship across tribal lines.

Among the multiplicity of ethnic groups, three tribes—the Hausa (in the north), the Igbo (in the east), and the Yoruba (in the west)—have dominated the socio-political and economic life of the country since 1950. Each controlled one of the three political regions into which the country was divided before independence, and still wields substantial power over that political entity. Other tribal or ethnic groups that have had substantial political and social influence on the nation include the Fulani and the Kanuri in the north, the Efik and the Ijaw in the east, and the Edo in the west.

In spite of people's recognition of the need for interethnic understanding and friendship, political wrangling and bitterness have plagued relationships among the ethnic groups, especially among the three major ones. These three have been particularly envious of one another over who has (or should have) the largest share of the national "cake"—political power and control of government, industrial and economic superiority, educational opportunities, and other social amenities. It was mainly this deadly envy manifested in intolerance and feelings of superiority that led to the 1966–69 civil war.

Surprisingly, the civil war, tribal animosity, and political strife appear to be directed at the tribes as entities rather than the individuals that make up the tribes. For even though the tribes have strong prejudicial attitudes toward one another, examples of strong friendship across tribal lines abound. Most important, these friendships exist not only among ordinary citizens, but also among political and industrial leaders. Two of the best-known friends of the first president of Nigeria, Dr. Nnamdi Azikiwe (an Igbo), are Chief Adeniran Ogunsanya (a Yoruba) and Alhaji Aminu Kano (a Hausa). It was probably the influence of Igbo friends that led the current president of the country, General Ibrahim Babangida (from the north), to the woman he eventually married, Maryam (an Igbo from the midwest). The first author of this chapter—an Igbo—has two very close friends. One is Urhobo; the other Yoruba.

The existence of such friendship formation in the face of strong tribal prejudices would thus appear to be determined by factors that cut across tribal lines. One set of these factors may be human behavioral qualities that distinguish between "good" and "bad" friends, irrespective of circumstances of birth. The question then arises: What are these qualities, and which of them prevail in Nigeria?

It must be noted that for Nigerians and other Africans the concept "friend" is not a constant. Its meaning and application change depending on whom one is talking about and to whom one is talking. Someone introduced as a friend to one person could be introduced as a brother to another person. It is unlikely that any culture-conscious Nigerian would introduce another Nigerian (irrespective of his/her tribe) to non-Nigerians as a friend. S/he is most likely to introduce that person as a brother or sister. However, if that Nigerian were in the midst of people of his/her own ethnic group, s/he would introduce that same person as a friend. Traditionally, the closer the blood relation between two people of the same sex who exhibit a close relationship, the less likely is it that the concept "friend" would be used to describe that relationship. This usage is based on the belief that a brother/sister is culturally more highly valued than a friend. This cultural assessment is reflected in an Igbo adage, "ozu sime oyi a naa," which is translated, "as soon as the corpse starts decomposing, friends disappear." This implies that only brothers and sisters endure until the very last. Other tribes have similar adages.

When a friend becomes very valuable, s/he is accorded an honorary brother/sister status; it is never the other way around. Though brothers or sisters may be very close, they do not become "friends." This is why one occasionally hears the statement, "He is no longer a friend—he is much more: he is now a brother." It is not that the culture has little regard for friendship; the importance of friendship, though well-recognized, is third after that of parents and brothers/sisters (of the same parents and of the extended family).

Friendship across sex lines is culturally suspect. In fact, it is openly discouraged, unless it involves young boys and very old women or young girls and very old men. The rationale for this is the necessity to protect the citizens against sexual temptations, which if given in to would lead to the violation of cultural norms and values concerning the sanctity of sex. It is said that friendship between opposite sex partners who are not culturally permitted to have sexual relationship is like "hiding a rat where a cat can get at it." (See Chapter 10 for a full treatment of culturally dictated values for sex in Nigeria.)

Because it is expected that these cultural variables are not the only ones that affect friendship formation in Nigeria, questions arise: What are the other variables and how do they relate to the friendship process in the Nigerian sociocultural environment?

The qualities Honesty and Responsibility are treated specially here. In everyday discussions, political speeches, academic exchanges, and even among co-workers and teenagers, these qualities are mentioned as the key to lasting friendship. This anecdotal evidence of their prevalence would seem to suggest a high degree of cultural value attached to them. It is thus important to discover if this normative ascription of value identifies theoretically important variables for friendship formation in Nigeria. Furthermore, it is important to discover the relationship between these traditional qualities and other variables.

Our basic concerns in this study can be summarized in the following formal research questions:

RQ1: *What are the most important friendship qualities (variables) in the Nigerian cultural environment?*

RQ2: *What is the relationship between friendship qualities (variables) and* ***Honest Person****?*

RQ3: *What is the relationship between friendship qualities (variables) and* ***Responsible Person****?*

Semantic markers for levels of friendship have been identified by research (see Chapter 3) as variables for levels or degrees of friendship. These markers are Acquaintance, Casual (Ordinary) Friend, Good (Close) Friend, and Best Friend.

Addressing these levels of friendship and a fifth level, Ideal Friend, we posit three related research questions.

RQ4: *What is the relationship between the Self and the semantic markers; in other words, do these markers represent increasing degrees of friendship for this culture?*

RQ5: *What are the entry level variables (those which predict initiation) and intensity variables (those which predict growth) in friendship?*

RQ6: *How much do individuals value the crucial entry and intensity variables in friendship?*

RQ7: *What are the respondents' perceptions of the relationships among the semantic marker variables?*

Methodology

Sample

The sample, chosen from a population of civil servants and graduate students from different parts of Nigeria, consists of 54 respondents (27 females and 27 males) purposely selected from eight ethnic groups (Hausa, Igbo, Yoruba, Fulani, Kanuri, Efik, Edo, and Ijaw) whose cultures are considered most pervasive among Nigerians. Ethnic groups were distributed throughout the sample as follows: 20 individuals of northern Nigerian ethnicity (Hausa, Fulani, and Kanuri); 20 individuals of eastern Nigerian ethnicity (Igbo, Efik, and Ijaw); and 14 individuals of western Nigerian ethnicity (Yoruba and Edo). The average age of the respondents, whose minimum level of education is high school, was 38 years, an age considered old enough for the individual to have felt the impact of pure traditional culture, yet young enough to have been influenced by encroaching Western values. (See Chapter 10 for a discussion of Nigerian value change.)

Data Collection/Measurement

The data were collected through a self-administered questionnaire. The questionnaire first asked respondents to list freely, in descending order of preference, 10 qualities that must be present in someone before they can consider entering into a friend relationship with that person. Such a listing produced two measures: the frequency of the listed qualities; and the frequency of each quality at each point on a scale of 1 (most preferred) to 10 (least preferred). For this latter measure, a value score was computed by reversing the ranks given by the respondents (so that no mention of qualities by some respondents would be reflected as true zeros), then by summing the rankings. The most highly valued qualities were thus identified by frequency and value scores. Some of the qualities mentioned by respondents were collapsed because of similarity in meaning. For example, "truthfulness" and "honesty" were collapsed into one concept—Honesty. "Smartness" and "intelligence" were collapsed into Intelligence; "hard work" and "resourcefulness" into Resourcefulness; and "dependability," "trustfulness," and "trustworthiness" into Trustworthiness.

Respondents were required to rate the distances of the valued qualities from the concepts Honest Person and Responsible Person and to rate the distance between the self (Real Self and Ideal Self) and each of the most valued qualities (and other variables in the analysis). These ratings were done in terms of perceived distance in cognitive space measured in points from 1 (extremely strong) to 20+ (extremely weak). In addition, they were asked to rate the distance of each of the most valued qualities in relation to the semantic-marker variables for increasing levels of friendship—Acquaintance, Ordinary Friend, Close Friend, and Best Friend—as well as the concept Ideal Friend. Finally, they were asked to rate the distances among the semantic markers. The measures obtained (Strength of Relationship points) served as indications of the values placed on each quality (variable) by respondents. The scale was interpreted as follows:

Points Apart	*Value*
1–3	extremely strong
4–6	very strong
7–9	strong
10–13	weak
14–17	very weak
18–20+	extremely weak

Table 6.1
Frequency Count, Percentage Scores, Value Scores, and Value Ranks of the Most Frequently Mentioned Qualities

Quality	*Frequency (%)*	*Value Score*	*Value Rank*
Tolerance	54 (100%)	303	2
Honesty	51 (94%)	465	1
Caring	49 (90.7%)	303	3
Trustworthiness	43 (79.6%)	217	5
Humor	42 (77.8%)	132	6
Intelligence	40 (74.1%)	230	4
Responsibility	28 (51.8%)	126	7
Religion	18 (33.3%)	123	8
Self-Discipline	18 (33.3%)	122	9
Resourcefulness	18 (33.3%)	97	10

Analyses, Results, and Discussion

Although only 10 friendship qualities were requested in the questionnaire, respondents were free to mention any qualities. In total, a list of 27 variables resulted. Many of the qualities were listed by few respondents. For example, Respect was listed by only 5 (9%) of the respondents; Boldness by 7 (12%); and Sociability by 10 (18%). The highest possible score was 54 (100%). Those qualities that did not score up to one-third of this total were eliminated. Those qualities that exceeded two-thirds of this total—mentioned by a majority of the respondents—are considered to be the crucial set of variables. Table 6.1 presents a list showing the frequency count, percentage scores, and value scores of the most frequently mentioned qualities.

The Frequency/Percentage tables that follow contain, in detail, the Strength of Relationship points (measured in cognitive-space distance) as perceived by the individual with regard to the relationship between friendship qualities and Honest Person and Responsible Person, between the self and semantic-marker variables, between friendship qualities and semantic-marker variables, between the self and friendship qualities, and among the semantic marker variables. (In these tables, percentages sum to less than 100% because not all respondents listed all qualities.)

Analyses

The thrust of these analyses is, of course, to explore the research questions raised in this chapter. These analyses provide an understanding of the friendship variables at work in Nigeria and their role in initiating and maintaining friendship. First, we identify the crucial variables (mentioned by two-thirds of the respondents). These variables—Tolerance, Honesty, Caring, Trustworthiness, Humor, and Intelligence—are the first set of variables used in this analysis. The second set of variables are the semantic markers that address questions of levels and intensity of interaction in friendship.

For questions that examine strength of relationship, the tables divide the scale into six levels, from extremely strong to extremely weak. This provides detailed levels of the strength of the relationships examined. For the particular purpose of these analyses, which are directed at determining the relative strength or weakness of the relationship rather than the level of strength, we divided the scale into two levels—Strong and Weak. In considering the results, therefore, all scores should be collapsed accordingly; positive levels of relationship classified as Strong, and negative levels as Weak.

Results and discussion for RQ1. What are the most important friendship qualities (variables) in the Nigerian cultural environment? Ten variables were mentioned by at least one-third of the respondents. Of these ten, six are considered crucial (mentioned by two-thirds). Tolerance was listed by 100% of the respondents and ranks second in value score. Honesty, listed by 94% of the respondents, ranks first in value. The remaining crucial variables in order of frequency are Caring (91%, rank 3), Trustworthiness (80%, rank 5), Humor (78%, rank 6), and Intelligence (74%, rank 4). (See Table 6.1.)

The two traditional friendship variables, Honesty and Responsibility, were both mentioned by the respondents. Though Honesty (94%, rank 1) is still extremely important, Responsibility (52%, rank 7) appears to have been superseded by other friendship qualities.

Results and discussion for RQ2. What is the relationship between friendship qualities (variables) and Honest Person? The data in Table 6.1 show that Honesty is clearly an important variable for Nigerian friendship. This traditional quality thus retains its place in cultural estimation. The thrust of RQ2, however, is not whether Honesty is still important, but rather the examination of the relationship between Honest Person and other friendship qualities. In other words, how do Nigerians perceive an honest person in relation to the other most valued friendship qualities? Table 6.2 presents these results. These respondents view an honest person as caring, trustworthy, tolerant, and somewhat humorous (in order of relationship strength), but not necessarily intelligent. All but one of the crucial variables are strongly related to Honest Person.

Results and discussion for RQ3. What is the relationship between friendship qualities (variables) and Responsible Person? The data in Table 6.1

Table 6.2
Strength of Relationship Between Honest Person and Friendship Qualities

	Extremely Strong	*Very Strong*	*Strong*	*Weak*	*Very Weak*	*Extremely Weak*
Tolerance	18 (33%)	4 (7%)	12 (22%)	13 (24%)	7 (13%)	—
Caring	41 (76%)	3 (6%)	5 (9%)	—	—	—
Trustworthiness	43 (80%)	—	—	—	—	—
Humor	16 (30%)	12 (22%)	—	—	3 (6%)	—
Intelligence	19 (35%)	—	—	15 (28%)	6 (11%)	—
Responsibility	18 (33%)	—	—	—	—	—
Religion	15 (28%)	3 (6%)	—	—	—	—
Self-Discipline	18 (33%)	—	—	—	—	—
Resourcefulness	9 (17%)	—	—	—	9 (17%)	—

Table 6.3
Strength of Relationship Between Responsible Person and Friendship Qualities

	Extremely Strong	*Very Strong*	*Strong*	*Weak*	*Very Weak*	*Extremely Weak*
Tolerance	20 (37%)	6 (11%)	11 (20%)	12 (22%)	—	—
Honesty	50 (93%)	1 (2%)	—	—	—	—
Caring	25 (46%)	12 (22%)	12 (22%)	—	—	—
Trustworthiness	31 (57%)	9 (17%)	3 (6%)	—	—	—
Humor	3 (6%)	5 (9%)	11 (20%)	23 (43%)	—	—
Intelligence	15 (28%)	14 (26%)	—	6 (11%)	5 (9%)	—
Religion	9 (17%)	—	—	9 (17%)	—	—
Self-Discipline	12 (22%)	6 (11%)	—	—	—	—
Resourcefulness	17 (31%)	1 (2%)	—	—	—	—

show that Responsibility as a traditionally valued friendship quality may be diminishing in its importance in contemporary Nigerian friendships. The focus of RQ3, however, is to examine the relationship between Responsible Person and other friendship qualities. In other words, how do Nigerians perceive a responsible person in relation to the other most valued friendship qualities? Table 6.3 presents these results. Responsible Person is very strongly associated with Honesty, signifying a close relationship between these two traditional friendship qualities. A responsible person is honest, caring, trust-

Table 6.4
Strength of Relationship Between the Self and Semantic-Marker Variables

	Extremely Strong	*Very Strong*	*Strong*	*Weak*	*Very Weak*	*Extremely Weak*
Real Self and . . .						
Acquaintance	2 (4%)	2 (4%)	—	5 (9%)	—	33 (61%)
Ordinary Friend	4 (7%)	—	—	10 (19%)	6 (11%)	27 (50%)
Close Friend	18 (33%)	9 (17%)	10 (19%)	6 (11%)	3 (6%)	8 (15%)
Best Friend	34 (63%)	4 (7%)	4 (7%)	9 (17%)	—	2 (4%)
Ideal Friend	45 (63%)	8 (15%)	—	3 (6%)	—	2 (4%)
Ideal Self and . . .						
Acquaintance	6 (11%)	6 (11%)	3 (6%)	—	—	35 (65%)
Ordinary Friend	3 (6%)	5 (9%)	—	5 (9%)	18 (33%)	21 (39%)
Close Friend	20 (37%)	13 (24%)	—	12 (22%)	5 (9%)	4 (7%)
Best Friend	32 (59%)	10 (19%)	9 (17%)	3 (6%)	—	—
Ideal Friend	46 (85%)	4 (7%)	—	—	—	—
Real Self	4 (7%)	16 (30%)	—	—	—	29 (54%)

worthy, tolerant, and somewhat intelligent (in order of relationship strength), but is not humorous. All but one of the crucial variables are strongly related to Responsible Person.

The weak relationship between Humor and Responsible Person may explain the apparent decline in the cultural value of Responsibility. Humor (78%, rank 6) was mentioned more often and ranked more highly in value than Responsibility (52%, rank 7). For these contemporary Nigerians, Humor is a more highly valued friendship quality than Responsibility. The two also have a weak relationship. It thus appears that Humor has superseded Responsibility as a salient and valued friendship quality.

Results and discussion for RQ4. What is the relationship between respondents and the semantic markers; in other words, do these markers represent increasing degrees of friendship for this culture? The results in Table 6.4 indicate that these semantic markers are salient levels for increasing friendship in Nigeria. For both Real Self and Ideal Self, each successive semantic marker is more strongly related. For Real Self, 70% of the respondents view Acquaintance as weakly related (61% rated it extremely weak); 80% view Ordinary Friend as weakly related (50% as extremely weak). The gap between Ordinary Friend and Close Friend appears to be the crucial transitional period for increasing friendship. With Close Friend, the relationship to Real Self is rated on the strong side of the scale. These ratings again increase toward the strong end of the continuum for Best Friend and Ideal Friend.

For Ideal Self, 65% of the respondents view Acquaintance as weakly related (all rated it extremely weak); 81% view Ordinary Friend as weakly related (39% as extremely weak). The gap between Ordinary Friend and Close Friend again appears to be the crucial transitional period for increasing friendship. With Close Friend, the relationship to Real Self is rated on the strong side of the scale. These ratings again increase toward the strong end of the continuum for Best Friend and Ideal Friend.

Real Self and Ideal Self are weakly related, indicating a self-actualization need that friendship may fulfill. Indeed, 85% of the respondents rated the relationship between Ideal Self and Ideal Friend as extremely strong, whereas only 63% rated the relationship between Real Self and Ideal Friend as extremely strong. We can conclude that the ideal friend is seen by Nigerians as resembling the self, especially the self one aspires to be.

Results and discussion for RQ5. What are the entry-level variables (those that predict initiation) and intensity variables (those that predict growth) in friendship? The crucial qualities were examined for their nature. All of these variables are very strongly related to Ideal Friend, providing more evidence of their salience and importance. Of the six variables (Tolerance, Honesty, Caring, Trustworthiness, Humor, and Intelligence), two were identified as entry-level variables and three as intensity variables. They were identified as such by their patterns of relationship strength with levels of friendship intensity. (See the results for RQ4, which establish that these semantic markers denote salient increasing levels of friendship.) Those variables whose perceived strength of relationship with the semantic markers remained relatively steady were identified as entry level variables. These are Humor and Intelligence. Those variables whose strength of relationship with the semantic markers increased with the friendship level were identified as intensity variables. These are Tolerance, Caring, and Trust. Tables 6.5a–e show these results.

Honesty shows an interesting pattern. The relationship between Honesty and friendship intensity gets weaker from Acquaintance to Ordinary Friend. In the transition to Close Friend, however, the relationship gains tremendous strength and then remains steady. As we saw for the relationship between the self and friendship levels, the gap between Ordinary Friend and Close Friend appears to be a crucial transition period. Because Honesty has been identified as a traditionally valued quality, the pattern for the other traditionally valued quality was examined. Responsibility shows a similar pattern. Although the relationship is on the strong side of the scale for both Acquaintance and Ordinary Friend, it is slightly stronger for Acquaintance; the strength of relationship increases dramatically for Close Friend, then

Tables 6.5a–e
Strength of Relationship Between Semantic-Markers and Friendship Qualities

Table 6.5a: Aquaintance

	Extremely Strong	*Very Strong*	*Strong*	*Weak*	*Very Weak*	*Extremely Weak*
Acquaintance and . . .						
Tolerance	9 (17%)	6 (11%)	15 (28%)	9 (15%)	15 (28%)	—
Honesty	10 (19%)	12 (22%)	—	5 (9%)	—	24 (44%)
Caring	13 (24%)	6 (11%)	—	6 (11%)	—	24 (44%)
Trustworthiness	10 (19%)	10 (19%)	—	18 (33%)	5 (9%)	—
Humor	12 (22%)	13 (24%)	4 (7%)	—	—	13 (24%)
Intelligence	8 (15%)	7 (13%)	10 (19%)	—	15 (28%)	—
Responsibility	10 (19%)	—	6 (11%)	4 (7%)	8 (15%)	—
Religion	—	6 (11%)	—	12 (22%)	—	—
Self-Discipline	3 (6%)	5 (9%)	7 (13%)	3 (6%)	—	—
Resourcefulness	5 (9%)	8 (15%)	—	3 (6%)	2 (4%)	—

Table 6.5b: Ordinary Friend

	Extremely Strong	*Very Strong*	*Strong*	*Weak*	*Very Weak*	*Extremely Weak*
Ordinary Friend and . . .						
Tolerance	14 (26%)	14 (26%)	6 (11%)	10 (19%)	10 (19%)	—
Honesty	10 (19%)	6 (11%)	—	10 (19%)	12 (22%)	13 (24%)
Caring	16 (30%)	8 (15%)	5 (9%)	10 (19%)	—	10 (19%)
Trustworthiness	13 (24%)	7 (13%)	10 (19%)	8 (15%)	5 (9%)	—
Humor	16 (30%)	9 (17%)	9 (17%)	3 (6%)	5 (9%)	—
Intelligence	10 (19%)	6 (11%)	—	5 (9%)	9 (17%)	10 (19%)
Responsibility	7 (13%)	8 (15%)	—	8 (15%)	6 (11%)	—
Religion	2 (4%)	6 (11%)	10 (19%)	—	—	—
Self-Discipline	—	3 (6%)	6 (11%)	6 (11%)	—	3 (6%)
Resourcefulness	—	3 (6%)	—	9 (17%)	—	6 (11%)

Table 6.5c: Close Friend

	Extremely Strong	*Very Weak*	*Strong*	*Strong*	*Very Weak*	*Extremely Weak*
Close Friend and . . .						
Tolerance	42 (78%)	10 (19%)	—	2 (4%)	—	—
Honesty	46 (85%)	5 (9%)	—	—	—	—
Caring	37 (69%)	3 (6%)	9 (17%)	—	—	—
Trustworthiness	30 (56%)	13 (24%)	—	—	—	—
Humor	14 (26%)	10 (19%)	5 (9%)	—	8 (15%)	5 (9%)
Intelligence	13 (24%)	9 (17%)	—	16 (30%)	2 (4%)	—
Responsibility	27 (50%)	1 (2%)	—	—	—	—
Religion	13 (24%)	5 (9%)	—	—	—	—
Self-Discipline	5 (9%)	10 (19%)	—	3 (6%)	—	—
Resourcefulness	13 (24%)	4 (7%)	—	1 (2%)	—	—

Table 6.5d: Best Friend

	Extremely Strong	*Very Strong*	*Strong*	*Weak*	*Very Weak*	*Extremely Weak*
Best Friend and . . .						
Tolerance	38 (70%)	10 (12%)	6 (11%)	—	—	—
Honesty	40 (74%)	11 (20%)	—	—	—	—
Caring	48 (89%)	1 (2%)	—	—	—	—
Trustworthiness	40 (74%)	3 (6%)	—	—	—	—
Humor	18 (33%)	21 (39%)	—	3 (6%)	—	—
Intelligence	22 (40%)	12 (22%)	6 (11%)	—	—	—
Responsibility	14 (26%)	10 (19%)	1 (2%)	3 (6%)	—	—
Religion	12 (22%)	6 (11%)	—	—	—	—
Self-Discipline	18 (33%)	—	—	—	—	—
Resourcefulness	18 (33%)	—	—	—	—	—

Table 6.5e: Ideal Friend

	Extremely Strong	*Very Strong*	*Strong*	*Weak*	*Very Weak*	*Extremely Weak*
Ideal Friend and . . .						
Tolerance	53 (98%)	1 (2%)	—	—	—	—
Honesty	51 (94%)	—	—	—	—	—
Caring	47 (87%)	2 (4%)	—	—	—	—
Trustworthiness	43 (80%)	—	—	—	—	—
Humor	28 (52%)	14 (26%)	—	—	—	—
Intelligence	40 (74%)	—	—	—	—	—
Responsibility	26 (48%)	—	2 (4%)	—	—	—
Religion	15 (28%)	3 (6%)	—	—	—	—
Self-Discipline	15 (28%)	—	3 (6%)	—	—	—
Resourcefulness	17 (31%)	1 (2%)	—	—	—	—

remains steady. No other variables show this pattern. Honesty and Responsibility appear to be a type of entry variable for close friendship levels.

Results and discussion for RQ6. How much do individuals value the crucial entry and intensity variables in friendship? This question examines how the respondents ranked the variables in value (what qualities they feel are most suitable for an ideal friendship) and how they see themselves in relation to the variables. This question is explored with frequency and value scores (see Table 6.1) as well as relationship strength between the self and each of the six crucial friendship qualities. (See Tables 6.6a and b.)

Table 6.1 shows that the six crucial variables rank as follows, beginning with the most highly valued: Honesty, Tolerance, Caring, Intelligence, Trustworthiness, and Humor. Tables 6.6a and b show how the respondents relate to the friendship qualities they chose—how these qualities are related to Real Self and Ideal Self.

All friendship qualities score on the strong side of the scale for both Real Self and Ideal Self. This indicates that the respondents' view of ideal friendship qualities parallels their view of qualities they see and aspire to in themselves. Some interesting differences can be seen between Real Self and Ideal Self that may help to explain the cultural value placed on these friendship qualities. Relationships of the qualities with Ideal Self are consistently stronger than those for Real Self. Extreme differences in the strength of relationship can be seen for Honesty, Trustworthiness, Intelligence, and Responsibility. The respondents aspire to higher levels of these variables than they see in their actual selves. These attributes can thus be presumed to be very highly valued culturally.

Table 6.6a and b
Strength of Relationship Between the Self and Friendship Qualities

Table 6.6a: Real Self

	Extremely Strong	*Very Strong*	*Strong*	*Weak*	*Very Weak*	*Extremely Weak*
Real Self and . . .						
Tolerance	31 (57%)	5 (9%)	15 (28%)	—	—	3 (6%)
Honesty	27 (50%)	4 (7%)	—	—	8 (15%)	12 (22%)
Caring	39 (72%)	5 (9%)	5 (9%)	—	—	—
Trustworthiness	24 (44%)	6 (11%)	—	3 (6%)	—	10 (19%)
Humor	30 (56%)	—	—	12 (22%)	—	—
Intelligence	12 (22%)	19 (35%)	—	5 (9%)	4 (7%)	—
Responsibility	12 (22%)	6 (11%)	—	—	—	—
Religion	5 (9%)	—	7 (13%)	6 (11%)	—	—
Self Discipline	12 (22%)	—	—	3 (6%)	—	—
Resourcefulness	10 (19%)	8 (15%)	—	—	—	—

Table 6.6b: Ideal Self

	Extremely Strong	*Very Strong*	*Strong*	*Weak*	*Very Weak*	*Extremely Weak*
Ideal Self and. . .						
Tolerance	30 (56%)	10 (19%)	11 (20%)	3 (6%)	—	—
Honesty	39 (72%)	11 (20%)	—	—	—	1 (2%)
Caring	28 (52%)	13 (24%)	8 (15%)	—	—	—
Trustworthiness	37 (69%)	6 (11%)	—	—	—	—
Humor	24 (44%)	10 (19%)	—	8 (15%)	—	—
Intelligence	37 (69%)	—	3 (6%)	—	—	—
Responsibility	11 (20%)	7 (13%)	10 (19%)	—	—	—
Religion	10 (19%)	3 (6%)	5 (9%)	—	—	—
Self-Discipline	10 (19%)	5 (9%)	—	3 (6%)	—	—
Resourcefulness	8 (15%)	10 (19%)	—	—	—	—

Results and discussion for RQ7. What are the respondents' perceptions of the relationships among the semantic-marker variables? The results in Table 6.7 address this question. These results, as do those in Table 6.4, show that Nigerians see these semantic markers as salient levels of friendship. They also show again a gap between casual relationships and more serious relationships. The gap again appears, as before, between Ordinary Friend and Close Friend. There is an extreme shift in the strength of relationship for higher

Table 6.7
Strength of Relationship Among Semantic-Marker Variables

	Extremely Strong	*Very Strong*	*Strong*	*Weak*	*Very Weak*	*Extremely Weak*
Acquaintance and . . .						
Ordinary Friend	10 (19%)	2 (4%)	—	7 (13%)	2 (4%)	31 (57%)
Close Friend	—	10 (19%)	2 (4%)	4 (7%)	4 (7%)	30 (56%)
Best Friend	2 (4%)	8 (15%)	—	9 (17%)	—	33 (61%)
Ideal Friend	4 (7%)	4 (7%)	—	5 (9%)	3 (6%)	37 (69%)
Ordinary Friend and . . .						
Close Friend	2 (4%)	5 (9%)	—	12 (22%)	—	31 (57%)
Best Friend	2 (4%)	4 (7%)	6 (11%)	9 (17%)	—	30 (56%)
Ideal Friend	2 (4%)	2 (4%)	—	9 (17%)	—	36 (67%)
Close Friend and . . .						
Best Friend	40 (74%)	6 (11%)	3 (6%)	—	4 (7%)	—
Ideal Friend	43 (80%)	4 (7%)	—	2 (4%)	—	3 (6%)
Best Friend and . . .						
Ideal Friend	44 (81%)	6 (11%)	4 (7%)	—	—	—

levels of friendship. These respondents seem to value closeness in friendship to such an extent that they distinguish very clearly between casual and close friendship levels.

Conclusion

This study has discussed the impact of culture on friendship formation and maintenance and the communication patterns that encourage and sustain friends; it has also identified the qualities that Nigerians see as most important in their quest to enter into and remain in friendships. The six crucial variables identified appear to have the greatest value for the respondents and would seem to have the greatest impact on friend relationships in Nigeria. An examination of the character of these variables reveals interesting patterns for Nigerian friendships. Tolerance, mentioned by every respondent, reflects the paradox of intertribal envy and intertribal friendship. Tolerance is a crucial attribute if intertribal friendships are to occur in an atmosphere of intertribal prejudice. Trustworthiness may also assist in forming intertribal friendships. Honesty, a traditionally valued trait, is very highly valued among these contemporary Nigerians. Responsibility, however, has lost some of the value it was traditionally accorded. Humor was mentioned by more respondents and is more highly valued than Responsibility; this may be a sign of encroaching Western values. Future research may provide greater insight into the character of these variables.

The developmental progression of friendship in Nigeria sharply distinguishes casual levels of relationship from close levels. That the distinctions were found to be especially prevalent for traditionally valued attributes may reflect some degree of discomfort with casual relationships; it may also reflect a high value placed on close relationships, such that they are entered into selectively. Indeed, given the strength of relationship among the higher levels of friendship, it appears that a crucial threshold arises between Ordinary Friend and Close Friend.

Although we have met the conditions we set out to achieve in this preliminary study, we must not fail to draw attention to one obvious limitation. The sample size and ethnic composition of our study, in relation to the size and composition of the Nigerian population, do not allow us to generalize to Nigerians beyond our sample characteristics (relatively young civil servants and graduate students from eight ethnic groups). Because the cultures of these groups are considered most pervasive among Nigerians, we have some small degree of generalizability. However, even though there is an underlying cultural trait that affects all ethnic groups, it is possible that a more representative sample (more ethnic groups and more respondents) could substantially alter the results we have obtained in this study. Our results must not be considered conclusive but must be tested further.

Other issues connected with the sampling include locale, social status, and education. Our sample was made up of educated, urban dwellers who were well exposed to Western influences. Future investigations should use suburban and rural respondents, examining them separately and together. Such studies would help to confirm or invalidate the results of this study and contribute to defining more clearly the nature of friendship in Nigeria. In addition, weak responses and nonresponses in our data make the results less conclusive. Our understanding of Nigerian friendship would be enhanced by studies designed to determine whether or not such weak relationships are ethnically based, and if so, which ethnic groups account for the differences.

Finally, we must draw attention to what appears to be a contradiction about honesty among most Nigerians. The very high value accorded honesty as a traditional and contemporary friendship quality stands in direct contrast to what can be anecdotally noted about most Nigerians' relationships—social, political and economic. Explicit behavior is in contrast to expressed attitude. As one respondent answered orally, when asked if he believed he were honest, "Honesty means being straightforward and truthful and non-deceptive in everything at all times. Everyone knows that and expects it from others. But only very few, if any, are that honest. To that extent I am not. But the fact that I am not does not detract from the fact that 'honesty is the best policy.'" Interesting patterns of Nigerian culture may be revealed with study into such accepted contradiction between attitudes and actions. Comparison with other cultures would provide further insight.

References

Atsumi, R. (1980). Patterns of personal relationships. *Social Analysis* 5:63–78.

Cushman, D. P., and D. D. Cahn (1985). *Communication in interpersonal relationships*. Albany, NY: State University of New York Press.

Cushman, D. P., B. Valentinsen, and D. Dietrich (1982). A rules theory of interpersonal relationships. In F. E. X. Dance (ed.), *Human Communication Theory* (90–119). New York: Harper and Row.

Gudykunst, W. B. (1985). An exploratory comparison of close intracultural and intercultural friendships. *Communication Quarterly* 33:270–83.

Gudykunst, W. B. (1989). Culture and the development of interpersonal relationships. In J. A. Anderson (ed.), *Communication yearbook 12* (315–54). Newbury Park, CA: Sage.

Gudykunst, W., and T. Nishida (1986). The influence of cultural variability on perceptions of communication behavior associated with relationship terms. *Human Communication Research* 13:147–66.

Moemeka, A. A. (1983). Socio-cultural environment of communication in traditional Nigerian societies: An ethnographic exploration. *Communicatio Socialis* 16:331–45.

Thompson, W., and R. Nishimura (1952). Some determinants of friendship. *Journal of Personality* 20:305–14.

Wright, P. H. (1978). Toward a theory of friendship based on a conception of self. *Human Communication Research* 4:196–207.

Yum, J. O. (1983). Social network patterns of five ethnic groups in Hawaii. In R. N. Bostrom (ed.), *Communication yearbook 7* (574–91). Beverly Hills, CA: Sage.

Yum, J. (1988). The impact of Confucianism on interpersonal relationships and communication patterns in East Asia. *Communication Monographs* 55:374–88.

7

Summary of Studies on the Theory of Friendship and Consideration of Implications

Anne Maydan Nicotera

This chapter serves first as a summary of the replications and extensions of friendship studies in Part II. (Chapter 13 contains Critiques of all the studies in this volume.) Following the summary, implications are considered for three categories across interpersonal communication: culture, conflict, and quality. These three categories correspond to Propositions 4–7 presented in Chapter 2.

Summary of Friendship Studies

Replication

In Chapter 4, Korn provides support for the general theoretic structure. With his American sample, he replicates the results of Chapter 3; the four hypothesized friendship levels are validated as stable semantic markers for increasing intimacy in the friend relationship. Also in support of the theory, deeper levels of intimacy are shown to be more closely associated with the real self and the ideal self. Chapter 4 provides support for Proposition 1 (see Chapter 2). Further, psychological support, trust, respect, and authenticity are established as variables whose increasing intensity will predict deeper levels of intimacy. Chapter 4 provides support for intensity variables in Proposition 3. Bahk, in Chapter 5, also replicates the semantic labels as distinct levels of intimacy in friendship. Bahk's attribute analysis compares American and

Korean culture on a single set of attributes; he does not attempt to establish their importance within each culture as intensity variables. In Chapter 6, Moemeka and Nicotera provide support for the basic theoretic structure in Nigeria. The semantic markers are upheld in yet another culture as tracing a theoretic progression to more intense levels of friendship, supporting Proposition 1. Their data suggest that within this progression, Nigerian culture imposes a distinct discrimination between casual and close friendships. Further, as opposed to similar studies and in support of Proposition 3, their data support the notion of entry and intensity rules for friendship, providing evidence that some attributes must be present for entry into friendship, whereas others must increase in intensity for the friendship to deepen.

Bahk performs the most stringent test of self-concept support. He provides clear conceptualizations of self-concept similarity, self-concept accuracy, perceived understanding, and perceived liking. His operationalizations are based on individual perceptions. Since self-concept support is a perceptual construct, this operationalization is not necessarily problematic. (This issue is addressed further in Chapter 13.) Bahk, supporting Proposition 1, convincingly establishes the importance of self-concept support in the development of friendship.

Extension

Korn directly tests the question of a universal theoretic structure for friendship development. His results do show evidence that the basic structure may be upheld cross-culturally, supporting Proposition 4. He verifies levels and dimensions of friendship development in Korean culture, providing evidence for the semantic markers for increasing friendship and for the attributes associated with friendship. In American and Korean friendships, self-concept appears to be a generative mechanism for relationship formation and growth, supporting Proposition 1. Although the question of theoretic universals was not a central part of his investigation, Bahk's data also show that the theoretic structure for the development of friendship can be applied cross-culturally. Moemeka and Nicotera (Chapter 6) provide data from Nigeria, not offering a cross-cultural comparison. However, when considered in light of the American and Korean data provided by Korn and Bahk, these data from Nigeria clearly support the cross-cultural application of the theoretic structure, supporting Proposition 4. Moemeka and Nicotera's finding of a distinction between casual and close friendships supports the use of such a measurement across cultures to determine cultural imperatives in the definition of friendship intensity. Ample evidence exists from these three studies to pursue this direction of research.

Bahk also expands the theory to explicate the intricacies of cross-sex friendship vis-à-vis same-sex friendships, providing support for Proposition

2 for different types of friendship. Most important, he illustrates that the basic theoretical structure is general enough to account for such differing relationship types, yet specific enough to provide explication of those types. In doing so, he shows how the theory can be more rigorously tested. Without doubt, he conducts the most stringent test appearing in this volume.

Both Korn's and Bahk's analyses of conversational penetration extend the theory by providing a true communication component. Korn's analysis is particularly heuristic. A host of new questions can be based on his data. Korn highlights potential differences between American and Korean friendships in the depth and breadth of their conversational topics. Bahk extends these questions with a deeper analysis of cross-cultural and gender differences. The penetration profiles provide strong bases for the explication of topical categories unique to the friend relationship in either or both cultures and topical categories whose intimacy may predict relationship level in either or both cultures. Bahk's data provides a strong base for similar explication of same- and cross-sex friendships. The general theory is in need of such a communication component. (This is further discussed in Chapter 13.) Bahk's factor analysis, yielding different results from the dimensional structure advanced by Taylor and Altman (1966) highlights the importance of further work in this area.

Implications Across Three Categories

Culture: Concerning Proposition 4

Interpersonal communication patterns differ from culture to culture. Rules that guide expectations and appropriateness of actions and responses are socially prescribed and thus differ according to the values imposed by the culture. The strength of the general theory to explicate friendship within cultures is evidenced by the homogeneity in the data from each culture in terms of the specified attributes. The diversity of the attributes across cultures illustrates the value of the theory in explicating the same general structure across cultures while discerning between cultures on specific attributes. Table 7.1 shows within-culture homogeneity and between-culture diversity of friendship, illustrating support of the studies for Proposition 4. The attributes listed in the table are obtained from the investigations in Part II as well as from the seminal investigations reported in Chapter 3.

Judgments of within-culture homogeneity are based on the level of agreement of the attributes that can be observed within the samples. Generally, the less diversity within the sample concerning a particular attribute, the higher the homogeneity. Commonalities can be seen among cultures, particularly between Korea and Nigeria. The American samples share only Trust as an attribute with the Nigerian sample. Commonalities between Korea and

Table 7.1
Homogeneity Within and Diversity Between Cultures on Friendship Attributes

	United States	*Korea*	*Nigeria*
Attributes and Level of Within-Culture Homogeneity	Trust (High)	Congeniality (Moderate)	Tolerance (High)
	Respect (High)	Sympathy (Moderate)	Honesty (High)
	Authenticity (High)	Unselfishness (Moderate)	Caring (High)
	Psychological Support (Low)	Responsibility (Moderate)	Trust (High)
		Honesty (Moderate)	Humor (Low)
		Generosity (High)	Intelligence (Low)
		Intelligence (High)	Responsibility (Moderate)

Nigeria include Honesty, Intelligence, and Responsibility, although differences in their homogeneity within each culture may be noted. Diversity among the three cultures is demonstrated in terms of the attributes that predict friendship formation and growth. Cushman and Kovacic (in press) note the implications of such intercultural diversity for the establishment and deepening of intercultural mate relationships. The same implications could be drawn for intercultural friendships. Diversity between cultures concerning the attributes necessary for friendship formation and growth complicate the development of intercultural friendship. Examination of such diversity has great potential to enhance our understanding of intercultural friendship.

Diversity is linked to communication interaction. The greater the diversity between cultures, the greater the impediment for intercultural friendship development. This is because the two individuals, in the attempt to initiate and/or develop the friendship, would be providing communication of support on different sets of attributes. Each individual's interaction need for friendship development would remain unfulfilled; a friendship would not grow. If individuals from different cultures are sufficiently interpersonally sensitive or culturally sensitive to recognize the needs of the other or the diversity of the cultures, these difficulties can be overcome and friendship may flourish.

Homogeneity within cultures is also linked to communication interaction. For attributes with a high degree of homogeneity, expressions of support for these attributes within the language must be tight. For example, in American culture, the attribute Trust has a high degree of homogeneity, whereas Psychological Support has a low degree. To develop a friendship, the dyad must precisely express their perception of trust for each other. However, psychological support may take many forms of expression. Stated from a receiver orientation, trust will only be recognized in precise expressions; whereas psychological support will be recognized in a wide variety of expressions.

Conflict: Concerning Propositions 5 and 6

Conflict in interpersonal interaction has been widely examined (e.g., Canary and Spitzberg, 1987, 1989; Conrad, 1983; Folger and Poole, 1984; Himes, 1980; Kilmann and Thomas, 1975, 1977; Papa and Natalle, 1989; Putnam and Wilson, 1982; Renwick, 1977; Sillars, 1980a, 1980b). Early work on conflict emphasized *conflict resolution*; conflict was seen as a destructive force to be avoided at all costs. In the 1960s the study of conflict began to take on a new focus; *conflict management* became the preferred term as definitions of conflict took on a healthy, positive aspect (Putnam and Wilson, 1982). Conflict is generally seen as an inevitable and potentially constructive part of human interaction (Putnam and Poole, 1987). Theory and research of conflict, therefore, is focused not on the destructive or constructive nature of the conflict itself, but on the destructive or constructive outcomes of attempts at conflict management.

Cushman (Cushman, 1989; Cushman and Kovacic, in press) discusses high- and low-quality conflict patterns for mate relationships. Generally, conflict patterns that reinforce the crucial attributes of the mate relationship result in increased intimacy and high relational quality. The same logic can be applied to friendship. Applying Cushman's (1989) explanation to the friend relationship provides a discussion that illustrates indirect support for Proposition 5; friends can be said to engage in conflict that is neither constructive nor destructive to the relationship. Such conflict does not threaten the crucial attributes for friendship. (Refer to Table 7.1 for lists of these crucial attributes for three cultures.) Provided that neither the conflict issue nor the interaction over the conflict threatens self-concept support on these attributes, the conflict has neither a constructive nor destructive impact on the friendship. For example, two American friends can repeatedly engage in conflict over the issue of legalized abortion. Provided that the interaction does not threaten their support of each other for the attributes of trust, respect, authenticity, or psychological support, the conflict will not impair their friendship. In fact, conflict interaction can enhance the friendship by providing the opportunity to express self-concept support on the crucial variables. For example, although one of the American friends may disagree with the other's opinion, s/he may express respect for the friend's conviction in defending his/her viewpoint on an emotionally laden and explosive issue.

Conflict issues or interaction that involve the crucial variables can damage the friendship (Proposition 5). As interaction over a conflict threatens self-concept support on the crucial variables, the friendship suffers. This argument is upheld for mate relationships by several theorists and researchers (Cushman, 1989; Cushman and Cahn, 1985; Cushman and Kovacic, in press; Genshaft, 1980; Levinger, 1980; Rands, Levinger, and Mellinger, 1981; Ritter, 1985; Ting-Toomey, 1983).

Further applying Cushman's (Cushman, 1989; Cushman and Kovacic, in press) explanation of mate relationship quality to friendship provides a discussion that illustrates indirect support for Proposition 6; conflict involving these crucial issues need not destroy the relationship. Conflict in low-quality relationships is characterized by the introduction of a complaint with negative affect; followed by confrontation, defensiveness, and/or cross-complaining; then by neutral or negative affect, reciprocated affect, and escalation or withdrawal (Cushman and Kovacic, in press). For example, in a low-quality American friendship, conflict interaction would begin as follows: "You returned my car with an empty gas tank. You know how I hate that!" A low-quality interaction would then continue: "I have never done that before, and I was in a hurry to get it back to you on time because you are so demanding about getting your things back. You really are stingy." Having threatened their mutual support on crucial variables (trust, respect, authenticity, and psychological support), the two are likely to increase their negative affect, escalate the dispute, and withdraw from the relationship. Once support is removed for the crucial variables, the friendship loses its basis; the pair is unable to solve the problem successfully.

Conflict in high-quality relationships is characterized by the introduction of a focused issue with neutral affect; followed by agreement on a preproportionalized issue with neutral or positive affect; then by mutual exploration of potential solutions; and finally by consensus and implementation of a solution (Cushman and Kovacic, in press). For example, in a high-quality American friendship, conflict interaction would begin as follows: "Although I appreciate your taking care not to damage my car when you borrow it, and returning it promptly, the gas tank was empty when it was returned, and I need to talk to you about this." A high-quality interaction would progress: "I did return it when I said I would, and I washed it before returning it, but I do remember that it usually has a full tank of gas when I borrow it." Having established the security of their mutual support on crucial variables (trust, respect, authenticity, and psychological support), the two are able to explore solutions and choose one to implement (Proposition 6).

The essential element for constructive handling of conflict that threatens support on the crucial attributes is the ability to proportionalize the problem (Cushman, 1989; Cushman and Kovacic, in press)—to define the problem in such a way that it does not threaten support on the crucial variables across the total relationship (Proposition 6). Little empirical work on conflict and friendship quality can be found; however, this argument finds support for mate relationships in the work of several theorists and researchers (Billingham and Sack, 1987; Birchler, Weiss, and Vincent, 1975; Cushman, 1989; Cushman and Cahn, 1985; Cushman and Kovacic, in press; Genshaft, 1980; Gottman, Markman, and Notarius, 1977; Noller, 1981; Rands et al., 1981; Ting-Toomey, 1983). The "complainer" must be able to express general self-concept support while making the specific and focused complaint; the "accused" must be able to accept both the general support and the specific complaint; and both must be willing to engage in a mutual search for an acceptable solution (Cushman, 1989; Cushman and Kovacic, in press). If the two are unable to proportionalize the problem, the complaint appears global and unfocused, thereby impairing general self-concept support on the crucial variables (Cushman, 1989; Cushman and Kovacic, in press). Without the basis of that general self-concept support, the friendship can be severely damaged (Proposition 5).

Quality of Relationship: Concerning Proposition 7

The final category of interpersonal communication to be examined is relationship quality. Given the studies of friendship in Part II, we will consider what constitutes quality from a communication point of view; the following discussion provides indirect support for Proposition 7. Quality is considered according to three characteristics: increasing intimacy, personal growth, and communication effectiveness. First, a quality friendship is characterized by an increase in intimacy or closeness over time (Gibbs, 1977; Hays, 1984). Frequent and consistent communication of self-concept support must be provided on the crucial attributes for the particular culture (see Table 7.1) in order for friendship to develop and deepen. The more frequently such support is communicated, the more the friendship deepens.

Second, a quality friendship is characterized by individuals' achievement of personal growth—learning and developing both within and outside the relationship (Cushman, 1979; Hays, 1984). This characteristic is greatly dependent on the homogeneity of crucial friendship variables (see Table 7.1). Cultures with high homogeneity around certain attributes allow less freedom for individual growth on those variables; personal growth within the relationship on those attributes may be thwarted by cultural impositions. In such cases the individual must look outside the friendship for growth in these areas while maintaining the attributes within the relationship. In cultures where homogeneity is high around crucial attributes, individual growth within the friendship must occur on other attributes—those that are not necessary for the development and maintenance of the friendship. For attributes with a low degree of homogeneity within the culture, growth within the relationship is less inhibited.

Finally, a quality friendship is characterized by effective communication of self-concept support, both directly and indirectly (Cushman, 1979; Cushman and Kovacic, in press; Crawford, 1977; Hays, 1984; Gibbs, 1977; LaGaipa, 1977). Friends can provide self-concept support for crucial attributes directly (as in "I respect you") or indirectly (as in "I respect people who do the things you do"). Further study of interpersonal penetration in friendships can illuminate the various topics within which indirect communication of self-concept support can take place. Effectively communicated self-concept support, whether direct or indirect, predicts relationship quality. In a quality friendship, each individual has a great degree of certainty about the other's opinion of him/her.

Conclusions

The investigations of friendship in Part II strengthen the theoretic structure and provide impetus for further study, clearly illustrating that theoretic development is far from exhausted. Most important, the studies provide support for Propositions 1–4. See Table 7.2 for a summary of direct support for the first four propositions.

Generally, these investigations provide for the theory: (1) compelling support for the basic developmental structure with self-concept support as the generative mechanism; (2) bases for revision and refinement both generally and specifically; and (3) bases for extension to other cultures, to different types of friendship, and to a communication component. The above discussion of implications across the categories of culture, conflict, and quality provides indirect support for Propositions 5–7, illustrating the myriad directions that may be taken by research in this area. Part IV advances these ideas: chapter 12 advocates a view of interpersonal relationships as cultural choice and presents a study to support that stance; chapter 13 provides critiques of the individual studies, assesses the current state of theoretic development gleaned from the studies, proposes theoretic advancement, and recommends research for further theoretic development. Prior to this analysis, however, we must explore studies of the mate relationship theory. Part III presents investigations of the mate relationship theory, summarizes their contributions to theoretic support and extension, and discusses implications across the same three categories of interpersonal communication.

Table 7.2
Direct Support for Propositions 1–4

	Proposition	*Supporting Research*
1.	Perceived self-concept support is the basis of interpersonal attraction.	Korn, Chapter 4; Bahk, Chapter 5; Moemeka and Nicotera, Chapter 6
2.	Different types of perceived self-concept support are the basis for different types of interpersonal relationships.	Bahk, Chapter 5
3.	Different types of self-concept support are the basis for *entry* into and increasing *intensity* of interpersonal relationships.	Korn, Chapter 4 (for intensity); Moemeka and Nicotera, Chapter 6
4.	The type and form of self-concept support is homogeneous by culture.	Korn, Chapter 4; Moemeka and Nicotera, Chapter 6

References

Billingham, R. E., and A.R. Sack (1987). Conflict tactics and the level of emotional commitment among unmarrieds. *Human Relations* 40:59–74.

Birchler, G. R., R. L. Weiss, and J. P. Vincent (1975). Multimethod analysis of social reinforcement exchange between maritally distressed and non-distressed spouse and stranger dyads. *Journal of Personality and Social Psychology 31:349–60.*

Canary, D. J., and B. H. Spitzberg (1987). Appropriateness and effectiveness perceptions of conflict strategies. *Human Communication Research* 14:93–118.

Canary, D. J., and B. H. Spitzberg (1989). A model of the perceived competence of conflict strategies. *Human Communication Research, 15:630–49.*

Conrad, C. (1983). Power and performance as correlates of supervisors' choice of modes of managing conflict: A preliminary investigation. *Western Journal of Speech Communication 47:218–28.*

Crawford, M. (1977). What is a friend? *New Society 42:116–17.*

Cushman, D. P. (1979). Communication in establishing, maintaining, and terminating interpersonal relationships. *Journal of Youth and Adolescence* 8:443–52.

Cushman, D. P. (1989). Communication in establishing, maintaining, and terminating interpersonal relationships: A study of mateship. In S. S. King (ed.), *Human communication as a field of study: Selected contemporary views* (87–104). Albany, NY: State University of New York Press.

Cushman, D. P., and Cahn (1985). *Communication in Interpersonal Relationships.* Albany, NY: State University of New York Press.

Cushman D. P., and B. Kovacic (in press). A rules perspective on communication theory. In F. L. Casmir (ed.), *Communication theory.* Albany, NY: State University of New York Press.

Folger, J. P., and M. S. Poole (1984). *Working through conflict: A communication perspective.* Glenview, IL: Scott, Foresman.

Genshaft, J. L. (1980). Perceptual and defensive style variables in marital discord. *Social Behavior and Personality* 8:81–84.

Gibbs, S. (1977). *A comparative analysis of friendship functions in six age groups of men and women.* Unpublished dissertation, Wayne State University, Detroit, MI.

Gottman, J., H. Markman, and C. Notarius (1977). The topography of marital conflict: A sequential analysis of verbal and nonverbal behavior. *Journal of Marriage and the Family* 39:461–477.

Hays, R. B. (1984). The development and maintenance of friendship. *Journal of Social and Personal Relationships* 1:75–98.

Himes, J. S. (1980). *Conflict and conflict management.* Athens, GA: University of Georgia Press.

Kilmann, R. H., and K.W. Thomas (1975). Interpersonal conflict-handling behavior as reflections of Jungian personality dimensions. *Psychological Reports* 37:971–80.

Kilmann, R. H., and K.W. Thomas (1977). Developing a forced-choice measure of conflict-handling behavior: The "MODE" instrument. *Educational and Psychological Measurement* 37:309–25.

LaGaipa, J. J. (1977). Testing a multidimensional approach to friendship. In S. Duck (ed.), *Theory and practice in interpersonal attraction* (249–70). London: Academic Press.

Levinger, G. (1980). Toward the analysis of close relationships. *Journal of Experimental Social Psychology* 16:510–44.

Noller, P. (1981). Gender and marital adjustment level differences in decoding messages from spouses and strangers. *Journal of Personality and Social Psychology* 41:272–78.

Papa, M. J., and E. J. Natalle (1989). Gender, strategy selection, and satisfaction in interpersonal conflict. *Western Journal of Speech Communication* 53:260–72.

Putnam, L. L., and M. S. Poole (1987). Conflict and negotiation. In F. M. Jablin, L. L. Putnam, K. H. Roberts, and L. W. Porter (eds.), *Handbook of organizational communication* (549–99). Newbury Park, CA: Sage.

Putnam, L. L., and C.E. Wilson (1982). Communicative strategies in organizational conflicts: Reliability and validity of a measurement scale. In M. Burgoon (ed.), *Communication yearbook 6* (629–52). Beverly Hills, CA: Sage.

Rands, M., G. Levinger, and G. D. Mellinger (1981). Patterns of conflict resolution and marital satisfaction. *Journal of Family Issues* 2:297–321.

Renwick, P. A. (1977). Effects of sex differences on the perception and management of conflict: An exploratory study. *Organizational Behavior and Human Performance* 16:143–55.

Ritter, K. Y. (1985). The cognitive therapies. *Journal of Counseling and Development* 64:42–44.

Sillars, A. L. (1980a). Attributions and communication in roommate conflicts. *Communication Monographs* 47:180–200.

Sillars, A. L. (1980b). The sequential and distributional structure of conflict interactions as a function of attributions concerning the locus of responsibility and stability of conflicts. In D. Nimmo (ed.), *Communication Yearbook 4* (218–35). New Brunswick, NJ: Transaction.

Taylor, D., and I. Altman, (1966). Intimacy-scaled stimuli for use in studies of interpersonal relations. *Psychological Reports 19*: 729–730.

Ting-Toomey, S. (1983). An analysis of verbal communication patterns in high and low marital adjustment groups. *Human Communication Research* 9:306–19.

Part III

Investigations of the Mate Relationship

8

Mate Relationship Entry, Intensity, and Communication Variables: A Preliminary Study

Donald P. Cushman and Dudley D. Cahn

Many communication scholars advocate a developmental approach, paying particular attention to how communicators develop, maintain, and dissolve interpersonal relationships (e.g., Baxter and Bullis, 1986; Baxter and Wilmot, 1983; Dillard and Witteman, 1985; Duck, 1988). Basic to an understanding of the role communicators play in the development of interpersonal relationships is the identification of key entry and intensity variables (Cahn, 1983, 1987). An intensity variable is incremental; its effects become stronger as a relationship develops. Entry variables, on the other hand, are defining in nature, for their effects are unique to a particular type of relationship and remain relatively constant throughout its development. Taking friendship as an example, trust, liking, and a helping orientation may function as entry variables because these terms distinguish friendship from other types of interpersonal relationships and are important for all degrees of intensity and at all stages of development (Cushman and Cahn, 1985).

The mate relationship—the development of intimacy over time in male–female interaction that clears the field of competitors (Karp, Jackson, and Lester, 1971)—is of particular interest to communication scholars. The mate relationship involves many social arrangements, some of which may be viewed as steps toward permanence. Mate relationships at all stages account for a great deal of intense happiness, satisfaction, and meaning in life (Cushman and Cahn, 1985).

The present study attempts to answer these questions: 1) What are some of the mate relationship entry variables? 2) What is at least one of the intensity variables that indexes the growth of a mate relationship? 3) What are some of the communication variables that facilitate the growth of a mate relationship?

Rationale and Hypotheses

The mate relationship is clearly different from other types of relationships such as friend, boss–employee, and doctor–patient relationships. A review of the research literature reveals that intelligence, physical attraction, and sex appeal may define mate relationships and function as entry variables (Cushman and Cahn, 1985; see also Chapter 3, this volume). When selecting a mate, one is attracted most to others of the opposite sex who one believes are about as intelligent, physically attractive, and sexually appealing as one believes onself to be (Duck, 1988).

H1: *As mate relationships become more permanent, intelligence, physical attraction, and sex appeal function as entry variables.*

A mate relationship grows more permanent as the couple achieves a deepening sense of commitment. The closer the other comes to one's ideal conception of a mate, the more likely one is to clear the field of competitors and feel committed to the relationship (Cushman and Cahn, 1985). Several researchers have attempted to discriminate between different degrees or levels of developing commitment in intimate male–female relationships. They found that Occasional Date, Steady Date, Engaged, and Spouse appear to mark distinct levels of increasing commitment (Bailey and Helm, 1974; Helm, Bailey, and Vance, 1977; see also Chapter 2, this volume).

H2: *As mate relationships become more permanent, Casual Date, Steady Date, Fiancé, and Spouse function as labels for identifiable developmental stages.*

Particular communication variables may facilitate the growth of a mate relationship. A review of the literature reveals that reciprocated affection, respect, and psychological-emotional support create conditions for the growth of a mate relationship (Crawford, 1977; Hill, Rubin, and Peplau, 1976; Krain, 1975; Murstein, 1976; Pam, Plutchik, and Conte, 1973; see also Chapter 2, this volume).

H3: *As mate relationships become more permanent, interpersonal communication in the form of reciprocal respect, affection, and psychological-emotional support facilitate development.*

Since the entry, intensity, and communication variables regarding the mate relationship probably vary among subcultures in the United States, research should take into consideration differences of opinion from at least two different sociocultural groups (Cahn, 1987). It would seem likely that whereas mainland Americans in upstate New York might agree on entry, intensity, and communication variables, members of a more heterogeneous group—for example, citizens of Hawaii—would reflect less agreement among themselves than mainland Americans. Hawaii consists of several distinctive and diverse ethnic groups, namely mainland Americans, Japanese, Chinese, Filipino, Korean, and Polynesian.

H4: *Mainland Americans in upstate New York tend to agree more on mate relationship entry, intensity, and communication variables than respondents in Hawaii.*

Method

Respondents

The United States mainland respondents consisted of 31 students enrolled in a communication class at an eastern university. The Hawaiian respondents consisted of 38 students enrolled in a communication class at the University of Hawaii.

Measurements

Data were gathered from the respondents using a metric scaling technique designed to measure cognitive space (Woelfel and Fink, 1980). More specifically, the technique measures perceived distance between concepts. The smaller the number of units between two measured concepts in cognitive space, the stronger the relationship is to the individual. The greater the number of units between two measured concepts, the weaker is the relationship. For example, if an individual perceives the relationship between love and hate as being 100 units apart (in cognitive space), the same individual may perceive the distance between love and liking as being only 30 units apart. The cognitive distance between any pair of concepts may be measured

Table 8.1
Measured Cognitive Distance Between Terms for Entry Variables in Mate Relationship

Entry Variables	*Casual Date*	*Steady Date*	*Fiancé*	*Spouse*
Intelligence				
Mainland group				
Mean	32	28	27	26
Std. Err.	6	6	7	7
Hawaiian group				
Mean	49	44	36*	37
Std. Err.	6	7	6	7
Physical Attraction				
Mainland group				
Mean	30	24	26	25
Std. Err.	6	5	7	7
Hawaiian group				
Mean	57	24*	25	25
Std. Err.	26	4	5	4
Sex Appeal				
Mainland group				
Mean	23	19	21	23
Std. Err.	5	5	7	9
Hawaiian group				
Mean	58	24*	25	23
Std. Err.	26	5	5	30

$^{*}p < .05$

in this manner. Theoretically, these paired measures are ratio scales because they have a true zero point (i.e., no perceived distance between concepts).

The following illustrates typical questions on the test. Respondents were asked, "If Acquaintance and Best Friend are 100 units apart, how far apart are Casual Date and Spouse?" Among the tested concepts were Fiancé, Spouse, Psychological Support, Casual Date, Affection, Sexually Appealing, Respect, Intelligent, Ideal Mate, Steady Date, and Physically Attractive.

Results

Regarding mate relationship entry variables, the results are shown in Table 8.1. The data from the United States mainland respondents show only 2 out of 12 statistically significant differences. The Hawaiian data show only 1 out of 12

Table 8.2
Measured Cognitive Distance Between Terms for Stages of Increasing Mate Relationship

	Casual Date	*Steady Date*	*Fiancé*	*Spouse*
Ideal Mate				
Mainland group				
Mean	74	42*	33*	24*
Std. Err.	6	6	9	6
Hawaiian group				
Mean	95	59*	28*	28*
Std. Err.	28	28	5	5

*$p < .05$

Table 8.3
Measured Cognitive Distance Among Three Forms of Interpersonal Communication Over Mate Relationship Stages

Communication Forms	*Casual Date*	*Steady Date*	*Fiancé*	*Spouse*
Respect				
Mainland group				
Mean	30	16*	11*	12
Std. Err.	6	5	5	6
Hawaiian group				
Mean	73	30*	16*	18
Std. Err.	23	6	3	11
Affection				
Mainland group				
Mean	58	20*	8	10
Std. Err.	19	6	5	5
Hawaiian group				
Mean	58	19*	9	11
Std. Err.	8	4	2	4
Psychological Support				
Mainland group				
Mean	45	19*	10	13
Std. Err.	6	5	5	7
Hawaiian group				
Mean	63	26*	23	15
Std. Err.	9	6	9	4

*$p < .05$

and reveal higher levels of heterogeneity or disagreement as indicated by the standard errors. Thus, the data tend to support the first hypothesis. Intelligence, physical attraction, and sex appeal tend to remain constant throughout the development of a mate relationship.

As for the identification of developmental stages, the results are shown in Table 8.2. The respondents from the continental United States show statistically significant decreases in the mean distances between each concept and Ideal Mate with acceptable levels of standard error in each pair of concepts. Thus, these data provide strong support for the second hypothesis. However, the Hawaiian data, though suggesting a similar trend, reveal no statistically significant difference for the cognitive distance between fiancé and spouse and a much higher degree of heterogeneity of difference of opinion for Casual Date and Steady Date.

The results of the third analysis concerning communication behavior are displayed in Table 8.3. For the perceived expressions of respect and affection, there is strong support for both groups. In the case of psychological support, the results are mixed. For the mainland American data, the trend is the same as for affection and respect, but in the Hawaiian data, no trend is discernible. At least for the mainland Americans, hypothesis three is supported, whereas for the Hawaiians it is only partially supported.

Regarding hypothesis four, differences between the mainland Americans and the Hawaiians are depicted in all three tables.

Discussion

Because this study employs a cross-sectional design, relies on self-report measures, and does not manipulate any theoretical processes under laboratory controlled conditions, the conclusions derived from these data are limited. Thus, at best the results of this study lend only preliminary support to the four hypotheses.

What distinguishes mate relationships from other types of interpersonal relationships? Here we found strong support from both groups for specific variables, with 21 of 24 measurements being consistent with the hypothesis and two of the three differences resulting from high measurement error. According to the results of this study, if one intends to form a mate relationship, physical attractiveness, sex appeal, and intelligence are the key defining characteristics at each stage of the relationship. They are qualitative in nature, and their importance remains constant throughout the stages of mate relationship development.

At each stage of a developing mate relationship, at least one variable grows stronger. Both the mainland American and the Hawaiian groups provide reasonable evidence that such a scale is useful in distinguishing levels of permanence. Results suggest that the mate relationship develops through identifiable stages—Casual Date, Steady Date, Fiancé, and Spouse.

Finally, the way one communicates verbally and nonverbally varies with the type of relationship. In both groups, respect, affection, and psychological support clearly differentiated the first three levels of commitment, but failed to separate fiancé from spouse. One possible reason for this is that neither group of respondents contained married couples; thus, the level of spouse could not be separated from the other levels on these dimensions because of a lack of marital experience. Future research is needed to resolve this issue. For the moment, however, it is clear that if a couple is interested in facilitating the growth of a mate relationship, they must manifest mutual respect, affection, and psychological support for one another.

More research is also needed on cultural differences regarding the role of communication in the mate relationship. The mainland American respondents showed greater agreement than the Hawaiian respondents on the mate relationship entry, intensity, and communication variables. That the Hawaiians expressed greater disagreement over some variables, failed to distinguish clearly between some concepts, and lacked significant differences in a few cases suggests that the concepts are truly culture-specific.

References

Bailey, R., and B. Helm (1974). Matrimonial commitment and date/ideal-date perceptions. *Perceptual and Motor Skills* 39:1245–46.

Baxter, L.A., and C. Bullis (1986). Turning points in developing romantic relationships. *Human Communication Research* 12:469–93.

Baxter, L., and W. Wilmot (1983). Communication characteristics of relationships with differential growth rates. *Communication Monographs* 50:264–72.

Cahn, D. (1983). Relative importance of perceived understanding in initial interaction and development of interpersonal Relationships. *Psychological Reports* 53:923–29.

Cahn, D. (1987). *Letting go: A practical theory of relationship disengagement and reengagement*. Albany, NY: State University of New York Press.

Crawford, M. (1977). What is a friend? *New Society* 42:116–17.

Cushman, D., and D. Cahn (1985). *Communication in interpersonal relationships*. Albany, NY: State University of New York Press.

Dillard, J., and H. Witteman (1985). Romantic relationships at work: Organizational and personal influences. *Human Communication Research* 12:99–116.

Duck, S. (1988). *Relating to others*. Chicago: Dorsey.

Helm, B., R. Bailey, and B. K. Vance (1977). Interpersonal commitment and self-concept support. *Journal of Social Psychology* 102:319–20.

Hill, C., Z. Rubin and L. Peplau (1976). Breakups before marriage: The end of 103 affairs. *Journal of Social Issues* 32:147–68.

Karp, E. S., J. Jackson, and D. Lester (1970). Ideal-self fulfillment in mate selection: A corollary to the complementary need theory of mate selection. *Journal of Marriage and the Family* 32:269–72.

Krain, M. (1977). Effects of love and liking in premarital dyads. *Sociological Focus* 10:249–62.

Murstein, B. I. (1976). *Who will marry whom?* New York: Springer.

Pam, A., R. Plutchik, and H. Conte (1973). Love: A psychometric approach. *Proceedings of the 81st Annual Convention of the American Psychological Association*, 159–60.

Woelfel, J., and E. Fink (1980). *Science and human communication: A theory of cultural processes.* New York: Academic Press.

9

Development of the Mate Relationship in Two Cultures: Theoretical Universals in the United States and Korea

Anne Maydan Nicotera

Cross-Cultural Comparison

Gudykunst (1989) asserts that general dimensions of interpersonal relations may be universal across cultures. A preliminary test of this claim would attempt to support in another culture a viable theory of interpersonal relationships that has been supported in the United States. Gudykunst (1989) also states that cross-cultural comparisons should always be theoretically based, because it is underlying theoretical dimensions that will remain universal. Two important contributions to such theoretic work are cross-cultural comparisons of social penetration (Gudykunst, 1983, 1985a, 1985c; Gudykunst, Chua, and Gray, 1987; Gudykunst and Nishida, 1983, 1984; Gudykunst, Nishida, and Chua, 1987; Gudykunst, Yang, and Nishida, 1985) and the preliminary work of Cushman and his associates as represented in this volume (also Cushman and Cahn, 1985; Cushman, Valentinsen, and Dietrich, 1982). A study was conducted in an attempt to crystallize and enrich the work of Cushman and his associates (see Part I, this volume, especially Chapter 3) and provide a basis for the advancement of the work on social penetration.

Theoretical Basis

Cushman and his associates have developed a theory of mate relationship development that attempts to describe and explain levels and dimensions of the mate relationship in America (Cushman and Cahn, 1985; Cushman, Valentinsen, and Dietrich, 1982). (See chapters 1 through 3 of this volume for explication and background of the general theory.) According to the theory, the mate relationship follows a developmental continuum: Casual Date, Steady Date, Fiancé, and Spouse. Cushman posits that social rules guide intimacy such that intimacy will deepen with increased accuracy of partners' perceptions of each other's real and ideal self-concepts. Further, as intimacy deepens, each partner will perceive that the other resembles his/her own real and ideal self-concept.

Intelligence, physical attractiveness, and sex appeal were established in chapters 3 and 8 as defining characteristics of the mate relationship. Theoretically, these dimensions are not expected to differ as level of intimacy increases. Respect, affection, and psychological support are the characteristics that theoretically discriminate the levels from one another. Deeper levels of intimacy will exhibit more intensity in these dimensions.

Seminal tests of the theory (see Chapter 3) find strong support for the hypothesis that the levels Casual Date, Steady Date, Fiancé and Spouse represent stable and significantly different semantic markers for increasing degrees of the mate relationship. The seminal study also finds that Intelligence, Physical Attractiveness, and Sex Appeal are defining characteristics of the mate role that do not vary with increasing degrees of intimacy.

Rationale for This Study

Cushman's concept of a developmental and topological process in mate relationship development is not unique. There is strong agreement among researchers from a variety of perspectives that interpersonal relationships are developmental and topological (see Chapter 2 of this volume for details). Few attempts have been made, however, to develop a measuring instrument that identifies stages in different cultures differentially or that allows for cross-cultural comparison without distortion. One approach that offers this potential and that has been used in the United States and Japan is the method followed by Cushman and his associates (Cushman and Nishida, 1984, unpublished study described in Cushman and Cahn, 1985; Chapter 3, this volume). The entry attributes in the instrument validated in the seminal study (see Chapter 3) include Intelligent, Physically Attractive, and Sexually Appealing. These attributes are included in the survey for verification. The primary task is to identify intensity variables from the theory

(Cushman and Cahn, 1985; Cushman, Valentinsen, and Dietrich, 1982) and from the literature (see Chapter 2); these are specified below.

Cushman and Nishida (1984, unpublished study described in Cushman & Cahn, 1985) pursued a similar strategy for a developmental theory in Japan. In-depth interviews with 35 college students located the following attributes: Common Values, Sound Health, Easy to Talk to, Intelligent, Affectionate, Honest, and Handles Money Well. Although levels of the mate relationship were not sought in the interviews, such research represents a promising approach to the development of a cross-cultural instrument. Independent verification of this study is another task of the present research.

Gudykunst and Nishida (1983) point out that a communication component is necessary to understand the process of development in the mate relationship. Here the research on social penetration finds its relevance. To provide a basis for the expansion of Cushman's theory, a set of social penetration questions (Altman and Taylor, 1973; Taylor and Altman, 1966) was included.

Hypotheses and Research Questions

Many theorists have posited specific stages and dimensions of the mate relationship development. These levels and dimensions need to be located with an instrument that permits cross-cultural comparison on a theoretical level while allowing for culturally divergent perceptions of specific attributes of interpersonal relations. The successful development of such an instrument would provide evidence for the validity of a method for exploration of Gudykunst's (1989) claim that general dimensions of interpersonal relations may be universal across cultures. Furthermore, use of such an instrument can provide a deeper understanding of relationship development in particular cultures. Thus, the study of interpersonal relationship development can be advanced both within and across cultures.

American Study

The focus of the study is to supplement the results of the seminal study in America (Chapter 3) by hypothesizing specific intensity variables for mate relationships. Many attributes of the mate relationship have been empirically verified in previous research (see Chapter 2). In order to draw upon the empirical strength of published research and to unite the work of Cushman and his associates with that of these scholars, semantic terms from this body of literature (see Chapter 2) were considered with the attributes used in the seminal study. A list of attributes of the mate relationship was generated. These attributes are Psychological Support, Emotional Support, Affection,

Trust, Commitment, Intimacy, Attachment, and Investment of Self in Relationship. The following hypotheses were generated.

H1: *Casual Date, Steady Date, Fiancé, and Spouse represent stable and significantly different semantic markers for increasing degrees of the mate relationship among the American sample.*

H2: *Psychological Support, Emotional Support, Affection, Trust, Commitment, Intimacy, Attachment, and Investment of Self in Relationship are dimensions of the mate relationship in the United States that increase in intensity as the relationship develops.*

Korean Study

Exploratory data from a Korean sample provided a theoretical cross-cultural comparison. Korea was chosen for the same theoretical reasons articulated by Korn (Chapter 4) and Bahk (Chapter 5). (See these chapters for discussions of the cultural disparities between Korea and the United States) Korean culture includes three types of mate relationship: arranged, nonarranged (love), and eclectic (a combination of arranged and love). To maintain contextual similarity to American mate relationships, Korean data collection efforts were focused on eliciting information about nonarranged mate relationships.

Following the procedure of Cushman and Nishida (1984, unpublished study described in Cushman and Cahn, 1985), 25 students were interviewed in Korea by a bilingual interviewer who is a native speaker of the Korean language. The interviews sought levels and dimensions of relationship development in nonarranged mate relationships. A questionnaire was developed from the Korean interviews with five levels and eight dimensions. The levels were Opposite-Sex Acquaintance, Opposite-Sex Friend, Lover, Engaged, and Spouse. The dimensions were Honest, Easy to Talk to, Assertive, Sound Health, Understanding, Intelligent, Attractive, and Handles Money Well. All of these labels, and those to follow, are back-translations from the Korean into English.

RQ1: *Do Opposite-Sex Acquaintance, Opposite-Sex Friend, Lover, Engaged, and Spouse represent stable and different semantic markers for increasing levels of the nonarranged mate relationship among the Korean sample?*

RQ2: *For the Korean sample, are the variables Honest, Easy to Talk to, Assertive, Sound Health, Understanding, Intelligent, Attractive, and Handles Money Well dimensions of the nonarranged* *mate relationship that increase in intensity as the relationship develops?*

Communication Component

In an attempt to provide a basis for future exploration of the role of communication in the mate-selection process, the following exploratory research question is examined. Penetration is defined as degree, depth, and breadth of intimacy, following the work of Taylor and Altman (Altman and Taylor, 1973; Taylor and Altman, 1966), Gudykunst (1985b), and Gudykunst and Nishida (1983). (See Chapter 5 for a discussion of social penetration.)

RQ3: *In a (nonarranged) mate relationship, do the Korean and the American samples each discuss specific, identifiable, and stable topics at differing levels of penetration?*

Method: Study 1

Sample

The American sample was drawn from a group of undergraduate students enrolled in a communication course at a moderate-sized northeastern university. The sample included 14 males and 25 females with an average age of 21 years. The average length of time the dating subjects had known their current dating partner was 2.4 years.

The Korean sample was drawn from a group of social sciences students at a Korean university. The Korean sample included 14 males and 23 females, with an average age of 21 years. The average length of time dating respondents knew their current dating partner was 3.2 years. Korean subjects were instructed to answer the questionnaire in regard to nonarranged relationships.

Questionnaires

Following the seminal work, both the American and Korean questionnaires contained a Galileo scale; they also contained a measurement of interpersonal penetration. Levels and dimensions for both the American and Korean samples were measured with the Galileo method, described in previous chapters. These data were analyzed with version 5.3 of the Galileo program.

Measurement of Interpersonal Penetration

Several questions were asked regarding the extent of subjects' interaction with their current dating partner. Measurement of interpersonal penetration was based on the work of Gudykunst (1985b), Taylor and Altman (1966), and Gudykunst and Nishida (1983). The questionnaire administered to the Korean sample was Taylor and Altman's (1966) original scale, which included 10 topics or dimensions, each comprised of three scale items. The dimensions were Relationships with Others (RL); Parental Family (PF); Love, Dating, and Sex (LDS); Physical Condition and Attractiveness (PC); School-Work (SW); Money–Property (MP); Own Marriage and Family (OM); Interests, Hobbies, and Habits (IH); Emotions and Feelings (EF); and Personal Attitudes, Values, and Evaluation (PV):

The American questionnaire was a variation of the Korean one, including 12 self-disclosure items explored in three dimensions: the extent to which the subject told his or her current dating partner within the topic; the extent to which the subject asked the particular other within the topic; and the extent to which the subject was told by the particular other within the topic. The respondents were instructed to rate each topic on each dimension on a 3-point scale, where 0 = I have told (asked/been told by) this person nothing about me (him/her); 1 = I (he/she) have (has) talked (asked) in general terms about this item; 2 = I (he/she) have (has) talked (asked) in full and complete detail about this item. The 12 topics were religion (RL), sexual morality (SM), how parents should deal with children (CH), pressures of studies (PS), ambitions/goals (AG), career choice (CC), what makes me furious (FR), what hurts my feelings (HF), what makes me proud of myself (PR), long-range health worries (HW), past illness (PI), and physical fitness efforts (PF).

Data Analysis

Differences between the mate relationship levels in Hypothesis 1 and RQ1 are operationalized as differences in their mean distances from Real Self and Ideal Self in the Galileo space, consistent with the theoretic structure described above. If the levels are different from one another in terms of those reference points, and if their ranges of uncertainty do not overlap, they are considered to represent different semantic markers. Range of uncertainty is assessed as the mean distance score plus or minus the standard error. A mate relationship level is considered to be stable if it has a distance score from any other variable with a small percent of error.

For the American sample, z-scores of mate relationship–level distances from Real Self, Ideal Self, dimension variables, and each other are used to assess statistical significance at the 0.05 level. Given that the levels have been validated in the United States in the past (see chapters 3 and 8 of this volume), tests of statistical significance are warranted. However, for the Korean investigation, the express purpose was to explore the efficacy of Cushman's theoretic structure across cultures. This is accomplished by assessing whether the posited Korean mate relationship levels are stable and whether they signify different levels of intimacy. Tests of statistical significance are considered to be premature in such an exploratory analysis.

The intensities of dimensions in H2 and RQ2 are operationalized by examining their closeness in the Galileo space to mate relationship levels, comparing mean distances of mate relationship levels using each mate relationship dimension in turn as point of reference. The same procedure for the levels in each culture is used to assess whether the dimensions signify different levels of the mate relationship and become more intense as the mate relationship increases in intimacy.

For the penetration items, the American data are analyzed by conducting t-tests between the means for all the topics within each dimension. T-tests are also conducted between dimension means for each topic. It is well established that the execution of such a large number of t-tests inflates the probability of Type I error. However, because of the exploratory nature of the research, an alpha level of 0.05 was maintained for significance. Such a procedure was followed to ensure the generation of an adequate number of topics for future research.

For the Korean penetration data on Taylor and Altman's (1966) measure of interpersonal penetration, the frequency score for each topic is computed as the mean of the frequency scores of the items in the topic; the intimacy score for each topic is computed as the mean of the intimacy scores of the items in the topic. An overall penetration score for each topic may be computed as the mean of the frequency score and the intimacy score. The exploratory nature of the Korean study makes it imprudent to calculate statistical significance among the topics for the Korean sample. As the research question regarding interpersonal penetration is exploratory, comparison of Korean mean penetration scores provides valuable insight for future research.

Results/Discussion: Study 1

Hypothesis 1

The first hypothesis posits that Casual Date, Steady Date, Fiancé, and Spouse represent stable and significantly different semantic markers for increasing

Table 9.1
Comparison of Mean Distances Between Mate Relationship Levels and Real and Ideal Self for American Sample, Study 1

	Casual Date	*Steady Date*	*Fiancé*	*Spouse*
Real Self	80.6	27.4	30.2	22.6
Std. Err.	28.9	4.6	6.1	5.5
% Err.	35.8	16.9	20.1	24.2
N =	37	36	37	37
Ideal Self	101.9	37.3	28.8	25.9
Std. Err.	34.5	5.8	7.1	7.1
% Err.	33.8	15.5	24.6	27.5
N =	35	35	35	36

degrees of the mate relationship among the American sample. Table 9.1 contains the means, standard errors, and percents of error for the distances of four semantic levels of the mate relationship from the concepts Real Self and Ideal Self. These results do not support the first hypothesis for the American sample. The large percent of error for Casual Date in its distance from Real Self shows it to be unstable. Though the errors for the remaining three show them to be relatively more stable in respect to Real Self, their ranges of uncertainty show that together they signify only two overlapping levels. The ranges of uncertainty for the concepts Steady Date and Spouse overlap with the range of uncertainty around Fiancé for the concept Real Self. For Ideal Self, high percent of error shows Casual Date to be unstable, and Fiancé and Spouse have overlapping ranges of uncertainty. In addition, z-scores reveal that the four levels are not significantly different from each other with either Real or Ideal Self as point of reference.

Z-scores of mean differences between the levels using each of the other levels as the point of reference reveal that Casual Date and Steady Date are significantly different when Spouse is the point of reference. Casual Date and Fiancé are significantly different, regardless of the point of reference. Casual Date and Spouse are significantly different only when Steady Date is the point of reference. Steady Date and Fiancé are not significantly different, nor are Steady Date and Spouse or Fiancé and Spouse, regardless of the point of reference.

The concepts Steady Date, Fiancé, and Spouse consistently signify only one level. The levels Casual Date, Steady Date, Fiancé, and Spouse are therefore considered to signify only two levels. The first hypothesis is not supported.

Table 9.2
Comparison of Mean Distances Between Mate Relationship Levels and Real and Ideal Self, Korean Sample

	Opposite-Sex Acquaintance	*Opposite-Sex Friend*	*Lover*	*Engaged*	*Spouse*
Real Self	92.4	54.5	36.7	29.1	17.4
Std. Err.	6.5	4.3	7.3	6.8	5.0
% Err.	30.6	36.4	22.7	30.0	22.2
N =	36	33	22	10	9
Ideal Self	65.5	47.9	40.0	16.0	8.0
Std. Err.	5.9	6.2	11.1	4.2	2.9
% Err.	17.1	26.5	7.4	13.3	14.3
N =	35	34	27	15	14

Research Question 1

Do Opposite-Sex Acquaintance, Opposite-Sex Friend, Lover, Engaged, and Spouse represent stable and different semantic markers for increasing levels of the nonarranged mate relationship among the Korean sample? Table 9.2 contains the means, standard errors, and percents of error for the distances of five semantic levels of the mate relationship from the concepts Real Self and Ideal Self. The results for the concept Real Self in Table 9.2 provide partial support for levels posited in the first research question. The percents of error indicate some instability. However, except for Lover and Engaged, these concepts represent different semantic markers for mate relationship levels. The ranges of uncertainty around Engaged and Spouse overlap by 0.1, but these results must be interpreted with caution, as the data for Engaged and Spouse contain many missing cases.

The results for the five levels with Ideal Self as point of reference also provide partial support for the posited levels. These data show a higher stability than is seen for Real Self. In addition, the ranges of uncertainty around Engaged and Spouse do not overlap with Ideal Self as the point of reference, and Opposite-Sex Friend and Lover are not different from each other in their respective distances from the concept Ideal Self.

Given the fact that Lover overlaps with Engaged for Real Self and with Opposite-Sex Friend for Ideal Self, the logic of this mate relationship level in the hypothesis is not upheld. Without Lover, the ranges of uncertainty around the remaining four concepts show that they signify different levels of intimacy for the mate relationship, following a uniform theoretical progression. The ranges of uncertainty around the levels Engaged and Spouse overlap slightly with Ideal Self as the point of reference, but these data have a high number of missing cases.

The data confirm the second research question for the Korean sample, except for the mate relationship level Lover. A different semantic signifier between Opposite-Sex Friend and Engaged seems warranted, as the conceptual jump between the two levels is illogical. The reader must keep in mind that the terms for these levels have been back-translated from the Korean. Connotations for these terms (such as "lover") in the United States cannot be used to judge connotations in Korea.

Hypothesis 2

The second hypothesis posits that Psychological Support, Emotional Support, Affection, Trust, Commitment, Intimacy, Attachment, and Investment of Self in Relationship are dimensions of the mate relationship in the United States that increase in intensity as the relationship develops. The data show a trend, such that the nine dimensions are closer to the higher levels of the mate relationship than they are to the lower levels, but given that the hypothesized mate relationship levels for the American sample are not supported, using them cannot validate or invalidate mate relationship dimensions. In fact, the data for the nine mate relationship dimensions further represents the lack of support for hypothesized American mate relationship levels. Extremely high percents of error show the instability of the levels as semantic markers.

Many of the ranges of uncertainty overlap, and for almost all variables, the differences among Steady Date, Fiancé, and Spouse are nonsignificant. Z-scores reveal that Casual Date and Steady Date are not significantly different from one another with any reference points; Steady Date and Fiancé are significantly different only with Attachment as a reference point; and Fiancé and Spouse are not different for any reference points. The second hypothesis cannot be adequately tested with this data. It must be retested with stable and significant relationship levels.

Research Question 2

For the Korean sample, are the variables Honest, Easy to Talk to, Assertive, Sound Health, Understanding, Intelligent, Attractive, and Handles Money Well dimensions of the nonarranged mate relationship that increase in intensity as the relationship develops? Table 9.3 contains the means, standard errors, and percents of error for the distances of the five hypothesized semantic levels of the mate relationship to eight mate relationship attributes or dimensions for the Korean sample. The results displayed in Table 9.3 lend

Table 9.3
Comparison of Mean Distances Between Mate Relationship Dimensions and Mate Relationship Levels, Korean Sample

	Opposite-sex Acquaintance	*Opposite-sex Friend*	*Lover*	*Engaged*	*Spouse*
Intelligent	60.3	53.3	39.1	23.3	21.1
Std. Err.	6.9	7.4	8.1	6.0	6.5
% Err.	22.9	30.1	4.2	33.3	23.1
N =	35	36	24	12	13
Attractive	69.1	54.3	38.0	29.2	28.4
Std. Err.	8.2	8.3	10.0	9.7	10.8
% Err.	28.6	22.9	9.1	8.3	15.4
N =	35	35	22	12	13
Honest	58.8	53.5	29.6	16.0	14.7
Std. Err.	5.7	8.3	8.1	5.5	5.4
% Err.	34.3	14.7	8.3	23.1	7.7
N =	35	34	24	13	13
Easy to Talk to	80.3	42.2	29.8	19.2	16.7
Std. Err.	19.9	6.0	8.3	5.8	6.6
% Err.	8.6	40.0	4.2	15.4	23.1
N =	35	35	24	13	13
Assertive	111.1	60.9	36.2	21.5	18.5
Std. Err.	56.4	11.6	8.6	6.4	6.5
% Err.	2.9	8.6	8.3	23.1	15.4
N =	35	35	24	13	13
Sound Health	62.5	51.1	35.2	23.3	20.7
Std. Err.	8.7	7.7	8.8	6.0	6.7
% Err.	26.5	31.4	4.5	38.5	16.7
N =	34	35	22	13	12
Understanding	59.6	51.2	39.3	24.4	24.0
Std. Err.	8.2	7.7	8.9	7.5	9.1
% Err.	22.9	22.2	12.5	16.7	23.1
N =	35	36	24	12	13
Handles Money Well	99.1	71.7	54.9	34.8	36.6
Std. Err.	27.8	8.6	11.0	10.3	10.9
% Err.	2.9	34.4	27.3	9.1	16.7
N =	35	32	22	11	12

little support to the mate relationship dimensions posed in the second research question. Fairly stable decreases in distance were seen for all attributes as relationship level increased, but ranges of uncertainty showed few levels to be different from one another. Opposite-Sex Acquaintance and Opposite-Sex Friend were only different from each other for the attributes Honest and Easy to Talk to. Opposite-Sex Friend and Lover were different for Honest, Assertive, Understanding, and Intelligent. Lover and Engaged were different for Easy to Talk to, Intelligent, and Attractive. Engaged and Spouse were different only for Sound Health. These dimensions may represent entry variables—those that distinguish this relationship type from other types—for Korean nonarranged mate relationships. Further research is needed to test this possibility.

Research Question 3: American Sample

In a mate relationship, does the American sample discuss specific, identifiable, and stable topics at differing levels of penetration? Table 9.4 contains the means, standard deviations, and *N*'s for all American topics across all dimensions. Topics and their abbreviations are identified in the methods section above.

Told dimension. T-tests (at alpha < 0.05) between topics in the *told* dimension indicated that subjects have told their dating partner significantly less about their religious views than about views on sexual morality, pressures of studies, ambitions/goals, or what makes them furious. They have told their date significantly more about religious views than about long-range health worries. Sexual morality has been told about significantly more than how parents ought to deal with children, career choice, long-range health worries, or past illness.

Respondents also report that they have told their dating partner significantly less about how parents ought to deal with children than about pressures of studies, ambitions/goals, what makes them furious, what hurts their feelings, what makes them proud, and physical fitness. They have told significantly more about pressures of their studies than about career choice, long-range health worries, or past illness. Ambitions/goals have been told about more than career choice, long-range health worries, or past illness. Career choice has been told about significantly less than what makes them furious and significantly more than long-range health worries.

In addition, subjects report that they have told their date significantly more about what makes them furious than about long-range health worries. They have told significantly more about what hurts their feelings than about long-range health worries or past illness. What makes them proud has also been told about significantly more than long-range health worries or past

Table 9.4
Mean Values of Topical Penetration, American Sample

	Told	*Asked*	*Been Told*		*Told*	*Asked*	*Been Told*
RL	1.39	1.31	1.28	*FR*	1.74	1.62	1.57
sd	.78	.73	.76	sd	.50	.49	.56
N =	39	38	39	*N* =	37	39	37
SM	1.74	1.50	1.58	*HF*	1.61	1.39	1.40
sd	.44	.69	.60	sd	.64	.71	.76
N =	39	39	38	*N* =	38	39	38
CH	1.23	1.18	1.29	*FR*	1.74	1.62	1.57
sd	.81	.79	.77	sd	.65	.68	.64
N =	39	39	38	*N* =	39	39	38
PS	1.74	1.55	1.47	*HW*	1.08	1.18	1.23
sd	.50	.72	.73	sd	.87	.83	.87
N =	39	38	38	*N* =	39	38	39
AG	1.67	1.72	1.62	*PI*	1.23	1.18	1.15
sd	.58	.46	.49	sd	.87	.83	.84
N =	39	39	39	*N* =	39	39	39
CC	1.42	1.59	1.66	*PF*	1.56	1.46	1.49
sd	.76	.50	.53	sd	.60	.68	.64
N =	38	39	38	*N* =	39	39	39

Note: Explanations for these abbreviations can be found on page 152.

illness. Finally, physical fitness has been told about more than long-range health worries or past illness.

Overall, topics that respondents have told their dates the most about are sexual morality and pressures of studies. Topics that they have told their dates the least about are long-range health worries, how parents ought to deal with children, and past illness.

Asked dimension. T-tests (at alpha < 0.05) on topics in the *asked* dimension revealed that subjects have asked their dating partner significantly less about their religious views than about ambitions/goals, career choice, or what makes them furious. They have asked significantly more about sexual morality than about how parents ought to deal with children or long-range health worries, but less than about ambitions/goals. They have asked about how parents ought to deal with children less than about pressures of studies, ambitions/goals, career choice, what makes them furious, what makes them proud, or physical fitness. They have asked about pressures in studies more than about long-range health worries or past illness.

Respondents have asked their dates more about ambitions/goals than about what hurts their feelings, what makes them proud, long-range health worries, past illness, or physical fitness. They have asked more about career choice than about what hurts their feelings, long-range health worries, or past illness. What makes them furious has been asked about more than what hurts their feelings, long-range health worries, or past illness. Finally, long-range health worries and past illness have been asked about less than what makes them proud or physical fitness.

Overall, the topic respondents have asked their dates the most about was ambitions/goals. Topics they have asked their dates the least about are long-range health worries and past illness.

Have been told dimension. T-tests (at alpha < 0.05) between topics in the *have been told* dimension revealed that subjects' dating partners have told them significantly less about their religious views than about sexual morality or ambitions/goals. Their partners have told them more about sexual morality than about how parents ought to deal with children, long-range health worries, or past illness. They have told them less about how parents ought to deal with children than about ambitions/goals, career choice, or what makes them furious. Pressures of studies have been told about more than past illness. Ambitions/goals have been told about more than what makes them proud, long-range health worries, or past illness.

Subjects report that their dates have told them more about career choice than about what hurts their feelings, what makes them proud, long-range health worries, or past illness. Long-range health worries and past illness have both been told about less than what makes them furious. Past illness has been told about less than what hurts their feelings, what makes them proud, or physical fitness.

Overall, the topic respondents report that their dates have told them the most about are ambitions/goals and career choice. The topic their dates have told them the least about is past illness.

Across dimensions. Comparison of the *told*, *asked*, and *have been told* dimensions reveals few significant differences. Subjects report (at alpha < 0.05) that they have told their dates about sexual morality more than they have asked them. They have told their dates about pressures of studies more than their dates have told them. They have told about what hurts their feelings more than they have asked about it or have been told about it.

Conclusions. Future research with college-age samples should focus on topics such as sexual morality, pressures of studies, ambitions/goals, and career choice to ascertain the patterns of interaction on these topics. Research should also explore whether topics discriminate among levels of dating

Table 9.5
Mean Scores for Intimacy and Frequency of Topics, Korean Sample

Topic	*Frequency Score*	*Intimacy Score*	*Topic*	*Frequency Score*	*Intimacy Score*
RL N =25	3.1	4.3	MP N = 23	1.8	2.6
PF N = 24	3.0	3.6	OM N = 22	2.6	3.7
LDS N = 25	3.8	4.2	IH N = 24	3.6	3.7
PC N = 24	3.2	3.6	EF N = 24	3.7	4.0
SW N = 25	4.0	4.3	PV N= 23	3.7	4.4

Note: Explanations for these abbreviations can be found on page 152.

relationships or discriminate dating relationships from other types of relationships. Topics that are not salient are long-range health worries, past illness, and how parents should deal with children.

Research Question 3: Korean Sample

In a mate relationship, does the Korean sample discuss specific, identifiable, and stable topics at differing levels of penetration? Table 9.5 contains the mean scores and *N*'s for intimacy and frequency of topics in the penetration profile for the Korean sample. The table contains topic-frequency scores and topic-intimacy scores. Topics and their abbreviations are identified in the methods section.

Results show that the Korean sample, like the American sample, differs across topical categories discussed in a mate relationship. On the frequency dimension, School–Work has a much higher mean compared to the other topics, whereas Money–Property and Own Marriage and Family have lower means relative to the others. On the intimacy dimension, Relationships with Others, Love, Dating and Sex, and Personal Values have higher means, whereas Money–Property has a lower mean. Given the consistency across the two dimensions, the efficacy of this scale for use in Korea is promising.

Conclusions: Study 1

The four hypothesized levels of the mate relationship for Americans are found to be stable and significantly different semantic markers for the mate relationship in the seminal investigation (see Chapter 3). However, the present American sample reveals little stability and no statistically significant differences. Because the theoretical structure had been supported previously, such results are troublesome. There are three probable reasons for the discrepancy. It may be that the patterns of mate relationships for undergraduate students have changed in the intervening years such that, though these patterns held true for the early 1980s sample, they did not hold true for the present (late 1980s) sample. If this is so, the thought guiding the study must be modified. It is also possible that one of the samples is not representative of the population of university students. The sample in the seminal studies was comprised of students in communication classes from the same university, making these comparable samples. A third possibility is that the phrasing on the measurement instrument created instability. Concepts apart from the mate relationship levels were not identical to the seminal investigation. To sort out which of these alternate explanations was most valid, another sample was drawn and administered a Galileo survey containing only Real Self, Ideal Self, and the four mate relationship levels. The results are presented below as Study 2.

Korean data strongly support the conceptual structure of Cushman's theory of the mate relationship for the pretested levels for the nonarranged mate relationship unique to the culture. When the Korean results are considered with past support for the theory in America, Gudykunst's (1989) claim of universal theoretic structures for interpersonal relationships across cultures is substantiated with empirical evidence. Korean mate relationship attributes are less clear.

The discovery of potential universal underlying theoretical processes in interpersonal relationships carries immense implications. First, it underscores the importance of theoretically based cross-cultural research. Second, culture itself becomes a viable theoretic variable. Third, specific findings about specific cultures are more meaningful when encompassed in global theoretic constructs. Moreover, there are obvious practical implications for international relationships, both business and personal.

Within this specific research, the Korean semantic level Lover exhibited some problems in its ability to discriminate from other levels. However, trends in the data indicated that a level exists between Opposite-Sex Friend and Engaged. It may be that the actual word used in the Korean survey was not reflective of the culture's semantic signifier. Future research should explore the possibilities of replacing "lover" with another term.

The present data are supportive but inconclusive for the relational levels Engaged and Spouse. The high number of missing cases indicates that many Korean respondents left these questions uncompleted. Additional data are needed to substantiate the trend these data exhibit.

The interpersonal penetration profile is a unique contribution to the study of communication in the mate-selection process. Trends in the Korean data suggest that topics of discussion differ from one another in the mate relationship in Korean culture. Interpersonal penetration specific to the mate relationship in Korea is considered to be an area worthy of future study.

American results indicate that this sample also differs across topical categories discussed in a mate relationship. Future research may build upon these findings not only by replicating them, but by comparing topical penetration in the mate relationship to other types of relationships, such as friendship at varying levels. The trends in the two data sets are an indication that social penetration theory is also viable cross-culturally, supporting the findings of Gudykunst and his associates (Gudykunst, 1983, 1985a, 1985c; Gudykunst, Chua, and Gray, 1987; Gudykunst and Nishida, 1983, 1984; Gudykunst, Nishida, and Chua, 1987; Gudykunst, Yang, and Nishida, 1985).

Method: Study 2

Sample

The sample for the second study was a group of 76 undergraduate students at the same university enrolled in an introductory-level communication course. The sample included 22 males and 54 females with an average age of 19 years.

Questionnaires

A Galileo questionnaire was administered containing only Real Self, Ideal Self, and the four hypothesized mate relationship levels. The data were analyzed with version 5.3 of the Galileo program.

Data Analysis

Hypothesis 1 is tested in the same way for the second American sample as for the first. Differences between the mate relationship levels in the hypothesis are operationalized by again using Real Self and Ideal Self as points of reference in the Galileo space and examining z-scores of mean differences.

It was decided a priori that if the data in Study 2 supported the results found in the seminal studies (see Chapter 3), it would be concluded that either the sample in Study 1 was unrepresentative or

Table 9.6
Comparison of Mean Differences Between
Mate Relationship Levels and Real and Ideal Self, Study 2

	Casual Date	*Steady Date*	*Fiancé*	*Spouse*
Real Self	60.0	50.9	31.9	32.5
Std. Err.	5.0	4.6	3.4	3.8
% Err.	8.3	9.0	10.6	11.6
N =	62	66	64	66
Ideal Self	82.1	62.0	47.7	45.7
Std. Err.	8.5	6.4	4.6	7.1
% Err.	10.4	10.2	9.6	15.5
N =	66	64	64	64

the questionnaire was unstable. If the data in Study 2 supported the results of Study 1, it would be concluded that either conceptions of the mate relationship had changed since the seminal study or that the sample (in Chapter 3) was unrepresentative.

Results/Discussion: Study 2

Hypothesis 1

The first hypothesis posited that Casual Date, Steady Date, Fiancé, and Spouse represent stable and significantly different semantic markers for increasing degrees of the mate relationship for the second American sample. Table 9.6 contains the means, standard errors, and percents of error for the distances of four semantic levels of mate relationship from the concepts Real and Ideal Self. The results provide partial support for the hypothesis. The low percents of error show all levels to be fairly stable semantic markers. With Real Self as the point of reference, Casual Date and Steady Date are seen as different levels, but z-scores showed that they are not significantly different from one another. Steady Date and Fiancé appear as different levels and their z-scores show them to be significantly different from one another. However, Fiancé and Spouse overlap to signify only one level.

The results for the point of reference Ideal Self also provide partial support for the hypothesis. All levels have relatively low percents of error, showing them to be relatively stable. In addition, Casual Date and Steady Date appear as different levels, and are shown by their z-scores to be significantly different from one another. Steady Date and Fiancé appear as different levels, but are not significantly different from one another. Fiancé and Spouse again overlap to signify only one level.

Z-scores of mean differences between the levels using the other levels as points of reference reveal that Casual Date and Steady Date are significantly different when Spouse is the point of reference. Casual Date and Fiancé are significantly different when Spouse is the point of reference. Casual Date and Spouse are significantly different when Fiancé is the point of reference. Steady Date and Fiancé are consistently significantly different. Steady Date and Spouse are significantly different with Casual Date as the point of reference. Fiancé and Spouse are significantly different with Casual Date as the point of reference.

Conclusions

The results of the second study provide more support for the hypothesized levels of the mate relationship in America than those of Study 1, but do not provide as much support as the results of the seminal study. It is possible that the phrasing on the questionnaire in Study 1 did indeed create instability, given that the second sample shows such a marked increase in stability.

When the results of Study 2 are considered in light of their stability, it appears that patterns of mate relationships for undergraduates at this university have indeed changed since the seminal data were gathered. Given that the hypothesized levels are not completely unsupported in Study 2, the theoretic structure guiding Cushman's research program need not be dramatically modified. It may be that the lack of marriage experience led subjects to view the levels Fiancé and Spouse as more similar than would a more experienced sample. Future research of the theory should use stratified sampling, being sure to include nondating individuals as well as those with casual relationships, those with steady relationships, those who are engaged, and those who are married.

Another possibility is that the increased acceptance of cohabitation may influence the way undergraduates view the mate relationship. With long-term cohabitation, Fiancé may cease to be a relevant concept as a level of the mate relationship. It would be fruitful to collect open-ended data and conduct interviews with today's undergraduates to assess the salience of the terminology. In addition, the original instrument should be administered to older samples and the results compared to those of an undergraduate group. A procedure such as discriminant analysis would ascertain whether certain perceptions of the mate relationship discriminate between older and younger groups. The second data set does not suggest that the theory is in need of drastic reconceptualization. It does, however, suggest that specific patterns of the mate relationship in America may be changing.

When considered with the Korean data set in Study 1, the data in Study 2 suggest that Korean and American patterns of the nonarranged mate relationship are not theoretically different from one another. Samples from both cultures show distinct patterns of mate relationship development that parallel one another. Perhaps most important, the findings of both Study 1 and Study 2 provide empirical basis for future cross-cultural comparisons in interpersonal communication using this theory and methodology, thus supporting Gudykunst's (1989) claim that basic theoretic structures for interpersonal relations may be universal across cultures.

References

Altman, I., and D. Taylor (1973). *Social penetration: The development of interpersonal relationships*. New York: Holt, Rinehart and Winston.

Cushman, D. P., and D. D. Cahn (1985). *Communication in interpersonal relationships*. Albany, NY: State University of New York Press.

Cushman, D. P., and T. Nishida (1984). *Mate selection in the United States and Japan*. Unpublished manuscript, State University of New York at Albany.

Cushman, D. P., B. Valentinsen, and D. Dietrich (1982). A rules theory of interpersonal relationships. In F. E. X. Dance (ed.). *Human communication theory* (90–119). New York: Harper and Row.

Gudykunst, W. B. (1983). Uncertainty reduction and prediction of behavior in low- and high-context cultures. *Communication Quarterly* 31:49–55.

Gudykunst, W. B. (1985a). Similarities and differences in perceptions of initial intracultural and intercultural encounters. *The Southern Speech Communication Journal* 49:49–65.

Gudykunst, W. B. (1985b). An exploratory comparison of close intracultural and intercultural friendships. *Communication Quarterly* 33:270–83.

Gudykunst, W. B. (1985c). The influence of cultural similarity, type of relationship, and self-monitoring on uncertainty reduction processes. *Communication Monographs* 52:203–17.

Gudykunst, W. B. (1989). Culture and the development of interpersonal relationships. In J. A. Anderson (ed.), *Communication yearbook 12* (315–54). Newbury Park, CA: Sage.

Gudykunst, W. B., E. Chua, and A. Gray (1987). Cultural dissimilarities and uncertainty reduction process. In M. L. McLaughlin (ed.), *Communication yearbook 10* (456–69). Newbury Park, CA: Sage.

Gudykunst, W. B., and T. Nishida (1983). Social penetration in Japanese and American close friendships. In R. N. Bostrom (ed.), *Communication yearbook 7* (592–610). New Brunswick, NJ: International Communication Association.

Gudykunst, W. B., and T. Nishida (1984). Individual and cultural influences on uncertainty reduction. *Communication Monographs* 51:23–36.

Gudykunst, W. B., T. Nishida, and E. Chua (1987). Perceptions of social penetration in Japanese-North American dyads. *International Journal of Intercultural Relations* 51:256–78.

Gudykunst, W. B., S. M. Yang, and T. Nishida (1985). A cross-cultural test of uncertainty reduction theory: Comparison of acquaintance, friend, and dating relationships in Japan, Korea, and the United States. *Human Communication Research* 11:407–54.

Taylor, D., and I. Altman (1966). Intimacy-scaled stimuli for use in studies of interpersonal relations. *Psychological Reports* 19:729–30.

10

The Mate Selection Process in Nigeria: A Preliminary Study of Cultural Impact, Communication Pattern, and Relationship Variables

Andrew A. Moemeka and Anne Maydan Nicotera

The mate relationship, the development of intimacy over time in male–female interaction, would appear to be a universal human phenomenon. Studies reported in chapters 3, 8, and 9 of this volume as well as in other works strongly attest to the existence of this opposite-sex relationship in the societies studied. Moreover, they give credence to the view (Gudykunst, 1989) that the mate relationship is a universal human phenomenon. Further evidence of the universality of this human behavior comes from existing (though unscientific) knowledge about the mate relationship vis-à-vis human societies. There is no known society in which marriage, as a cultural norm, is taboo or in which intimate relationships between people of the opposite sex are explicitly forbidden.

The conditions under which this important human act occurs differ from society to society. In addition to the studies cited above, Barnlund (1975), Gudykunst, Yang, and Nishida (1985), Gudykunst and Nishida (1986), and Yum (1988) discuss differences in the mate-selection process among societies. These differences can be explained by cultural norms, historical backgrounds, economic and political realities, and the impact of social interaction between and among societies. A people's experiences ultimately determine the philosophical base of their behavior, their communication pattern and system, and therefore determine the nature of the rules and norms of interpersonal relationships. For example, the concept of mate selection in the West (with its philosophy of pronounced individualism) implies, and in fact demands, freedom of choice by prospective mates. Such freedom of choice is frowned upon in Africa, where the philosophy of communalism enshrines the supremacy of the community. Girlfriend and boyfriend relationships in the West involve sexual intercourse because sex is merely seen as part of life. In Nigeria and other African countries, the culture holds sex as sacrosanct and therefore forbids premarital sex.

Purpose and Rationale

The far-reaching differences in the norms and rules for engaging in the universal behavior of mate selection warrant the separate and detailed study of each society. Such study can reveal the factors at work in the development, growth, and maintenance or termination of mate relationships in individual societies. The existing literature on the mate relationship contains no information from the African continent. Because intercultural communication is fast becoming a cornerstone of international understanding and world peace, the investigation of social forces that underlie systems of interpersonal relationships in various parts of the world, such as this preliminary study undertakes, is of great value.

The study is preliminary in two respects. First, it addresses only one (albeit a significant one) of the more than 50 independent countries on the continent of Africa. If there is an underlying philosophical base for communication and human relationships in all of Africa (Moemeka, 1983), then further study of other countries is necessary for researchers to be able to make any categorical statement about mate relationships on the continent. Second, the study is aimed at identifying variables (see Chapter 8, this volume) that are considered integral to the formation and maintenance of male–female relationships, as well as determining the importance attached to each variable. Identification of these variables is considered basic to an understanding of the role communicators play in the development of interpersonal relationships (Cahn, 1983; 1987).

Cultural Background

General Cultural Background

Nigeria is a multiethnic society with about 300 distinct tribes, three of which—the Hausa, the Igbo, and the Yoruba—have dominated the sociopolitical and economic environments of the country since independence from Great Britain in 1960. Although there are about 200 tribes in the north, the Hausa language is spoken by practically everyone in that part of the country. Political hegemony, however, is held by the Fulani, who are reputed to have leadership qualities admired by the largely Moslem population of the north. The Igbos, until quite recently, dominated in the east, where there are about 50 different tribes. The Yoruba dominated in the west, which has about 30 ethnic groups. Other tribes that have had substantial political and social influence on the nation include the Kanuri in the north, the Efik and the Ijaw in the east, and the Edo in the west.

In an investigation into the sociocultural environment of communication in Nigeria (Moemeka, 1983), we found that in spite of the multiplicity of ethnic groups and some fundamental tribal differences, there is a common underlying philosophical base that seems to explain how Nigerians (and indeed Africans in general) communicate, and why they communicate the way they do. The characteristics of this philosophical base—Supremacy of the Community, Sanctity of Authority, Utility of the Individual, Respect for Old Age, and Religion as a Way of Life—necessarily have direct a impact on mate relationship formation and maintenance.

Specific Cultural Background: The Mate Relationship

Relationships between boys and girls and between young adults of the opposite sex are not alien to Nigeria. Cat-calls and nonverbal signs by boys indicate interest in girls whom they admire and would want to have as mates. The extensive use of occulesics by girls to draw attention to themselves or to reciprocate the "distant" advances of boys have also been part of the acceptable norms related to male–female relationships. Still, the Western concept of girlfriend/boyfriend relationships is alien to traditional culture and remains culturally forbidden. Traditionally common and still culturally upheld in rural areas is something nearer the concept of "escort"—called *"Amariya"* by the Hausa, *"Onitiju"* by the Yoruba, and *"Ogacha"* by the Igbo. These terms literally mean "it will mature," implying that the girl in the relationship is not yet old enough or ready for marriage and therefore a sexual relationship. This tradition has underlying cultural imperatives. First, entering into this relationship was expected to lead ultimately to marriage. Anyone who did not have marriage in mind was regarded as of questionable character. S/he was watched very carefully. Second, virginity was held sacrosanct (with particular reference to the girl) until the ritual and drama of marriage were concluded. A relationship between a boy and a girl was therefore strictly platonic. The boy was expected to protect the girl against anything or anybody (including himself) that could bring her into social or cultural disrepute.

The relationship between a boy and a girl was expected to be carried on without any physical body contact. The boy visited with the girl in the home of her parents. During such visits, which could take place every night for years, the girl sat apart from the boy; they did not touch each other, let alone hug or kiss. They were hardly ever left alone. A parent of the girl (usually the mother) and/or other members of the family joined in conversations, which could be about anything but love and sex. In the course of such conversations—always led by the oldest person present—personalities, attitudes, behaviors, aspirations, and character were determined. Only the boy was required to visit the girl and her parents; girls were forbidden to visit with boys, unless it was the traditional visit—an act to show the community that the girl was now the "boy's woman" to marry.

In the not-too-distant past, boys escorted "their girls" to the stream or to the farm. They even traveled miles to meet their girls returning from neighborhood markets. All this was a mark of love and concern for the safety of the girls they "carried in their hearts." Most important, such acts of escort were meant to sound strong notes that the escorting mates meant business—marriage—and therefore had "cleared the field."

Cultural imperatives and the behaviors that derived strength from them have begun to break down over the last 20 years in urban areas. First, relationships between opposite-sex teenagers and young adults began to be entered into purely for their own sake. However, care was still taken to avoid sexual intercourse, especially if it was fairly obvious that there was not going to be a marriage between the pair. This caution was necessary because it was a cultural disgrace—and still is in the rural communities that constitute about 80% of the land area and 85% of the population of the country—for a girl and her parents and a sign of a lack of integrity on the part of the boy if the virginity sign was not seen on the girl's wedding night. The girl could be sent back in shame to her parents the following morning.

The next stage in the degeneration of cultural imperatives of the mate relationship is the culturally unapproved but steady adoption of the Western model of that relationship. Currently, mate relationships among educated teenagers and young adults—especially those living in urban and suburban areas—are based on the Western model, which does not merely allow sexual intercourse, but explicitly expects it. These actions are steadily radiating into the rural communities.

Nigerian society frowns upon this "going-the-whole-hug" type of mate relationship before marriage for two reasons. First, it is seen as an immoral and shameless, with sex for its own sake degrading one of the most valued gifts of providence to humanity—the power of procreation. Second, it is believed to deaden the feeling of love and affection between couples. After sharing all that there is to share before marriage, it is believed that young couples get bored with each other soon after marriage because they did not leave anything to imagination or delay any satisfaction. The culturally expected result is divorce, which is also frowned upon and seen as a disgrace to the families of the couple.

Because remarriages are rare, the culture encourages the practice of what the Igbos call "Mgba" ("Ale" in Yoruba), a particular mate relationship between two consenting adults. This relationship occurs primarily between widows and widowers but is also permitted between widows and married men. The concept for the relationship comes near the concept "concubine" in English, except that it does not involve cohabitation; the woman lives separate from the man. A sexual relationship is a prime requirement; also very important is economic support by the man for the woman and her children.

Marriage is no longer arranged as it was in earlier times. However, because it is generally seen as an act between two extended families represented in the marrying couple, mere verbal consent of parents is still not considered enough. There must be consensus among members of each extended family and agreement between the two extended families before marriage is contracted. Whether or not such consensus and agreement are reached depends primarily on the perception of the moral probity, health history, and economic status (in that order of priority) of each extended family. Secondarily, it depends on the perception of the degree of respect possessed by each of the contracting mates, and of obedience on the part of the female partner.

Therefore, culturally speaking, the most important qualities for permitting and upholding the mate relationship in Nigeria are Honesty (moral probity), Wealth (evidence of or the likelihood of economic security), and Health (the absence of contagious diseases among the extended family e.g., leprosy; "conspicuous" diseases such as epilepsy; physical deformities such as blindness; biological problems such as impotence and barrenness; and psycho-physiological problems such as mental illness). The two other variables are Respect, which is a reciprocal variable (required of both parties), as are Honesty and Health, and Obedience, which is a nonreciprocal variable, as is Economic Security. Obedience is required only of the woman, just as Economic Security is required only of the man.

The remaining questions, expressed formally, are the research questions for this investigation:

RQ1: Do the culturally specified qualities for ideal mates—Moral Probity, Good Health, Economic Security, Respect, and Obedience—rate highly in the opinion of prospective mates?

RQ2: Is there a shift of emphasis between the culturally prescribed values for mate relationship qualities and the values of contemporary interacting males and females?

Semantic markers for levels of the mate relationship have been identified by research (Bailey and Helm, 1974; Helm, Bailey, and Vance, 1977; Krain,

1975) as variables for levels or degrees of mate relationship. These markers are Casual Date, Regular Date, Steady Date and Spouse. Addressing these levels of the mate relationship, we posit four related research questions.

RQ3: What is the relationship between respondents and the semantic markers; in other words, do these markers represent increasing degrees of intimacy for this culture?

RQ4: What are the entry-level variables (those that predict initiation) and intensity variables (those that predict growth) in contemporary mate relationships?

RQ5: How much do individuals value the crucial entry and intensity variables in mate relationships?

RQ6: What are the respondents' perceptions of the relationships among the semantic marker variables?

Method

Sample

The sample, chosen from a population of civil servants and graduate students from different parts of Nigeria, consisted of 54 respondents (27 females and 27 males) purposely selected from eight ethnic groups (Hausa, Igbo, Yoruba, Fulani, Kanuri, Efik, Edo, and Ijaw) whose cultures are considered most pervasive among Nigerians. The average age of the respondents, whose minimum level of education was high school, was 38 years. This age range was considered old enough for respondents to have felt the impact of pure traditional culture, yet young enough to have been influenced by encroaching Western values.

Measurement

A self-administered questionnaire was used for data collection. The questionnaire was, in structure and content, a replica of that which has been used in preliminary studies of mate relationship in the United States (chapters 3 and 8, this volume), Korea (Chapter 9, this volume), and Yugoslavia (Foldy, Danielsen, and Cushman, 1988). The questionnaire first asked respondents to list in descending order of preference 10 qualities that they consider important for entering into and maintaining a viable mate relationship. This was expected to produce two measurements: the frequency of 10 listed qualities (variables); and the frequency of each quality (variable) at each point on a scale of 1 (most preferred) to 10 (least preferred). For this latter measure, a value score was computed by reversing the ranks given by the respondents (so that no mention of qualities by some respondents would be reflected as true zeros), then by summing the rankings. The most highly valued qualities were thus identified by frequency and value scores. Some of the qualities mentioned by respondents were collapsed because of similarity in meaning. For example, Being a Catholic, Being a Protestant, and Being Religious were collapsed into one concept—Religion (which was later dropped). Also collapsed into one concept—Trustworthiness—were Dependability, Trustfulness, and Trustworthiness. A third example was the collapsing of Beauty, Handsomeness, Attractiveness, and Fair-Complexion into Good Looks.

Respondents were also required to rate the distance between the self and each of the most valued qualities in terms of perceived distance in cognitive space measured in points from 1 (nearest) to 20+ (farthest). In addition, they were asked to rate each of the qualities in relation to semantic marker variables—Casual Date, Regular Date, Steady Date, and Spouse. These were directed at obtaining a measure of the strength of relationship as an indication of the value placed on each quality by respondents. The nearer a variable or variables, the stronger the relationship. Responses therefore also pinpointed Strength of Relationship points: 1) between respondents and valued qualities (variables); and 2) between each of the valued qualities (variables) and each semantic-marker variable as perceived by the individual on a scale of 1 (strongest) to 20+ (weakest). The scale was interpreted as follows:

Points Apart	*Value*
1–2	Extremely strong
3–6	Very Strong
7–10	Strong
11–14	Weak
15–18	Very Weak
19–20+	Extremely Weak

Analyses, Results, and Discussion

Although each individual listed only 10 qualities, respondents were not restricted in their choice of qualities; the list was very long. However, many of the qualities mentioned were low in frequency count. For example, Wealth appeared only 5 times (9%) and Health only 10 times

Table 10.1
Frequency Count, Percentage Scores, Value Scores, and Value Ranks of the Most Frequently Mentioned Qualities

Quality	*Frequency (%)*	*Value Score*	*Value Rank*
Good Looks	54 (100%)	247	4
Love/Affection	52 (96%)	384	2
Honesty	52 (96%)	414	1
Politeness	39 (72%)	145	7
Intelligence	37 (69%)	261	3
Caring	37 (69%)	124	9
Tolerance	34 (63%)	132	8
Hard Work	33 (61%)	157	6
Respect	26 (48%)	100	11
Trustworthiness	25 (46%)	211	5
Open-Mindedness	18 (33%)	109	10
Humor	17 (31%)	68	12

(19%). The highest possible score was 54 (100%). Those qualities that did not score up to one-third of this total (except for Humor, which scored 17) were eliminated. Those qualities that exceeded two-thirds of this total are considered to be the crucial set of variables—mentioned by a majority of the respondents. Table 10.1 presents a list showing the frequency count, percentage scores, and value scores of the most frequently mentioned qualities.

The Frequency/Percentage tables that follow contain, in detail, the Strength of Relationship points (measured in cognitive-space distance) as perceived by the individual with regard to the relationship between the self and mate relationship qualities, between the self and semantic-marker variables, among the semantic-marker variables, and between mate relationship qualities and semantic-marker variables. (In these tables, percentages sum to less than 100% because not all respondents listed all qualities.)

Analyses

The thrust of these analyses is, of course, to explore the research questions raised in this chapter. Adequate answers to the questions will provide a clear understanding of what mate relationship variables are at work in Nigeria and of their role in initiating and maintaining male–female relationships. Because the frequency counts show the place of each variable in the mate relationship vis-à-vis the respondents, we are able to pinpoint the most important variables (mentioned by two-thirds of the respondents). These variables—Good Looks, Love/Affection, Honesty, Politeness, Caring, and Intelligence—are the first set of variables we have used in this analysis. They are used mainly to answer questions related to cultural stability and/or change in mate relationship practices (RQs 1 and 2). The second set of variables is the semantic markers, which address questions of levels and intensity of interaction in mate relationships (RQs 3 through 6).

For questions that examine Strength of Relationship, the tables divide the scale into six levels, from extremely strong to extremely weak. For the particular purpose of these analyses, which are directed at determining the relative strength or weakness of a relationship rather than the level of strength, we divided the scale into two levels—strong and weak. In considering the results, therefore, all scores should be collapsed accordingly, with positive levels of relationship classified as strong, and negative levels as weak.

Results and discussion for RQ1. Do the culturally specified qualities for ideal mates—Moral Probity, Good Health, Economic Security, Respect, and Obedience—rate highly in the opinion of prospective mates? The data show that many qualities specified by the respondents as desirable by the culture were accepted by the respondents. Honesty (Moral Probity) was listed by 96% of the respondents and Respect by 48% (see Table 10.1). Although dropped from the analyses because of low frequency, Health (19%) and Wealth (9%) were mentioned by some respondents, indicating that for these individuals cultural imperatives appear to be operating.

Cultural imperatives of Respect for the Aged, Sanctity of Authority, and the Supremacy of the Community as well as the impact of religious injunctions (Moemeka, 1983) may explain why respondents accepted qualities specified by the culture. Presumably, even individuals with doubts about the authenticity or the relevance of such variables for him/herself could not deviate from the norm. Indeed, this culture-directed choice remains the norm in rural Nigerian communities, bolstered by the adage: "The extent to which the elderly can see, the youth will not be able to match even if they climb the tallest palm tree." Relationships between boys and girls in rural communities usually lead to marriages; and virtually all these marriages endure. It is not surprising, therefore, that even in urban areas the young appear to conform to the demands of the culture for mate relationship qualities. There may be sufficient evidence of positive results from such conformity that few individuals question the demands.

The culturally specified variables appear to be (especially in rural communities) both entry-level and intensity variables. They are used to determine whether a relationship should be entered into and in deciding whether it is progressing satisfactorily. The relationship intensifies largely to the extent that the culturally specified requirements are met.

Results and discussion for RQ2. Is there a shift of emphasis between the culturally prescribed values for mate relationship qualities and the values of contemporary interacting males and females? The answer is a resounding "yes." Although some culturally prescribed values hold, others have been superseded or replaced by new values. Of the five culturally prescribed variables, only one—Honesty (96%, rank 1)—still ranks high among these urban dwellers. Respect, although mentioned by 48% of the respondents, is ranked at 11 in value; only Humor (31%, rank 12) ranks lower. Love/Affection (96%, rank 2), Intelligence (69%, rank 3), and Good Looks (100%, rank 4) appear to have replaced Health (19%, no rank) and Economic Security (9%, no rank). Trustworthiness (46%, rank 5), Hard Work (61%, rank 6), Politeness (72%, rank 7), Tolerance (63%, rank 8), Caring (69%, rank 9), and Open-mindedness (33%, rank 10) appear to have superseded Respect (48%, rank 11) in value and to have replaced Obedience. (See Table 10.1.) Although Honesty is still most valued, the value of Respect has diminished. Health and Economic Security seem to have lost their salience, and Obedience seems to have been completely wiped out of the contemporary urban value system.

To many viewers of the Nigerian scene, the high value attached to honesty by the respondents is a reflection of the often-talked about difference between perception (attitude) and behavior. First, Nigerian citizens, like most people around the globe, have lapses of honesty in terms of economic and political issues. Still, Nigerians adhere to a strong belief in honesty. This partly explains the high rating of this variable as a mate relationship quality. Second, a distinction is usually made between attitudes toward economic and political transactions and those toward intimate relationship transactions. In intimate relationships, Nigerians expect their mates to be honest in both "words and actions" and feel obligated to do the same to sustain the relationship. This reciprocal expectation was also reflected in the rating of the distance between self and honesty. (This is addressed under RQ5. See Table 10.4).

The shift of emphasis from Economic Security, Health, Respect, and Obedience to Love/Affection, Intelligence, Politeness, Tolerance, and Caring appears to reflect a shift of emphasis from blind conformity to cultural demands to self-determined criteria based on personal aspirations and expectations—very prevalent among the educated and/or urbanized. Our sample was chosen from this group of Nigerians. The devaluation of economic security can be explained from two angles. First, only women were likely to have mentioned this variable; men do not require it of their female partners. Culturally, it is still expected that men must provide for their families. The second reason for the low frequency of this variable is the economic status

Table 10.2
Strength of Relationship Between the Self and Semantic Markers

	Extremely Strong	*Very Strong*	*Strong*	*Weak*	*Very Weak*	*Extremely Weak*
Self and . . .						
Casual Date	—	13 (24%)	1 (2%)	—	4 (7%)	30 (56%)
Regular Date	9 (17%)	15 (28%)	6 (11%)	—	—	20 (37%)
Steady Date	21 (39%)	8 (15%)	9 (17%)	—	—	12 (22%)
Spouse	47 (87%)	—	—	—	—	2 (4%)

of the respondents. Nearly half of them were middle-income earners; the rest were graduate students, invariably with some justified hope of a high standard of living. This is true of both male and female respondents.

Results and discussion for RQ3. What is the relationship between respondents and the semantic markers; in other words, do these markers represent increasing degrees of intimacy for this culture? Table 10.2 summarizes the analysis of this question. Sixty-three percent of the respondents rated a weak relationship between the self and Casual Date. This weak relationship decreases as one moves to more intimate relationship markers, indicating that these semantic markers are salient levels of intimacy for this culture. It would appear from these results that the culture still has a strong, albeit subtle, hold on individuals' attitudes. Traditionally, casual mate relationships are not permitted; regular dating is allowed only if it is seen as a prelude to marriage. Table 10.2 indicates that Nigerians may still hold on to these cultural injunctions, viewing casual relationships as weakly related to the self. More germane to this study, the results in Table 10.2 indicate that these semantic markers represent salient levels of increasing intimacy.

Results and discussion for RQ4. What are the entry level variables (those that predict initiation) and intensity variables (those that predict growth) in contemporary mate relationships? The crucial qualities were examined for their nature. Of these six variables (Good Looks, Love/Affection, Honesty, Politeness, Intelligence, and Caring), three were identified as entry-level variables and three as intensity variables. They were identified as such by their patterns of relationship strength with levels of mate relationship intensity. (See the results for RQ3, which establish that these semantic markers denote salient increasing levels of intimacy.) Those variables whose perceived Strength of Relationship with the semantic markers remained relatively

Tables 10.3a–d
Strength of Relationship Between Semantic Markers and Mate Relationship Qualities

Table 10.3a: Casual Date

	Extremely Strong	*Very Strong*	*Strong*	*Weak*	*Very Weak*	*Extremely Weak*
Casual Date and . . .						
Good Looks	18 (33%)	22 (41%)	9 (17%)	—	—	3 (6%)
Love/Affection	2 (4%)	8 (15%)	14 (26%)	—	—	26 (48%)
Honesty	6 (11%)	4 (7%)	10 (19%)	—	3 (6%)	27 (50%)
Politeness	24 (44%)	3 (6%)	6 (11%)	—	—	5 (9%)
Intelligence	23 (42%)	3 (6%)	5 (9%)	—	2 (4%)	4 (7%)
Caring	—	—	—	10 (19%)	—	23 (43%)
Tolerance	2 (4%)	15 (28%)	1 (2%)	—	2 (4%)	14 (26%)
Hard Work	10 (19%)	5 (9%)	2 (4%)	—	—	16 (30%)
Respect	12 (22%)	6 (11%)	4 (7%)	—	—	3 (6%)
Trustworthiness	3 (6%)	6 (11%)	—	—	—	16 (30%)
Open-Mindedness	3 (6%)	3 (6%)	5 (9%)	—	—	5 (9%)
Humor	3 (6%)	14 (26%)	—	—	—	—

Table 10.3b: Regular Date

	Extremely Strong	*Very Strong*	*Strong*	*Weak*	*Very Weak*	*Extremely Weak*
Regular Date and . . .						
Good Looks	27 (50%)	5 (9%)	8 (15%)	—	—	8 (15%)
Love/Affection	26 (48%)	10 (19%)	10 (19%)	—	—	6 (11%)
Honesty	25 (46%)	17 (31%)	5 (9%)	—	—	1 (2%)
Politeness	12 (22%)	15 (28%)	9 (17%)	—	1 (2%)	—
Intelligence	15 (28%)	8 (15%)	10 (19%)	—	—	6 (11%)
Caring	15 (28%)	6 (11%)	13 (24%)	—	2 (4%)	6 (11%)
Tolerance	7 (13%)	15 (28%)	2 (4%)	—	1 (2%)	8 (15%)
Hard Work	11 (20%)	1 (2%)	8 (15%)	—	2 (4%)	9 (17%)
Respect	—	13 (24%)	10 (19%)	—	—	3 (6%)
Trustworthiness	12 (22%)	8 (15%)	5 (9%)	—	—	—
Open-Mindedness	13 (24%)	5 (9%)	—	—	—	—
Humor	2 (4%)	15 (28%)	—	—	—	—

Table 10.3c: Steady Date

	Extremely Strong	*Very Strong*	*Strong*	*Weak*	*Very Weak*	*Extremely Weak*
Steady Date and . . .						
Good Looks	22 (41%)	19 (35%)	8 (15%)	—	—	3 (6%)
Love/Affection	31 (57%)	19 (35%)	2 (4%)	—	—	2 (4%)
Honesty	22 (41%)	16 (30%)	3 (6%)	—	—	1 (2%)
Politeness	9 (17%)	10 (19%)	6 (11%)	—	—	4 (7%)
Intelligence	16 (30%)	18 (33%)	2 (4%)	—	—	—
Caring	20 (37%)	10 (19%)	7 (13%)	—	—	—
Tolerance	17 (31%)	12 (22%)	2 (4%)	—	3 (6%)	—
Hard Work	14 (26%)	8 (15%)	9 (17%)	—	2 (4%)	—
Respect	15 (28%)	1 (2%)	1 (2%)	6 (11%)	—	3 (6%)
Trustworthiness	21 (39%)	4 (7%)	—	—	—	—
Open-Mindedness	10 (19%)	3 (6%)	2 (4%)	—	2 (4%)	1 (2%)
Humor	10 (19%)	7 (13%)	—	—	—	—

Table 10.3d: Spouse

	Extremely Strong	*Very Strong*	*Strong*	*Weak*	*Very Weak*	*Extremely Weak*
Spouse and . . .						
Good Looks	34 (63%)	16 (30%)	—	—	—	—
Love/Affection	42 (78%)	10 (19%)	—	—	—	—
Honesty	35 (65%)	5 (9%)	—	—	—	—
Politeness	27 (50%)	9 (17%)	3 (6%)	—	—	—
Intelligence	31 (57%)	6 (11%)	—	—	—	—
Caring	31 (57%)	5 (9%)	—	—	—	—
Tolerance	30 (56%)	4 (7%)	—	—	—	—
Hard Work	22 (41%)	11 (20%)	—	—	—	—
Respect	15 (28%)	3 (6%)	3 (6%)	—	—	5 (9%)
Trustworthiness	23 (43%)	2 (4%)	—	—	—	—
Open-Mindedness	6 (11%)	8 (15%)	—	—	—	4 (7%)
Humor	12 (22%)	15 (28%)	7 (13%)	—	—	—

steady—Good Looks, Politeness, and Intelligence—were identified as entry-level variables. Those variables whose Strength of Relationship with the semantic markers increased with the intimacy level—Love/Affection, Honesty, and Caring—were identified as intensity variables. Tables 10.3a–d show these results.

Table 10.4
Strength of Relationship Between the Self and Mate Relationship Qualities

	Extremely Strong	*Very Strong*	*Strong*	*Weak*	*Very Weak*	*Extremely Weak*
Self and . . .						
Good Looks	18 (33%)	28 (52%)	5 (9%)	1 (2%)	—	—
Love/Affection	28 (52%)	9 (17%)	11 (20%)	—	—	4 (7%)
Honesty	40 (74%)	9 (17%)	2 (4%)	—	—	—
Politeness	23 (43%)	13 (24%)	3 (6%)	—	—	—
Intelligence	26 (48%)	10 (19%)	1 (2%)	—	—	—
Caring	23 (43%)	6 (11%)	6 (11%)	—	—	2 (4%)
Tolerance	26 (48%)	5 (9%)	3 (6%)	—	—	—
Hard Work	26 (48%)	7 (13%)	—	—	—	—
Respect	16 (30%)	7 (13%)	1 (2%)	—	—	—
Trustworthiness	17 (31%)	5 (9%)	—	—	—	3 (6%)
Open-Mindedness	10 (19%)	5 (9%)	3 (6%)	—	—	—
Humor	10 (19%)	5 (9%)	2 (4%)	—	—	1 (2%)

Here, once again, there seems to have been a change from culturally prescribed values. Traditionally, there was no distinction between entry-level and intensity variables. All the mate relationship qualities served as both, intensifying only to the extent that traditional expectations for each quality were met. In modern times there is a clear distinction between those variables that signal the entry into a mate relationship and those that signal the intensification of that relationship. Good looks, politeness, and intelligence are qualities that signal entry. As perceptions of love, honesty, and caring increase, the relationship intensifies.

The presence of this distinction in the mate relationship process can be attributed to education and modernization, which emphasize rational thinking and choice on the part of the individual, making it justifiable to evaluate a relationship on the basis of distinctive qualities rather than on culturally imposed expectations.

Results and discussion for RQ5. How much do individuals value the crucial entry and intensity variables in mate relationships? This question seeks to find out how the respondents ranked the variables in value (their perception of what qualities are most suitable for an ideal mate relationship) and how they see themselves in relation to the variables. This question is explored with frequency and value scores (see Table 10.1) as well as Strength of Relationship between the self and each of the six mate relationship qualities.

Table 10.1 shows that of the six crucial variables, Honesty, Love/Affection, Intelligence, and Good Looks are most highly valued. Table 10.4 shows

Table 10.5
Strength of Relationship Among Semantic Marker Variables

	Extremely Strong	*Very Strong*	*Strong*	*Weak*	*Very Weak*	*Extremely Weak*
Casual Date and . . .						
Regular Date	2 (4%)	7 (13%)	12 (22%)	—	1 (2%)	14 (44%)
Steady Date	—	9 (17%)	6 (11%)	6 (11%)	3 (6%)	27 (50%)
Spouse	—	14 (26%)	5 (9%)	—	—	33 (61%)
Regular Date and . . .						
Steady Date	9 (17%)	13 (24%)	12 (22%)	—	—	11 (20%)
Spouse	7 (13%)	15 (28%)	5 (9%)	—	1 (2%)	15 (28%)
Steady Date and . . .						
Spouse	32 (59%)	4 (7%)	8 (15%)1	—	—	3 (6%)

how the respondents relate to the mate relationship qualities they chose—how important these qualities are in their view of themselves. All mate relationship qualities score on the strong side of the scale. This indicates that the respondents' view of ideal mate relationship qualities parallels their view of qualities they see in themselves.

Results and discussion for RQ6. What are the respondents' perceptions of the relationships among the semantic marker variables? The results in Table 10.5 address this question. These results, like those in Table 10.2, show that Nigerians see these semantic markers as salient levels of intimacy. They also show again a gap between casual relationships and more serious relationships. The Strength of the Relationships among Regular Date, Steady Date, and Spouse does not mean that regular daters go directly to going steady and getting married. Perhaps because the culture does not condone casualness in dating, prospective mates determine their intent for permanence quite early, either disengaging (if they do not like what they see) or dating more regularly in preparation for marriage (if conditions are favorable). Regular dating seems to be a sign of serious intent for marriage. Nigerians seem to distinguish very clearly between casual and serious relationships.

Conclusion

This study has helped to identify 12 qualities most commonly applicable to the mate relationship in Nigeria. From these, we have identified the six most crucial variables. These crucial variables are not those specified by traditional culture as most desirable. However, there is ample evidence of the subtle hold of the culture on the people's idea of what the ideal mate should be and what qualities make for the presence and sustenance of a mate relationship. It would appear that Nigerians entering into mate relationships desire the best of two worlds. Though they do not seem eager to shield their culture from foreign influences, neither do they seem to favor a disintegration of their culture. They enjoy the comfort of the protection traditional culture provides, as well as the freedom of choice Western values permit. Striking a balance between the two may or may not be a continuing problem for relating partners.

This potential problem is just one issue raised by this preliminary investigation. Resolving the issue would require an investigation into what social forces are brought to bear on decisions as to where meeting the demands of the culture ends and safely applying Western values begins. Other issues raised and for which follow-up studies are necessary include the following:

1. Determining empirically the present state of mate selection process in rural communities as against urban communities.
2. Determining whether or not frequency, value, and Strength of Relationship scores are ethnically based or cut across culture; if ethnically based, locating the ethnic group or groups that account for them.
3. Determining empirically if there are gender differences in variable preference and in the level of willingness to infuse Western values to the mate-selection process.

This study has provided relevant information from the continent of Africa—conspicuously absent from the literature on interpersonal relationships. The study shows some similarities and differences between American and Nigerian culture, which chapter 11 addresses.

References

Bailey, R. C., and B. Helm (1974). Matrimonial commitment and date/ideal date perceptions. *Perceptual and Motor Skills* 39:245–46.

Barnlund, D. (1975). *Public and private self in Japan and the United States: Communicative styles in two cultures*. Forest Grove, IL: International Scholarly Book Services.

Cahn, D. D. (1983). Relative importance of perceived understanding in initial interaction and development of interpersonal relationships. *Psychological Reports* 53:923–29.

Cahn, D. D. (1987). *Letting go: A practical theory of relationship disengagement and reengagement*. Albany, NY: State University of New York Press.

Foldy, J., S. Danielsen, and D. P. Cushman (1988). The characteristics of mates and the communication pattern involved in initiating mate relationships in American culture as compared to Yugoslavian culture. *Informatologia Yugoslavica* 20:147–54.

Gudykunst, W. B. (1989). Culture and the development of interpersonal relationships. In J. A. Anderson (ed.), *Communication yearbook 12* (315–54), Newbury Park, CA: Sage.

Gudykunst, W. B., and T. Nishida (1986). The influence of cultural variability on perception of communication behavior associated with relationship terms. *Human Communication Research* 13:147–66.

Gudykunst, W. B., S. M. Yang, and T. Nishida (1985). A cross-cultural test of uncertainty reduction theory: Comparison of acquaintance, friend and dating relationships in Japan, Korea and the United States. *Human Communication Research* 11:407–54.

Helm, B., R. Bailey, and B. Vance (1977). Interpersonal commitment and self-concept support. *The Journal of Social Psychology* 102:319–20.

Krain, M. (1975). Communication among marital couples at three stages of dating. *Journal of Marriage and the Family* 37:609–18.

Moemeka, A. A. (1983). Socio-cultural environment of communication in traditional Nigerian societies: An ethnographic exploration. *Communicatio Socialis* 16:331–45.

Yum, J. (1988). The impact of Confucianism on interpersonal relationships and communication patterns in East Asia. *Communication Monographs* 55:374–88.

11

Summary of Studies on the Theory of the Mate Relationship and Consideration of Implications

Anne Maydan Nicotera

This chapter, parallel to Chapter 7, serves first as a summary of the replications and extensions of mate relationship studies in Part III. (Chapter 13 contains critiques of all the studies in this volume.) Following the summary, implications are considered for three categories across interpersonal communication: culture, conflict, and quality. These categories correspond to Propositions 4–7, presented in Chapter 2.

Summary of Mate Relationship Studies

Replication

In Chapter 8, Cushman and Cahn provide support for the theoretic structure. With their American sample, they replicate the results of Chapter 3; the four hypothesized mate relationship levels are validated as semantic markers for increasing mate relationship. In support of the theory, deeper levels of intimacy are shown to be more closely associated with the real self, the ideal self, and the ideal mate. Chapter 8 provides support for Proposition 1. Further, in support of Proposition 3, intelligence, physical attraction, and sex appeal are established as entry variables for the mate relationship, whereas respect, affection, and psychological support are shown to be intensity variables whose increase predicts deeper levels of intimacy. In Chapter 10, Moemeka and Nicotera provide support for the basic theoretic structure in Nigeria. The semantic markers are upheld in yet another culture as tracing a theoretic progression to more intense levels of the mate relationship (supporting Proposition 1). Their data suggest that within this progression, Nigerian culture imposes a distinct discrimination between casual and close levels of mate relationship, as it does for friendship. These Nigerian data also support the notion of entry and intensity rules for the mate relationship, providing further evidence that some attributes must be present for entry into a mate relationship whereas others must increase in intensity for the relationship to deepen (supporting Proposition 3).

Nicotera (Chapter 9) calls the semantic labels into question. The American data in her first study do not provide support for four hypothesized mate relationship levels as semantic markers of mate relationship intensity. The second American data set provides only limited support. The second data set supports the basic theoretic structure for increasing degrees of the mate relationship in relation to real and ideal self-concept. However, the data do not verify the specific semantic labels for those levels. Nicotera's data were collected in the same region as Cushman and Cahn's but more recently, providing some credence to her contention that patterns of mate relationships may be changing. The proposition that self-concept support is the basis for interpersonal relationships (Proposition 1) remains secure.

Extension

Cushman and Cahn's (Chapter 8) extension is to compare a homogeneous mainland American sample with a heterogeneous Hawaiian sample. Their expectation that members of the heterogeneous sample will be more diverse in their responses, showing less agreement for the distances between mate relationship concepts, is borne out. Both samples uphold the basic premises of the theory. However, the heterogeneous Hawaiian sample is distinctly more diverse in its distance judgments—so much so that the concept Psychological Support is not upheld as an intensity variable. The specific semantic labels for mate relationship levels and the character of dimensions may indeed, as Cushman and Cahn claim, be culture-specific. Their greatest contribution to the theory's extension is the preliminary evidence that the basic theoretic structure is valid across sub-cultural lines (supporting Proposition 4).

Nicotera (Chapter 9) directly tests the question of a universal theoretic structure for mate relationship development. Her results do show evidence that the basic structure may be upheld cross-culturally. In the United States, and in Korean nonarranged mate relationships, self-concept appears to be a generative mechanism for relationship formation and growth (Proposition 1). Cushman and Cahn's (Chapter 8) results provide some evidence that the structure also holds for the heterogeneous subculture in Hawaii. Moemeka and Nicotera (Chapter 10) provide data from Nigeria, not offering a cross-cultural comparison. However, when considered in light of the data provided by the other studies, these data from Nigeria clearly support the cross-cultural application of the theoretic structure (Proposition 4). The distinction found between casual and close mate relationships supports the use of such measurement across cultures to determine cultural imperatives in the definition of mate relationship intensity. Because the particular semantic labels show some instability in all of these data sets, it cannot be conclusively determined that the specific theoretic structure is truly universal. Clearly, however, enough evidence exists to pursue research in this direction.

Nicotera's (Chapter 9) contributions to the basic theory include preliminary evidence of a culturally universal general theoretic structure, preliminary data for the development of culture-specific levels and dimensions for nonarranged mate relationships in Korea, and the basis for extending the theory into the realm of social penetration. The penetration profiles for American and Korean mate relationships provide a starting point for the explication of topical categories unique to the mate relationship (perhaps "entry" topics) and topical categories whose intimacy may predict relationship level (perhaps "intensity" categories). The general theory is in need of such a communication component. For the mate relationship, Nicotera provides the basis for such expansion.

Implications Across Three Categories

Culture: Concerning Proposition 4

Rules that guide expectations and appropriateness for actions and responses in mate relationships are socially prescribed, and thus differ according to cultural values. As illustrated for friendship in Chapter 7, the power of the general theory to explicate the mate relationship within cultures is evidenced by the homogeneity in the data from each culture in terms of the specified attributes. Further, the diversity of the attributes across cultures illustrates the value of the theory in explicating the same general structure across cultures while discerning between cultures on specific attributes. Table 11.1 illustrates within-culture homogeneity and between-culture diversity of mate relationships, providing support of the studies for Proposition 4. The attributes listed in Table 11.1 are obtained from the investigations in Part III as well as from the seminal investigations reported in Chapter 3. Because of the inconclusive nature of Nicotera's (Chapter 9) study, results for Korea are not included in this table.

Table 11.1
Homogeneity Within and Diversity Among Cultures on Mate Relationship Attributes

	United States	*Hawaii*	*Nigeria*
Entry Variables			
Level of within-culture homogeneity	Intelligence (High), Physical Atttractiveness (High), Sex Appeal (High)	Intelligence (High), Physical Attractiveness (Moderate), Sex Appeal (High)	Good Looks (High), Politeness (Moderate), Intelligence (High)
Intensity Variables			
Level of within-culture homogeneity	Respect (High), Affection (High), Psychological Support (High)	Respect (Moderate), Affection (High), Caring (High)	Affection (High), Honesty (Moderate)

Judgments of within-culture homogeneity are based on the level of agreement of the attributes that can be observed within the samples. Generally, the less diversity within the sample concerning a particular attribute, the higher the homogeneity. Commonalities and differences can be seen among cultures. For entry variables, Physical Attractiveness (Good Looks in Nigeria), and Intelligence are universal. Sex Appeal is shared by the American mainland and Hawaiian samples, and Politeness is unique to Nigeria. For intensity variables, Affection is shared by all three cultures. Honesty and Caring are unique to Nigeria. Although the mainland American and Hawaiian samples share Respect, the level of within-culture homogeneity is lower for the Hawaiians. Cushman and Kovacic (in press) note the implications of intercultural diversity for the establishment and deepening of intercultural mate relationships. As discussed in Chapter 7 for friendships, diversity between cultures concerning the attributes necessary for mate relationship formation and growth complicate the development of intercultural mate relationships. Examination of such diversity has great potential to enhance our understanding of intercultural mate formation.

Diversity is linked to communication interaction. The greater the diversity between cultures, the more difficult intercultural mate relationship development would be. In the attempt to initiate and/or develop a mate relationship, two individuals of diverse cultures provide communication of support on different sets of attributes. Whereas these three cultures are fairly similar for entry variables, others have been shown to be more diverse. (See Cushman and King, 1991; Cushman and Kovacic, in press; Foldy, Danielsen, and Cushman, 1988; Ju, Chapter 12, this volume.) For an intercultural mate relationship to begin and develop, each individual must be sensitive to the different expectations of the other.

Homogeneity within cultures is also linked to communication interaction. For attributes with a high degree of homogeneity, expressions of support for these attributes within the language must be tight. For example, in American culture, the entry and intensity attributes have high levels of homogeneity. For successful initiation of a mate relationship, partners must precisely express their perceptions of intelligence, physical attractiveness, and sex appeal for each other. For successful growth of the relationship, the dyad must precisely express their perceptions of respect, affection, and psychological support for each other. However, in the Hawaiian subculture, expressions of respect may take more forms.

Conflict: Concerning Propositions 5 and 6

Conflict in interpersonal interaction and in mate relationships has been widely examined (e.g., Barry, 1970; Canary and Spitzberg, 1987, 1989; Feldman, 1982; Folger and Poole, 1984; Hennon, 1981; Himes, 1980; Huber, 1984; Kilmann and Thomas, 1975, 1977; Papa and Natalle, 1989; Putnam and Wilson, 1982; Renwick, 1977; Rogers, Millar, and Bavelas, 1985; Sillars, 1980a, 1980b). As discussed in depth in Chapter 7, current theory and research of conflict is focused not on the destructive or constructive nature of the conflict itself, but on the destructive or constructive outcomes of conflict management attempts.

Cushman (Cushman, 1989; Cushman and Kovacic, in press) discusses high- and low-quality conflict patterns for mate relationships. Generally, conflict patterns that reinforce the crucial attributes of the mate relationship result in increased intimacy and high relational quality; such a discussion can provide indirect support for Proposition 5. Mates can be said to engage in conflict that is neither constructive nor destructive to the relationship. Such conflict does not threaten the crucial attributes for mate formation and development. (Refer to Table 11.1 for lists of these crucial attributes for three cultures.) Provided that neither the conflict issue nor the interaction over the conflict threatens self-concept support on these attributes, the conflict has neither a constructive nor destructive impact on the relationship. For example, two American mates can repeatedly engage in conflict over political ideology. Provided that the interaction does not threaten their support of each other for the attributes of intelligence, physical attraction, sex appeal, respect, affection, or psychological support, the conflict will not impair the relationship. In fact, conflict interaction can enhance the relationship by providing the opportunity to express self-concept support on the crucial variables. For example, although he disagrees with his mate, an American man may express his appreciation for the intelligence of her argument and his respect for her conviction.

Conflict issues or interaction that involve the crucial variables can damage the relationship (Proposition 5). As interaction over a conflict threatens self-concept support on the crucial variables, the relationship suffers. This argument is supported by several theorists and researchers (Cushman, 1989; Cushman and Cahn, 1985; Cushman and Kovacic, in press; Genshaft, 1980; Levinger, 1980; Rands, Levinger, and Mellinger, 1981; Ritter, 1985; Ting-Toomey, 1983). Conflict over entry variables threatens the basic support for the other as a person who is desirable as a mate (Cushman, 1989). Conflict over intensity variables threatens support for the level of intimacy in the relationship (Cushman, 1989); discussion of these issues can provide support for Proposition 6.

Conflict that threatens self-concept support on the crucial variables need not destroy the relationship (Cushman, 1989; Cushman and Kovacic, in press). As discussed for friendship (Chapter 7), conflict in low-quality relationships is characterized by the introduction of a complaint with negative affect; followed by confrontation, defensiveness, and/or cross-complaining; then by neutral or negative affect, reciprocated affect, and escalation or withdrawal (Cushman and Kovacic, in press). For example, in a low-quality American mate relationship, conflict interaction would begin as follows: "You are an incredible slob. I can't stand to look at you. Why can't you clean yourself up?" A low-quality interaction would then continue, "I am not a slob. Besides, you're not exactly a prizewinner. You're too picky." Having threatened their mutual support on several crucial variables (physical attraction, sex appeal, respect, and affection), the two are likely to increase their negative affect, escalate the dispute, and withdraw from the relationship. Removing support from these crucial variables jeopardizes both the basis for the relationship and its level of intimacy.

Conflict in high-quality relationships is characterized by the introduction of a focused issue with neutral affect; followed by agreement on a preproportionalized issue with neutral or positive affect; then by mutual exploration of potential solutions; and finally by consensus and implementation of a solution (Cushman and Kovacic, in press). For example, in a high-quality American mate relationship, conflict interaction would begin as follows: "You always look so good when you go out. I know you like to relax on the weekend; I wish you would try to look good for me when we are at home." A high-quality interaction would progress, "I do like to relax on the weekend, and I know you hate these messy old clothes. It's nice that you want me to look good, but I need to loosen up once in a while." Having secured support on crucial variables that define the other as a desirable mate (physical attraction and sex appeal) and maintain the level of intimacy (respect and affection), the two are able to explore solutions and choose one to implement (Proposition 6). The essential element for constructive handling of conflict that threatens support on crucial attributes is the ability to proportionalize the problem (Cushman, 1989; Cushman and Kovacic, in press) so that it does not threaten self- concept support across the whole relationship (Proposition 6). This idea is supported by the work of several scholars (Billingham and Sack, 1987; Birchler, Weiss, and Vincent, 1975; Cushman, 1989; Cushman and Cahn, 1985; Cushman and Kovacic, in press; Genshaft, 1980; Gottman, Markman, and Notarius, 1977; Noller, 1981; Rands et al. 1981; Ting-Toomey, 1983). (See Chapter 7 for a discussion of this issue.)

Quality of Relationship: Concerning Proposition 7

The final category of interpersonal communication to be examined is relationship quality. Given the studies of the mate relationship in Part III, we will consider what constitutes quality from a communication point of view; the following discussion provides indirect support for Proposition 7. Quality, like friendship in Chapter 7, is considered according to three characteristics: increasing intimacy, personal growth, and communication effectiveness. First, a quality mate relationship is characterized by an increase in intimacy or closeness over time (Montgomery, 1981; Rettig and Bubolz, 1983; Spanier and Lewis, 1980). Frequent and consistent communication of self-concept support must be provided on the crucial attributes for the particular culture (see Table 11.1) in order for a mate relationship to be initiated and to grow. The more frequently such support is communicated for entry variables, the more quickly a mate relationship is established. The more frequently support is communicated for intensity variables, the more quickly the relationship deepens.

Second, a quality mate relationship is characterized by individuals' achievement of personal growth—learning and developing both within and outside the relationship (Cushman, 1979; Fincham and Bradbury, 1989; Montgomery, 1981; Spanier and Lewis, 1980). This characteristic is greatly dependent on the homogeneity of crucial variables (see Table 11.1). Cultures with high homogeneity around certain attributes allow less freedom for individual growth on those variables; personal growth within the relationship on those attributes may be thwarted by cultural impositions. In such cases the individual must look outside the mate relationship for growth in these areas while maintaining the attributes within the relationship. In cultures where homogeneity is high around crucial attributes, individual growth within the mate relationship must occur on other attributes—those that are not necessary for the definition, maintenance, and growth of the mate relationship. For attributes with a low degree of homogeneity within the culture, growth within the relationship is less inhibited.

Finally, a quality mate relationship is characterized by effective communication of self-concept support, both directly and indirectly (Aguirre and Kirwan, 1986; Cushman, 1989; Cushman and Cahn, 1985; Cushman and Kovacic, in press). Mates can provide self-concept support for crucial attributes directly (as in "I think you're smart") or indirectly (as in "The way you fixed that broken drawer was very clever and inventive"). Further study of interpersonal penetration in mate relationships can illuminate the various topics within which indirect communication of self-concept support can take place. Whether direct or indirect, effectively communicated self-concept support predicts relationship quality. In a quality mate relationship, each individual has a great degree of certainty about the other's opinion of him/her.

Conclusion

The general theory of mate relationship development is far from complete. Most important, however, the investigations provide support for Propositions 1, 3, and 4. Because only one type of relationship is studied, these studies alone cannot support Proposition 2. However, considering together the results of these studies and the studies in Part II, Proposition 2 gains support. See Table 11.2 for a summary of direct support for the first four propositions.

Generally, the studies in Part III provide for the theory: 1) support for the basic developmental structure, with self-concept as the generative mechanism; 2) bases for revision and refinement both generally and specifically; and 3) bases for extension to other cultures as well as for the extension of a communication component. The discussion of implications across the categories of culture, conflict, and quality provides indirect support for Propositions 5–7, showing the variety of directions that may be taken by research in this area. Part IV advances these ideas with two chapters: the first advocates a view of interpersonal relationships as cultural choice and presents a study to support that stance; the second provides critiques of the individual studies,

Table 11.2
Direct Support for Propositions 1–4

Proposition	*Support provided by:*
1. Perceived self-concept support is the basis of interpersonal attraction.	Cushman and Cahn, Chapter 8; Nicotera, Chapter 9; Moemeka and Nicotera, Chapter 10
2. Different types of perceived self-concept support are the basis for different types of interpersonal relationships.	*Together with investigations of friendship (Part II):* Cushman and Cahn, Chapter 8; Nicotera, Chapter 9; Moemeka and Nicotera, Chapter 10
3. Different types of self-concept support are the basis for *entry* into and increasing *intensity* of interpersonal relationships.	Cushman and Cahn, Chapter 8; Moemeka and Nicotera, Chapter 10
4. The type and form of self-concept support is homogeneous by culture.	Cushman and Cahn, Chapter 8; Nicotera, Chapter 9; Moemeka and Nicotera, Chapter 10

assesses the current state of theoretic development gleaned from the studies, proposes theoretic advancement, and recommends research for further theoretic development.

References

Aguirre, B., and P. Kirwan (1986). Marriage order and the quality and stability of marital relationships: A test of Lewis and Spanier's theory. *Journal of Comparative Family Studies* 17:247–76.

Barry, W. A. (1970). Marriage research and conflict: An integrative review. *Psychological Bulletin* 73:41–54.

Billingham, R. E., and A. R. Sack (1987). Conflict tactics and the level of emotional commitment among unmarrieds. *Human Relations* 40:59–74.

Birchler, G. R., R. L. Weiss, and J. P. Vincent (1975). Multimethod analysis of social reinforcement exchange between maritally distressed and non-distressed spouse and stranger dyads. *Journal of Personality and Social Psychology* 31:349–60.

Canary, D. J., and B. H. Spitzberg (1987). Appropriateness and effectiveness perceptions of conflict strategies. *Human Communication Research* 14:93–118.

Canary, D. J., and B. H. Spitzberg (1989). A model of the perceived competence of conflict strategies. *Human Communication Research* 15:630–49.

Cushman, D. P. (1979). Communication in establishing, maintaining, and terminating interpersonal relationships. *Journal of Youth and Adolescence* 8:443–52.

Cushman, D. P. (1989). Communication in establishing, maintaining, and terminating interpersonal relationships: A study of mateship. In S. S. King (ed.), *Human communication as a field of study: Selected contemporary views* (87–104). Albany, NY: State University of New York Press.

Cushman, D. P., and D. D. Cahn (1985). *Communication in interpersonal relationships*. Albany, NY: State University of New York Press.

Cushman, D. P., and S. S. King (1991). *The mate selection process in Bolivia.* Unpublished manuscript, State University of New York at Albany.

Cushman D. P., and B. Kovacic (in press). A rules perspective on communication theory. In F. L. Casmir (ed.), *Communication Theory*. Albany, NY: State University of New York Press.

Feldman, L. (1982). Dysfunctional marital conflict: An integrative interpersonal-intrapsychic model. *Journal of Family and Marital Therapy* 8:295–308.

Fincham, F., and T. Bradbury (1989). Perceived responsibility for marital events: Egocentric or partner-centric bias? *Journal of Marriage and the Family* 51:27–35.

Foldy, J., S. Danielsen, and D. P. Cushman (1988). The characteristics of mates and the communication pattern involved in initiating mate relationships in American culture as compared to Yugoslavian culture. *Informatologia Yugoslavica* 20:147–54.

Folger, J. P., and M. S. Poole (1984). *Working through conflict: A communication perspective*. Glenview, IL: Scott, Foresman.

Genshaft, J. L. (1980). Perceptual and defensive style variables in marital discord. *Social Behavior and Personality* 8:81–84.

Gottman, J., H. Markman, and C. Notarius (1977). The topography of marital conflict: A sequential analysis of verbal and nonverbal behavior. *Journal of Marriage and the Family* 39:461–77.

Hennon, C. (1981). Conflict management within cohabitation relationships. *Alternative Lifestyles* 4:467–86.

Himes, J. S. (1980). *Conflict and conflict management*. Athens, GA: University of Georgia Press.

Huber, C. H. (1984). Cognitive considerations of coping with marital conflict. *American Mental Health Counselors Association Journal* 6(2):71–78.

Kilmann, R. H., and K. W. Thomas (1975). Interpersonal conflict-handling behavior as reflections of Jungian personality dimensions. *Psychological Reports* 37:971–80.

Kilmann, R. H., and K. W. Thomas (1977). Developing a forced-choice measure of conflict-handling behavior: The "MODE" instrument. *Educational and Psychological Measurement* 37:309–25.

Levinger, G. (1980). Toward the analysis of close relationships. *Journal of Experimental Social Psychology* 16:510–44.

Montgomery, B. M. (1981). The form and function of quality communication in marriage. *Family Relations* 30:21–29.

Noller, P. (1981). Gender and marital adjustment level differences in decoding messages from spouses and strangers. *Journal of Personality and Social Psychology* 41:272–78.

Papa, M. J., and E. J. Natalle (1989). Gender, strategy selection, and satisfaction in interpersonal conflict. *Western Journal of Speech Communication* 53:260–72.

Putnam, L. L., and C. E. Wilson (1982). Communicative strategies in organizational conflicts: Reliability and validity of a measurement scale. In M. Burgoon (ed.), *Communication yearbook 6* (629–52). Beverly Hills, CA: Sage.

Rands, M., G. Levinger, and G. D. Mellinger (1981). Patterns of conflict resolution and marital satisfaction. *Journal of Family Issues* 2:297–321.

Renwick, P. A. (1977). Effects of sex differences on the perception and management of conflict: An exploratory study. *Organizational Behavior and Human Performance* 16:143–55.

Rettig, K., and M. Bubolz (1983). Interpersonal resource exchanges as indicators of quality marriages. *Journal of Marriage and the Family* 45:497–509.

Ritter, K. Y. (1985). The cognitive therapies. *Journal of Counseling and Development* 64:42–44.

Rogers, L. E., F. E. Millar, and J. Bavelas (1985). Methods for analyzing marital conflict discourse: Implications of a systems approach. *Family Process* 24:175–87.

Sillars, A. L. (1980a). Attributions and communication in roommate conflicts. *Communication Monographs* 47:180–200.

Sillars, A. L. (1980b). The sequential and distributional structure of conflict interactions as a function of attributions concerning the locus of responsibility and stability of conflicts. In D. Nimmo (ed.), *Communication yearbook 4* (218–35). New Brunswick, NJ: Transaction.

Spanier, G. B., and R. A. Lewis (1980). Marital quality: A Review of the seventies. *Marriage and Family Living* 42:825–39.

Ting-Toomey, S. (1983). An analysis of verbal communication patterns in high and low marital adjustment groups. *Human Communication Research* 9:306–19.

Part IV

Integration and Critical Appreciation

12

Mate Selection as Cultural Choice: Reflections on Findings in China, Japan, and Korea

Yanan Ju

Mate selection as a cultural choice has probably been implied—if not explicitly asserted, much less theorized—in many cultural-anthropological studies of cultures, modern or more traditional. However, this very interesting and important perspective has largely been missing from the literature on mate selection. Mate selection theorists have been predominantly Western-biased, their work heavily laden with Western values; they have generated theories and models with a discernable imprint of "free choice." Their studies, therefore, may have reduced significance for more traditional, non-Western cultures.

This chapter is designed to sensitize researchers to cultural differences in mate selection, a point still very much neglected in ongoing research trends. It does not seek to diminish the importance of psychological, social psychological, communication or other approaches, nor does it ignore what other researchers have accomplished using various disciplinary approaches or theoretical assumptions. The suggestion here is simply that many of the theories and models on mate selection apply only in certain societies, or perhaps only in the society where the theory was generated, and are largely irrelevant in other cultures. Mate selection researchers and theorists, as in other social sciences and humanities, must constantly test the validity and applicability of a theory across cultures.

The assertion of mate selection as a cultural choice is based on some of the findings of a major cultural change survey completed in China before the Tiananmen Square incident, and an in-depth interview study conducted in

Qingpu County on the outskirts of Shanghai. The following pages provide a discussion of the conceptual framework within which the survey was designed, followed by a brief account of the research methods. Then follows a report on the findings in China, compared with some of the results in similar surveys conducted in Japan and Korea. The chapter concludes with a discussion of the implications of the findings and an argument that future theory development should adequately consider the notion of mate selection as a cultural choice.

Conceptual Framework

Mate selection, it should be noted, is only part of the theme of the cultural change survey in China and the two similar surveys in Japan and Korea. Major findings of the China study are reported in Chu and Ju (in press). The larger framework employed for the whole research project also holds true for the subtopic of mate selection.

The Conceptualization of Culture

Despite general agreement that the concept of culture is evasive, scholars have never ceased in their attempt to define it with a gamut of theoretical perspectives or research methodologies. Kroeber and Kluckhorn (1952) identified 164 definitions of culture from which they developed their own conceptualization: "Culture is a product; is historical; includes ideas, patterns, and values; is selective; is learned; is based upon symbols; and is an abstraction from behavior and the products of behavior" (157). Chu (Chu 1979, 1985; Chu and Ju, in press) views culture as consisting of three major components in the life of any self: first, the social relations between the individual self and his/her significant others; second, materials and objects in the physical environment that the self relies on for survival and that, through the extent of technology, mediate social relations; and third, ideas, including ideology, values, and religious beliefs—both cognitive and evaluative—that influence the way the self perceives the social and physical environments and sets priorities for social relations and the pursuit of materials and objects in the physical environment.

Mate selection, which will lead to a mate relationship and possibly marriage, is part of the first component of social relations between the individual self and his/her significant others. In other words, mate selection is by nature a cultural action. This cultural action, like all others, is determined by the cultural values and beliefs a particular "mate selector" holds. Following the logic implied in Chu's cultural model, a person's cultural values and beliefs are largely the product of his/her physical environment. Given that different cultures have different relational patterns, value and belief systems, and physical environments, the way people select their mate must be different across cultures. It is therefore argued that mate selection is a cultural choice.

Cultural Change as a Constant

Though cultural differences—including mate-selection process differences—are informed by a horizontal comparison, cultural change is constantly reported as a result of efforts to reevaluate a culture's whole way of life over a certain historical period of time. When culture is conceptualized using Chu's framework, as consisting of three major components, cultural change is observed mainly by examining the dynamics of a culture's social relational patterns, value and belief systems, and material and technological developments.

Cultural change is a dynamic process in the sense that it is never-ending; it is a result of interactions among a culture's three components; and it is demonstrated in individual and institutional responses. With cultural change as a constant in mind, mate selection can be viewed as a cultural action following a set of nonstatic criteria, participating in interactions of the three cultural components, and changing its procedures as well as content as part of individuals and institutions' responses to the overall changes in the larger society. It may therefore be argued that mate selection as a relational pattern that changes over time as the larger cultural system changes is, again, a cultural choice.

Method

Sampling and Sample Composition

The China study drew a stratified probability sample of 2,000 respondents, including 1,199 from metropolitan Shanghai, 304 from the two towns in Qingpu County on the outskirts of the city, and 497 from 20 villages in four of the 20 rural districts in the same county. We divided the 10 districts in Shanghai into two strata. The upper stratum consisted of five districts previously under the rule of the International Settlements (administered by the British), the French Concession, and the Japanese Concession before they were returned to Chinese jurisdiction following World War II. These districts used to have better roads, better housing and higher living standards than the other districts, which belonged to the lower stratum. It was later found, surprisingly, that the higher and lower strata were in fact about the same as far as their average income was concerned. The egalitarian policy adopted in China since 1949 has eliminated the class-based income differentiation of the old society.

For cross-tabulations, the total sample was classified into three income groups: 20.1% with average monthly income (in Chinese Yuan) below Y59, 46.% from Y60 to Y89, and 33.7% earning Y90 and above. For educational level, the sample was classified into three groups: approximately 22.9% low (8.9% up to some elementary school and 13.9% elementary school graduation), 38.4% middle (junior high school), and 38.7% high (28.3% senior high school and 10.4% college).

Age was measured at six levels: under 20, 20–29, 30–39, 40–49, 50–59, and 60–65. Again for the purpose of cross-tabulations, the sample was divided into three age groups: younger group (29 years and under), middle group (30–49), and older group (50–65). Because we included in our sample only those who were literate, the rural subsample was much younger than their urban counterparts. Though fewer than one in five in the Shanghai sample was in the younger age group, as many as 44.3% of the rural respondents were in that group. In the Shanghai subsample, over a third were 50 or older, as compared to only 6.2% in the villages. In the sample the two genders were about evenly represented. In the Japan and Korea studies the samples were drawn, respectively, from the metropolitan Tokyo area and the larger Seoul area in the belief that the data generated would be more comparable. Given the limited resources, both samples were smaller than the Shanghai sample.

Instruments

The Shanghai survey instrument consisted of 185 questions, some having as many as 11 subitems. Altogether, there were 360 items. Most of the questions had multiple-choice answers; a few were open-ended. Given the conceptual framework, the questions, arranged in three sections of family life, organizations, and society, were focused on relational patterns (including the mate relationship), values and beliefs (including mate-selection criteria), and some material aspects of the society.

The survey instrument was developed through lengthy and thorough discussions and consultations with prominent scholars in the field and revised after a pretest had been conducted. The instruments used in Korea, Japan, and later Taiwan were all based on our Shanghai questionnaire with the deletion or modification of some items.

The Shanghai instrument contained six questions on the topic of the mate relationship:

1. Of the following factors, which three are most important for young people when they select a marriage partner? (The factors provided were looks; education; occupation; work ability; family financial

condition; family social position; common interests; emotional compatibility; high moral standards; love; age; other—please specify.)

2. If a man and a woman are in love, and they live together before their marriage is registered, what do you think about this situation? (Three choices: all right; not right; other—please specify.)
3. If you have a daughter, and she carries on with several boyfriends before she gets married, what would you think about this? (Three choices: would permit; would not permit; other—please specify.)
4. If you have a son, and he carries on with several girlfriends before he gets married, what would you think about this? (Three choices as above.)
5. If you have a daughter, will you let her find her own mate or find one for her? (Three choices: find one for her; let her find her own mate; other—please specify.)
6. If you have a son, will you let him find his own mate or find one for him? (Three choices as above.)

All six questions were repeated in the Korea instrument. The Japan instrument used only the first two.

Procedures

In the pretest conducted in Shanghai, people put in a face-to-face interview situation were reluctant to answer questions they thought were sensitive. Assurance of anonymity did not seem to alleviate their hesitation. Because of the nature of the political climate in China, after considerable discussion it was decided to use the small-group, self-administered approach. At each group session, one faculty member and one or two graduate assistants from Fudan University of Shanghai were present to answer questions that respondents might wish to ask. The questionnaires, when completed and returned, were randomized to ensure complete anonymity. In contrast, Japanese data-collection used the face-to-face interview survey method. In Korea the respondents were allowed to take the questionnaires and complete them at home.

Findings

Focusing on the mate-selection criteria question asked in all our three studies ensures the comparability of the research findings. In each of the three questionnaires, respondents were given a list of 11 criteria and asked to pick three that were most important among young people today. Though they were also free to write in other criteria not on the list, very few people did

Table 12.1
Shanghai Respondents' Choices for the Three Most Important Criteria for Mate Selection in Order of Descending Importance

1.	High Moral Standards	47.4%
2.	Emotional Compatibility	45.3%
3.	Common Interests	39.9%
4.	Education	34.8%
5.	Looks	27.3%
6.	Work Ability	26.8%
7.	Love	22.6%
8.	Age	14.7%
9.	Family Financial Condition	14.4%
10.	Occupation	11.2%
11.	Family Social Position	7.6%

so. Analysis was therefore based on the 11 criteria provided. Respondents were asked about their perceptions, rather than their own personal criteria, so that all respondents could answer the question regardless of their own marital status.

Shanghai Results

Table 12.1 presents Shanghai respondents' choices arranged in order of descending importance. Most astonishing was the finding that Family Social Position, traditionally the single most important criterion in mate selection in China, is now considered the least important of all. A familiar Chinese saying states, "Dragon matches dragon, phoenix matches phoenix, and rats go to little holes." In the past it was not important whether it was arranged for a woman to marry a sick, dying, or insane man; it was crucial that the two families matched each other in their social position. (This finding reflects the depth of sociocultural changes Chinese society has been undergoing since the 1949 revolution. Cultural change in itself is not the issue here, but rather to show that mate-selection criteria are inextricably intertwined with the dynamics of a culture.)

Family Social Position as a mate-selection criterion was inherited in a very peculiar way by a people who experienced radical social changes in the first two or three decades after the founding of the People's Republic. A Party cadre, or even an ordinary staff member in a state-owned enterprise, was required to report to his or her work unit on the family background of the person s/he intended to marry. Official approval had to be obtained for the marriage. A person who bypassed this procedure risked punishment by the authorities. A cadre who honestly reported that the person to be married was from, say, a former rich peasant's family would usually be advised to stay away if s/he wished to further advance in his/her career. Those who were bold enough to ignore such advice might be moved to a less desirable job or position. People were encouraged to marry those with a revolutionary family background or of a peasant-worker origin. On the other hand, children from families that belonged to any of the condemned classes usually had a difficult time finding a marriage partner outside their own condemned circles; few people would want to be dragged down to such a low social status through marriage. Free mate selection was a naive, if not harmful, idea in those days.

The inhumane practice of selecting marriage partners based on classes was stopped soon after the reform years began in the early 1980s—another abrupt social change. What came as a surprise was that only 7.6% of our survey respondents picked Family Social Position as one of the three most important mate-selection criteria. It was a surprise because the change was so fast and so thorough. With other cultural changes, this criterion may again become strong in the future. As a reflection of social and cultural change, this low value for Family Social Position strongly supports the idea that mate-selection criteria are closely related to social and cultural dynamics.

As expected, the most highly endorsed criterion was High Moral Standards, which, in the Chinese context, would mean "highly reliable." In a culture where divorce is still very much frowned upon, it is only reasonable that one would choose someone highly reliable. Age was also an important factor. Those who were in the 50–65 age group were far more likely (62.4%) to see this as an important criterion than the younger (below 29) and middle groups (30–49) (about 42% each). The difference was 20%. There was no difference between the younger and middle groups. These findings suggest a residual effect of cultural indoctrination in traditional Chinese society. Most of the people in the older group grew up in traditional China before the founding of the People's Republic in 1949. High moral standards were still very important for the selection of a marriage partner. For most people in the middle and younger groups, socialization did not begin until after 1949. In the many mass criticism campaigns that took place during the lifetime of the middle group, what counted was not moral standards, but ideological reaffirmation and tenacious ability for mere survival. Even though those in the younger group did not have such intensive experience with the criticism campaigns, they grew up in a cultural environment where moral standards had already been diluted.

A most intriguing finding had to do with Western cultural influence. The more heavily one was exposed to Western culture, the less likely one was to recognize High Moral Standards as an important mate-selection criterion.

Among those least exposed, 52.4% mentioned this criterion—twice as many as the 25.5% among those most heavily exposed. Most of those heavily exposed to Western culture were young. Given the finding that there was no difference between the middle and young groups in their choice of High Moral Standards as an important criterion, it seems an acceptable explanation that Western ways of life seen in Western television programs and Hollywood films had a cultural effect.

One cultural behavior is particularly noteworthy. The term Emotional Compatibility was endorsed by 45.3% of the respondents, and Love chosen by a moderate 22.6%. This confirms the expectations under which the questionnaire was designed. Emotional Compatibility is generally considered a subdued Chinese way of saying "love"; merely uttering the word "love" is too romantic for an average Chinese.

> The expression "I love you" sounds foreign and formal in Chinese, and consequently is rarely used. Indeed, there are Chinese intellectuals who use the English words for "love" and "kiss," even in their most intimate moments, because they sound less strange than their Chinese equivalents. Such people glumly insist that Chinese is simply not a language for lovers. (Kristof, 1991, p. A4)

The assertion that Chinese is "simply not a language for lovers" lacks both theoretical and empirical basis. In fact, it is more likely that Chinese shy away from such romantic (in the Chinese sense) terms as "love" and "kiss" not because the Chinese language lacks such characters but because their culture does not encourage their use in daily life. It is more a cultural phenomenon than a linguistic issue. The way people use the language—a cultural process—certainly defines the way they love and the way they select mates—again a cultural process.

Cultural Comparisons

Chinese, Japanese and Korean cultural traditions share the Confucian root. We know that these three East Asian cultures have been undergoing fundamental cultural changes in the last four decades or so, albeit in quite different directions. We also know that both the Japanese and Korean ways of life (but certainly not the Chinese), in the process of industrialization, have been under heavy American influence. How do these three Confucian cultures compare in their perceptions of mate-selection criteria?

We now take a look at the contemporary Japanese and Korean criteria of mate selection. Tables 12.2 and 12.3 present these results, listed in the order of descending popularity. The comparison here implies much more

Table 12.2
Japanese Respondents' Choices for the Three Most Important Criteria for Mate Selection in Order of Descending Importance

1.	Love	64.4%
2.	Emotional Compatibility	53.8%
3.	High Moral Standards	46.0%
4.	Work Ability	35.4%
5.	Occupation	22.6%
6.	Family Financial Condition	21.5%
7.	Common Interest	21.1%
8.	Age	6.8%
9.	Education	6.4%
10.	Looks	4.3%
11.	Family Social Position	2.7%

Table 12.3
Korean Respondents' Choices for the Three Most Important Criteria for Mate Selection in Order of Descending Importance

1.	Work Ability	59.9%
2.	Love	56.4%
3.	Looks	38.6%
4.	Occupation	35.6%
5.	High Moral Standards	31.3%
6.	Family Financial Condition	29.9%
7.	Emotional Compatibility	14.2%
8.	Age	9.2%
9.	Education	6.8%
10.	Family Social Position	5.1%
11.	Common Interest	2.2%

than we are able to discuss here. One striking similarity among the three cultures is the fact that Family Social Position, which was traditionally the single most important criterion for mate selection for all of them, is now least important, though for different reasons. In China revolution and successive ideological campaigns to promote an egalitarian society seem to be the catalyst for the change. That the Japanese and Koreans no longer care much about their mates' family social position is probably the result of industrialization and modernization, which have helped promote such ideologies as social equality and fair competition, concepts that contradict the notion of Family Social Position.

One striking difference between the Chinese on the one hand and the Japanese and Koreans on the other is that whereas the former, like their parents and grandparents, shy away from such "glamorous" words as "love", the latter no longer want to conceal their most intimate feelings. As is shown above, Love tops the list of the Japanese criteria of mate selection, and the Koreans see Love as the second-most important criterion. Language is not a satisfactory or appropriate explanation. Like Chinese, both Japanese and Korean may be said to be languages "not for lovers." Still, the users of either language now say that love is an important criterion for mate selection. The explanation, therefore, should come from a consideration of cultural changes that have occurred in both Japan and Korea. In this particular respect Japan and Korea seem to have become less traditional than China.

Among the three cultures, Korea appears to have become the most radical in terms of the intensity of change. It is not surprising to find Koreans choosing Work Ability as the top criterion for mate selection. This simply reflects the competitive nature of contemporary Korean society. After World War II Korea was one of the poorest nations in the world. Over the past two decades or so, as a result of the hard work of its people, Korea has overcome its lack of natural resources and achieved a real annual growth rate of over 9% in GNP (Yoo and Lee, 1987). Korea's top three mate selection criteria, Work Ability, Love, and Looks, seem to suggest that Koreans have become a people who work hard and play hard, an obvious departure from Confucian influence.

The Koreans and Chinese are different regarding the top three criteria; Japan stands in the middle, sharing two criteria with the Chinese and one with the Koreans. The Japanese appear to be as spiritually and morally oriented as the Chinese, except that the former have become more "romantic" than the latter. Besides the fact that both the Japanese and Koreans see Love as an important mate-selection criterion, they have more in common with each other than each has with the Chinese in their perceptions of such factors as Occupation and Family Financial Condition. This is understandable because Japan and Korea both have market-oriented economies where jobs and money are crucial for survival and family development. In China Family Financial Condition and Occupation received the weakest endorsement, exceeding only Family Social Position. Family Financial Condition and Occupation carry little significance: In China, where there are few rich people, a renowned professor and a peddler selling tea-leaf eggs on the street earn about the same amount of money—perhaps less for the professor. It is not likely that these criteria would become important unless the society changes its very nature of egalitarianism.

Discussion

The findings on mate-selection criteria in contemporary China, Japan, and Korea, and how such criteria may change along with changes in the larger cultural environment, suggest that mate selection is indeed a process where cultural choice is exercised. The findings focus on mate selection criteria, not on mate selection as a process. However, the fact that these criteria exhibit change in response to larger cultural changes confirms the suggestion that mate selection is a dynamic cultural process where the relational pattern is very much controlled by cultural forces. It is therefore argued that mate selection is not only an individual process, but is also a cultural process.

Filter and Stage Models of Mate Selection

Having emphasized mate selection as a cultural process, we are now in a position to review some of the existing mate-selection theories. Our purpose is to discuss their cultural limitations and raise sensitivity to cultural variables. Therefore, our discussion focuses on filter and stage theorists, a group that represents the better-developed Western theories in the field.

Cushman's three-stage filter. We will begin with Cushman and his associates' three-stage theory of mate selection. Researchers in this volume have used their theoretical variables as a tool with which to locate cultural differences. From a self-concept and rules perspective, Cushman and his associates treat mate selection as a three-stage filtering process, which involves a field of availables, a field of approachables, and a field of reciprocals (Cushman and Cahn, 1985; Cushman, Valentinsen, and Dietrich, 1982; for a full discussion, see Chapter 1). The endeavor of this chapter is not to examine microscopically mate selection as a process; it is simply to sensitize researchers in this predominantly Western-oriented area to cultural variables that, once introduced in the research framework, can raise the study to a more culturally (or historically) substantive level. The findings reported in the previous pages support the notion of mate selection as a general cultural process; they also relate in a meaningful way to Cushman and his associates' conceptualization of mate selection (Cushman and Cahn, 1985; Cushman and Kovacic, in press; studies in this volume). For example, Cushman and his associates also propose a set of criteria in each of the three fields, which include intelligence, physical attraction, and sexual appeal (Cushman and Cahn, 1985).

Like other mate-selection models, this theoretical framework is very much built on the Western notion of free individual choice. Were the model applied to traditional Chinese culture, where people have had no free choice in marriage or many other social affairs, certainly both the field of approachables and the field of reciprocals, if measured using numerical terms, would be close to zero. Few Chinese would be allowed to approach an opposite-sex person to initiate a mate relationship; culturally, the other person would be considered immoral were s/he to respond favorably to such an attempt. Were the Cushman three-stage model applied to contemporary Chinese culture, where limited individual choice has become possible, intervening cultural variables would result in three fields that would probably look quite different from those found in other cultures. This suggests that the three-stage process model, if used to study cultural differences, could become a vigorous and viable model.

Cushman and his associates, as well as the authors in this volume, have provided evidence regarding cultural differences in using mate-selection entry rules as opposed to intensity rules (in this essay the term "rules" is comparable to "criteria"), though further studies are needed to confirm findings in selected cultures. Table 12.4 presents the first half of Cushman and Kovacic's (in press) cultural comparisons of the mate-selection process using entry and intensity rules. The reader may also note the comparable rules revealed by the studies in this volume for Hawaii (Chapter 8), Korea (Chapter 9), and Nigeria (Chapter 10).

An elaborate comparison analysis is pending, as more focused studies in the use of entry and intensity rules in mate selection in China, Japan, and Korea are needed. To make research findings more comparable, variables must be carefully selected. It is difficult to compare our findings in China, Japan, and Korea with those of Cushman and his associates presented in the Table 12.4 because the categories in these separate studies were quite different. What should be emphasized, however, is that some of the existing Western-biased mate-selection models could be further enriched by adding manageable cultural variables or simply by testing in different cultural contexts, as evidenced by efforts using the Cushman three-stage model to investigate cultural differences.

Kerckhoff and Davis's filters. Kerckhoff and Davis (1962) identify two filtering factors—value consensus and need complementarity—as having a significant impact on the mate formation process. They found value consensus to be significant only for short-term couples, whereas for long-term couples need complementarity was more important. They report that social status variables operate early in a relationship, value consensus later, and need complementarity still later. Kerckhoff and Davis's work represents an early academic effort to identify significant variables affecting the mate-selection and formation process.

These filtering factors are unquestionably useful categories with which to investigate the mate-formation process not only in Western societies but

Table 12.4
Cultural Comparisons of Mate Selection Processes Using Entry and Intensity Rules

	United States	*Yugoslavia*	*Bolivia*
Entry rules	Intelligent; Physical attraction	Intelligent; Attractive; Sexually appealing	Intelligent; Passionate; Good looking
Intensity rules	Respect; Affection; Psychological support	Likeable; Tolerant; Right interests; Sense of humor; Trustful	Understanding; Responsible; Trustworthy; Respectful Loving
Research citation	Valentinsen, Cushman, & Schroeder (1981; see Chapter 3); Cushman &Cahn, Chapter 8, this volume	Foldy, Danielsen & Cushman, (1988)	Cushman & King (1991)

in non-Western cultures. However, to what extent these factors would operate in what stage may vary from culture to culture. Take the social status factor as an example. As discussed in the previous pages, while family social position was the single most important mate-selection criterion in traditional China, it has become the least important today. This suggests that the way these factors operate changes as the culture changes. In this sense, what factors operate in what stage to what extent can hardly be persistent, much less common in different cultures. Drawing conclusions such as "value consensus is only significant for short-term couples and need complementarity is significant for long-term couples" would immediately become problematic if the theory were tested in a culture other than the one in which it was developed.

Lewis's PDF. Following Kerckhoff and Davis's work, Lewis (1972; 1973) proposes a developmental framework for the analysis of Premarital Dyadic Formation (PDF), which involves six steps: perceiving similarities, achieving pair rapport, inducing self-disclosure, role-taking, achieving interpersonal role fit, and achieving dyadic crystallization. This appears to be a natural relationship-formation process, but in actuality the process does not always unfold as the theory postulates. When a theory concerning an often irrational and unpredictable human process tested in actual life situations, the results can be very discouraging. When tested in a different cultural environment, the results could make no sense at all. It seems that Lewis's framework may have a lower degree of applicability in other cultures than Kerckhoff and Davis's model because of the former's more clearly defined stage categories. Another problem is the nonobservance of the suggested sequence, particularly when the sequence involves as many as six steps. A scientifically postulated sequence may have very limited applicability to real-life situations.

Murstein's SVR. Murstein's (1970; 1974; 1976) SVR theory—referring to Stimulus, Value, and Role—is another three-stage process. The initial phase of a relationship, according to Murstein, is the Stimulus stage, where potential relational partners make their move based on information that does not come from interaction; the information has only "stimulus values." During the Value stage, relational partners use verbal interaction to determine their value compatibility. The Role stage is said to involve perceived role fit, personal adequacy, and sexual compatibility. Murstein's SVR model has intuitive appeal, but its viability may be brought into question when it is applied in a non-Western culture, such as Chinese culture. The category of sexual compatibility in the Role stage, for example, is hardly testable or even meaningful in today's China where premarital sex is frowned upon and considered culturally inappropriate or even immoral in the more remote rural areas. It seems that whereas broad categories may be relatively applicable across cultures, lower-level variables and more refined examination could be problematic cross-culturally.

Knapp's stages. Knapp's (1978) theory, which may not specifically be identified as a mate-selection theory, breaks the development of interpersonal relationships, including mate relationships, into ten stages: Initiating, Experimenting, Intensifying, Integrating, Bonding, Differentiating, Circumscribing, Stagnating, Avoiding, and Terminating. The first five stages are relevant to mate relationship formation. Like most stage theories, Knapp's has intuitive appeal. However, the model has no empirical support. In real-life situations, things are simply not that orderly or predictable. If a couple skips or reverses any stage or stages to cement a relationship, or if there are too many exceptions to the step-by-step progress, the usefulness and viability of the theory is immediately brought into question.

In contemporary Chinese culture, where personal free choice is still very much limited, Bonding, which comes as the fifth stage in Knapp's model, may well be the second or even the first. People may, for various cultural, social, economic, or political reasons, lock themselves into a mate relationship before anything happens in order to be "safe." Whether the bonding is tight or loose is another issue; so long as the relationship is ritualistically bonded, they feel they are safe. Any rigidly set sequential process, as in the case of Knapp's theory, has cross-cultural pitfalls. Ironically, the more stages a stage theory identifies and the more scientific it looks, the less applicable it becomes to other cultural contexts.

Nofz's FTA. As opposed to Knapp's and others' multistep sequential process approach, Nofz (1984) focuses on the "modes" in which relational partners manage their relationship. Three such modes are identified: Fantasy, Testing, and Assessment (FTA). Fantasy is a way of perceiving the partner; it is primarily built upon internalized expectations which the self assumes will automatically be fulfilled by the partner. In the Testing mode, the self's and/or the partner's orientations to values, sex roles, and other variables are clarified through interactive episodes. Assessment refers to conscious evaluation of the rewards and costs involved in the relationship, based on the social exchange theory.

Because the three modes are fairly general and broad and are nonsequential, Nofz's model seems to be widely applicable. Moreover, Nofz himself claims that his FTA theory is a response to the alleged possibility that essential qualities that give a relationship its permanence may be operating differently from one dyad to another. This seems to suggest that his model may have a better chance in non-Western cultures.

Implications for Mate-Selection Theorizing

The critique of the above six theories is informal—occasionally even intuitive. The underlying "tool" of the criticism is the notion that mate selection is a process where cultural choice is exercised. The next task is to lay out some of the implications for mate-selection theorizing that may be drawn from the discussion of recent findings as to mate-selection criteria in China, Japan, and Korea, and from the brief critique of existing Western mate-selection theories. The conclusions are tentative and need to be tested in future research. Based on the theory that mate selection is a cultural choice, recent research findings relating to the area, and several mate-selection theories, the following suggestions might be helpful to researchers and students of mate selection and marriage in their future theory development, particularly in attempts to formulate culturally universal theories.

The notion of free individual choice. Mate selection, probably the most important decision in one's life, reflects some of the most fundamental cultural values and beliefs of a society. The notion of free individual choice has little meaning if it is divorced from the larger sociocultural context. Free individual choice (the term itself a Western creation) undeniably makes more sense in Western cultures than in many of the more traditional cultures. However, even in so-called free Western societies, free individual choice is limited by many sociocultural parameters and contingencies. Action theorists agree that people have only "some degree of choice among alternatives" (Cushman and Kovacic, in press).

Mate-selection theorists may choose to study such alternatives, or the forces that influence a person's choice, but it is crucial for a theorist to keep in mind that a person's choice is limited. It is equally important to remember that such limitations vary from culture to culture. In some cultures, free individual choice is so limited as to be practically nonexistent. Although some mate selection theorists do inquire into limitations that influence choice, the kinds of limitations they talk about are primarily psychological—from within the person rather than from without. Cushman's three-stage theory is unique in that it does both: its field of approachables and field of reciprocals mainly involve a person's psychological restraints, while its field of availables does touch spacio-temporal contingencies, which are outside a person's direct control. A more flexible and culturally sensible mate-selection theory or model should be constructed on the notion of limited free individual choice.

Cultural variables. Viewing mate selection as a cultural choice would lead one to consider cultural variables in theorizing. These would include cultural values, attitudes and beliefs, patterned behaviors, customs, rituals and symbols, verbal and nonverbal systems, and other ways of life. Employing cultural theories of mate selection, like reclaiming a fertile piece of land, would almost guarantee a rich harvest. Cultural variables are particularly useful for comparative mate-selection researches, as the China–Japan–Korea comparison has implied.

Cultural change. Culture changes over time, as does mate selection in a culture. Theories are no more than symbolic representations of realities. Such representations should change along with perceived changes in realities. A theory is useless, to say the least, if it does not reflect the changed realities. We do not know the average life expectancy of a social science theory—though we tend to believe that it is becoming shorter and shorter. One way to extend a theory's life is to allow sufficient room for variations introduced simply by time. Another way to keep a theory alive is to add new findings, or rather new thinking based on new findings, to the original formulation, like adding amendments to the United States Constitution. Theorists who specifically see mate selection as a cultural choice need not worry about losing their job; they probably need to go back to the real world every five years to check on new developments and to see if their original symbolic representation still makes sense.

Cultural specificity. Mate-selection theories do not have to be universally applicable across all cultures; they can be culture-specific, provided the specificity is clear. A peculiar phenomenon in social science is that many theorists assume their theories are universally true when they are only culture-specific or even subculture-specific. Perhaps it is arrogance, or, to be more generous, cultural ignorance that makes many theorists unable or unwilling to admit their cultural specificity. The solution is simple: If a theory applies, for example, only to middle-class America, then it should be specified as such. Admitting cultural specificity does not weaken a theory. In fact, it strengthens it. On the other hand, if a theorist does intend to develop a universally applicable theory, his/her variables or categories must be broad enough to be applicable to a wide range of cultural contexts. For example, Cushman's three-stage theory and Kerckhoff and Davis' two-factor model seem to have a higher degree of applicability across cultures than Lewis' PDF theory or Knapp's ten- stage theory. The broader the research variables are, the more widely applicable the theory.

Sequences in the mate-selection process. Sequences of mate selection—not only the order of the sequence, but also the duration and importance of each sequential element—have serious cultural implications. A widely applicable mate selection sequence should follow three guidelines: 1) the sequence should not involve too large a number of stages or phases; 2) the sequential order should not be rigidly set to exclude possible variations; and 3) the duration and importance of each phase should be stated in such a way as to allow cultural variations.

References

Chu, G. C. (1979). Communication and cultural change in China: A conceptual framework. In G. C. Chu and F. L. K. Hsu (eds.), *Moving a mountain: Cultural change in China* (2–24). Honolulu: The University Press of Hawaii.

Chu, G. C. (1985). The changing concept of self in contemporary China. In A. J. Marsella, G. DeVos, and F. L. K. Hsu (eds.), *Culture and self: Asian and Western perspectives* (252–79). New York: Tavistock Publications.

Chu, G. C., and Y. A. Ju (in press). *The Great Wall in ruins: Communication and cultural change in China*. Albany, NY: State University of New York Press.

Cushman, D. P., and D. Cahn (1985). *Communication in interpersonal relationships*. Albany, NY: State University of New York Press.

Cushman, D. P., and S. S. King (1991). *The mate selection process in Bolivia*. Unpublished manuscript, State University of New York at Albany.

Cushman, D. P., and B. Kovacic (in press). A rules perspective on communication theory. In F. L. Casmir (ed.), *Communication theory*. Albany, NY: State University of New York Press.

Cushman, D. P., B. Valentinsen, and D. Dietrich (1982). A rules theory of interpersonal relationships. In F. E. X. Dance (ed.), *Human communication theory* (90–119). New York: Harper and Row.

Foldy, J., S. Danielsen, and D. P. Cushman (1988). The characteristics of mates and the communication pattern involved in initiating mate relationships in American culture as compared to Yugoslavian culture. *Informatologia Yugoslavica* 20:147–54.

Kerckhoff, A. C., and K. E. Davis (1962). Value consensus and need complementarity in mate selection. *American Sociological Review* 27:295–303.

Knapp, M. (1978). *Social intercourse: From greeting to goodbye*. Boston: Allyn and Bacon.

Kristof, N. D. Love, the starry-eyed kind, casts spell on China. *New York Times*, 6 Mar. 1991, A4.

Kroeber, A. L., and C. Kluckhorn (1952). *Culture: A critical review of concepts and definitions*. Cambridge, MA: The Peabody Museum of American Archaeology and Ethnology, Harvard University.

Lewis, R. A. A. (1972). A developmental framework for the analysis of premarital dyadic formation. *Family Process* 11:17–48.

Lewis, R. A. A. (1973). A longitudinal test of a developmental framework for the analysis of premarital dyadic formation. *Journal of Marriage and the Family* 35:16–25.

Murstein, B. I. (1970). Stimulus-value-role: A theory of marital choice. *Journal of Marriage and the Family* 37:265–81.

Murstein, B. I. (1974). Clarification of obfuscation on computation: A reply to criticism of the SVR theory of marital choice. *Journal of Marriage and the Family* 36:231–34.

Murstein, B. I. (1976). *Who will marry whom?* New York: Springer.

Nofz, M. P. (1984). Fantasy-testing-assessment: A proposed model for the investigation of mate selection. *Family Relations* 33:273–81.

Valentinsen, B., D. P. Cushman, and L. E. Schroeder (1981, May). *The friend and mate formation processes: Testing a rules theory*. Paper presented at the annual meeting of the International Communication Association, Minneapolis, MN.

Yoo, S. and S. M. Lee (1987). Management style and practice of Korean chaebols. *California Management Review* 24 (4):95–110.

13

Where Have We Been, Where Are We, and Where Do We Go?

Anne Maydan Nicotera

Interpersonal Relationships as Cultural Choice

Friendship as Cultural Choice

Before turning to a consideration of the questions that make up the title of this chapter, we must ground our multicultural view of interpersonal relationships. In Chapter 12, Ju argues for a view of mate selection as cultural choice, defining mate selection as a cultural action. With the evidence provided by the studies in Part II, the same argument can be made for friendship. Following Chu's (Chu, 1979, 1985; Chu and Ju, in press) three-fold definition of culture (see Chapter 12), friendship is part of the first component of social relations between the self and significant others. Further, the physical environment and the culture's ideology, respectively, mediate and set priorities for social relations. Finally, following the logic set forth in Chapter 12, changes in friendship patterns will be observed as the larger cultural system changes. As Ju succinctly states, such patterns of change can also be defined as cultural choice.

Moemeka and Nicotera (Chapter 6) provide preliminary evidence for the viability of applying a cultural-choice framework to friendship. Through testing the traditionally valued friendship attributes honest and responsible, their data show that contemporary values for friendship may have departed from traditional Nigerian values. Specifically, Responsible—traditionally highly valued—is neither a crucial nor highly valued variable according to their measurement. Other attributes, perhaps Humor, may have replaced Responsible as a valued trait. These authors claim that encroaching Western values are at the root of such change. This explanation fits Ju's (Chapter 12) cultural choice framework. Following the framework, as Western values exert a change in Nigerian culture, friendship patterns can be expected to change accordingly. Of course, a more comprehensive study comparing the friendship values of rural and urban Nigerians is necessary to substantiate the claim that friendship patterns are changing as the culture changes. Changes in the culture attributable to Western influences would begin in urban areas; cultural differences between rural and urban areas would be expected to correspond with differences in friendship patterns.

Entry and Intensity Variables

Following the logic of a cultural-choice framework, friend and mate relationships are seen as dependent on two crucial sets of variables—both of which arise from cultural imperatives. These variables are, of course, entry and intensity variables. The theoretic structure is multicultural because it predicts the general pattern of relationship initiation and growth, yet does not dictate the specific character of the crucial variables. First, before a dyad can enter into a friend or mate relationship, they must perceive each other as having the basic attributes of a friend or mate (dictated by the culture) and must provide self-concept support to each other on those variables. Second, for the relationship to deepen, they must perceive each other as having increasingly intense levels of a set of key attributes (dictated by the culture) and must provide self-concept support to each other on those variables. The work presented in this volume presents a set of basic tools with which to locate these crucial attributes in different cultures.

Where We Have Been: Critique of the Studies

Scope: What Have We Done?

Development of two ideas. This book fosters the development of two important ideas. First, a theoretic basis has been found. In Chapter 2, seven empirically confirmable propositions were derived from Cushman's general conceptual theory (Cushman and Cahn, 1985; Cushman, Valentinsen, and Dietrich, 1982; see Chapter 1) and a review of the literature. The studies presented in this volume provide direct support for Propositions 1–4 and indirect support for Propositions 5–7. These propositions and their security are considered in some detail below.

Second, a methodological basis has been developed that allows the location of crucial relationship attributes in any culture without cultural bias. The method thus has the potential to be used across cultures without Western or American bias. (See Ju, Chapter 12, for a full discussion of this issue.) Another contribution of the method is that it has a communication bias. The attribute-location process can discern the crucial relationship attributes for different relationship types and different cultures. Levels of homogeneity within cultures reveal the degree of precision with which self-concept support for these attributes must be communicated. The degree to which communication of support for the attributes is direct or indirect can be illuminated with penetration profile analyses. Finally, the method forms the basis for broadening into other areas. Similar methodologies can be applied far beyond the narrow scope of interpersonal relationship development.

Substance of the studies. In a variety of cultures, the studies in this volume delineate relational levels, identify crucial attributes for friendship and/or the mate relationship, and support the location of these attributes with the method. A few of the chapters also conduct interpersonal penetration analyses that may provide the basis for studies of indirect communication of self-concept support.

Foremost in importance, the studies provide a basis for the multicultural application of the theory. Crucial attributes for interpersonal relationship initiation and growth are identified in a wide variety of cultures. Regardless of the sample size or the specific method used to measure these attributes, a high degree of homogeneity within the cultures is observed. Ju's (Chapter 12) finding of a similar pattern with his enormous sample lends credence to the other studies' locations of attributes. These studies show, above all else, that the same general framework for relationship growth and formation can be applied cross-culturally. They provide both a theoretic and a methodological basis for doing so, while allowing the theory to encompass specific attributes for relationship formation and growth that differ from culture to culture.

Friendship studies. Korn's (Chapter 4) study of friendship tests the theorized levels of friendship and extends this test to Korean friendship. Chapter 4 provides direct support for Propositions 1, 3, and 4. Bahk's (Chapter 5) study delves into the explication of friendship levels and self-concept support cross-culturally and cross-sexually, providing direct support for Propositions 1 and 2. Both friendship studies provide an extension into conversational penetration, providing a basis for direct investigation of Proposition 7. Moemeka and Nicotera (Chapter 6) locate levels and attributes in Nigerian culture, give some evidence for the existence of entry and intensity variables in friendship, and furnish some evidence of the impact of cultural imperatives on friendship formation. Chapter 6 provides direct support for Propositions 1, 3, and 4.

Mate relationship studies. Cushman and Cahn (Chapter 8) test levels of the mate relationship in two subcultures, and provide direct support for Propositions 1, 3, and 4. Nicotera (Chapter 9) tests levels of the mate relationship and extends this test to Korean mate relationships, providing direct support for Propositions 1 and 4. Her extension also follows Korn and Bahk into the realm of conversational penetration. Moemeka and Nicotera (Chapter 10) locate mate relationship levels and crucial attributes in Nigerian culture. Chapter 10 directly supports Propositions 1, 3, and 4.

Friend and mate studies together. When all six of the studies are considered together, direct support can be found for Proposition 2. Together the studies also identify crucial attributes of the friend and mate relationships that may be used as the basis for further investigation into the communication of self-concept support and its role in relational development in several cultures. Bahk's study provides insight into the ways in which self-concept support may be manifested in both relationship types.

Conceptualizations

The studies presented in this book share conceptual definitions of their key variables. All conceptualizations are consistent with the theory and each other. Friend and mate are two forms of interpersonal relationships conceptualized as coordination systems, the function of which is to develop and maintain consensus on individual self-concepts (Cushman, Valentinsen, and Dietrich, 1982). Self-concept support is that validation of (consensus on) self-concept. Intimacy (or depth) of interpersonal relationships is thus conceptualized as the intensity of self-concept support—particularly on attributes defined as intensity variables. Korn, Bahk, and Nicotera (Chapters 4, 5, and 9, respectively) conceptualize interpersonal penetration as the degree, breadth, and depth of communication between two relationship partners.

Bahk (Chapter 5) provides a more thorough conceptualization of self-concept support. He investigates its different forms: self-concept similarity, self-concept accuracy (perception of other's self-concept), perceived understanding, and perceived liking. All of these are conceptualized perceptually.

Operationalizations

Relationship levels. To test relationship levels, all authors operationalize the distinction between levels as their distances from the self in cognitive space. This is an excellent operational definition of intimacy; more intimate levels will be cognitively closer to the self. The problem is that the operationalizations of real and ideal self may preclude conclusions about self-concept support as theorized. Real self and ideal self have specific conceptual definitions (see Chapter 1). In most of these studies, however, they are operationalized by the subjects' perceptions of those terms. The operationalization of the level distinctions is not affected by this problem. However, caution must be used in interpreting the results; it cannot be assumed that the subjects' perceptions of their real and ideal selves fully operationalize the theory of self-concept upon which the theory is based. More work is needed to confirm this part of the theory adequately.

A comment about Bahk's use of cognitive distance between the self and relationship levels is necessary. He correctly notes a weakness in the measure: that the results from different groups of people with different perceptions of the base concept (i.e., neighbor) cannot be strictly compared and tested. As he does not use the Galileo program, he is correct. This criticism, however, is not applicable to studies that do use Galileo. In a true Galileo, the reference pair and its distance are given to the subjects. The reference pair is also included in the survey as a paired comparison. The program then compares the distances for the reference pair given by the subjects to the standardized distance for that pair. This distance is then standardized, and all other distances are calibrated to this standardization (Woelfel and Fink, 1980). Bahk's analysis does not include this standardization. The Nigerian studies (Chapters 6 and 10) compute cognitive distance on a scale that ranges from strong to weak. These studies illustrate yet another specific method that can be used to estimate cognitive distances. However, these data are also lacking the standardization of a criterion pair.

Relationship attributes. Cognitive distance is also used to operationalize the attributes of friend and mate relationships as they compare to the levels of intimacy. This operationalization is an excellent way to determine intensity variables. However, it is lacking in its ability to determine entry variables unique to the relational type, unless concepts that represent other relational types are also included in the study. When a fixed set of attributes is tested, the representativeness of that set to the true domain of attributes for that relationship type is unknown. Studies that use attributes generated by the sample (e.g., the Nigerian studies) are less susceptible to this problem, because the sample's generation of attributes effectively defines the domain of attributes for the relationship type. Also, since the several studies in the book that investigate different relationship types can be considered together, critique of the domain for entry variables may be a minor point. However, it does warrant further investigation.

Self-concept support. Bahk's (Chapter 5) operationalizations of the specific self-concept support variables are excellent. The other studies are not as rigorous in their definition of self-concept support. Bahk uses specific measures with past evidence of reliability and validity. However, the conceptualizations and operationalizations of these variables are perceptual; the validation of self-concept is defined in terms of the individual's perception of that support. Therefore, operationalizations of self-concept similarity, self-concept accuracy, perceived understanding, and perceived liking are perceptually based. Without a dyadic base, this information is necessarily incomplete.

Interpersonal penetration. Korn, Bahk, and Nicotera (Chapters 4, 5, and 9, respectively) operationalize interpersonal penetration using some form of Taylor and Altman's (1966) scale. This scale has been widely used, and its reliability and validity have been previously established (Altman and Taylor, 1973; Taylor and Altman, 1966). Bahk's factor analysis, however, warrants a reexamination of the dimensionality of the scale; his factors differ from the dimensions advocated by its authors (Altman and Taylor, 1973; Taylor and Altman, 1966). Furthermore, the weakness in this measure is that it operationalizes *perceptions* of conversational penetration. We cannot draw conclusions about the actual depth and breadth of communication from any of these data. That is not to say that the penetration profiles are meaningless. They can and do provide useful perceptual information upon which to base future research of actual interactions between members of different relational types and levels.

Sampling

The studies in this volume primarily rely on college student samples. Though we cannot generalize beyond this population, we must not assume that such sampling diminishes the work. It is in college that we develop the greatest number of friendships—and the most enduring. College-age is also when most individuals marry, or begin their relationships with their future mates. Regrettably, the population of that same age that does not attend college remains untapped.

Research that samples different age groups and college-age populations not in school can, of course, strengthen the program of research presented herein. As with all social research, college student samples must be supplemented with other types of samples to generalize more widely. However, for study of relationship development, college student samples are highly appropriate. At that time in our lives we are most active in developing friendships and mate relationships. The college experience, like almost no other, provides constant opportunity to meet and spend time with a great number of one's peers. From the close proximity of living quarters and the semester-to-semester shift of classmates to the overwhelming number of organized social activities, the college campus offers a seemingly boundless field of availables. This is a perfect setting in which to study relationship development.

Where We Are: The Current Status

A Critical Assessment of the Theory

Other theories of relationship development (see Chapter 2 for a full review) can be encompassed in four categories. First, theories of *attraction* attempt to account for the processes that lead individuals to strike up a relationship (e.g., for friendship, Duck, 1973; for the mate relationship, Udry, 1963). Second, theories of *attributes* offer descriptions of the relational type as distinct from other types (e.g., Indvik and Fitzpatrick, 1986; for friendship, Parks, 1977; for the mate relationship, Pam, Plutchik, and Conte, 1973). Third, theories of *stages* offer descriptions of the discrete levels of deeper intimacy reached as the relationship develops (e.g., for friendship LaGaipa, 1977; for the mate relationship, Knapp, 1978). Finally, theories of *growth* offer descriptions of the movement of relationships between those levels of intimacy (e.g., for friendship, Wright, 1969, 1978; for the mate relationship, Baxter and Bullis, 1986).

The general theory of relational development posited by Cushman and his associates (Cushman and Cahn, 1985; Cushman, Valentinsen, and Dietrich, 1982) does all four of these things and more. As a general framework, the theory proposes a three-stage filter—fields of availables, approachables, and reciprocals. Between the field of availables and the field of approachables, the theory delineates entry variables, those dimensions or attributes of friend and mate relationships that distinguish relationship types. Several of these attributes have been identified and upheld in empirical tests appearing in this book. The recognition of these attributes by at least one of the pair accounts for the attempt to initiate a relationship. When self-concept support on these attributes is provided by both parties, the relationship begins, and the pair moves to the field of reciprocals.

Within the field of reciprocals, the theory delineates discrete levels of intimacy. These levels have been identified and upheld in empirical tests appearing in this book. To account for growth to deeper levels of intimacy, the theory delineates intensity variables, which co-vary with the intimacy of the relationship. Several of these attributes have also been identified and upheld in empirical tests appearing in this book.

Using the filtering framework, the theory conceptually unites the four basic processes of relational development identified by other theories—attraction, attributes, stages, and growth. However, the general theory is much more than mere consolidation of past theory. It provides a deeper integration of those theoretical descriptions; description is secondary to explanation, prediction, and control. Self-concept is proposed as the basic explanatory device for interpersonal relationships. The general theory is grounded in a view of human beings as conscious goal-directed actors engaged in coordination systems (interpersonal relationships), the function of which is to develop and maintain consensus on individual self-concepts. As such, the processes of relational formation and development center around the development, presentation, and validation of individual self-concepts (Cushman, Valentinsen, and Dietrich, 1982).

Self-concept is the generative mechanism for relational formation and growth. All the subprocesses and variables are conceptualized and grounded in the self-concept. (See Chapter 1 for a full explanation of the theory). Where other theories of relational development stop at mere description, Cushman and his associates (Cushman and Cahn, 1985; Cushman, Valentinsen, and Dietrich, 1982) probe more deeply to the generative processes that manifest themselves on the surface as attraction, attributes, stages, and growth. Self-concept is the mechanism that drives these generative processes.

Security of the Propositions

Proposition 1. Perceived self-concept support is the basis of interpersonal attraction. This proposition is supported by the research literature of four decades (see Chapter 2). This tremendous support confirms the basic definition of interpersonal relationships as coordination systems that function to develop and maintain consensus on individual self-concepts (Cushman and Cahn, 1985; Cushman, Valentinsen, and Dietrich, 1982). Further, every study in this book supports this fundamental idea. From this body of work, it can be confidently stated: An individual will be interpersonally attracted to those whom s/he perceives to provide him/her with self-concept support.

Proposition 2. Different types of perceived self-concept support are the basis for different types of interpersonal relationships. The literature that defines attributes of friend and/or mate relationships (see Chapter 2) provides some support for this idea. However, consideration of the studies in this book provides the most compelling support. For example, Chapters 4 and 9 (Korn and Nicotera, respectively) show differences in the bases for friend and mate relationships in Korea. Moemeka and Nicotera (Chapters 6 and 10) demonstrate the different bases for friend and mate relationships in Nigeria. Bahk (Chapter 5) shows differences in the bases for different types of friendships (same-sex, opposite-sex, intracultural, and intercultural).

There may be contradictions over the specific character of the crucial attributes for a particular culture; further, not all cultures have been studied. Even though the specific character of the crucial attributes is debatable, from this body of work it can be confidently stated: If perceived self-concept support is assumed to be the basis for interpersonal relationships, then different types of relationships are based on different types of perceived self-concept support.

Proposition 3. Different types of self-concept support are the basis for entry into and increasing intensity of interpersonal relationships. From the studies in this book, variables can be identified that mark entry into a relationship; other variables can be identified that co-vary with the intimacy of the relationship. We can conclude from the body of work presented herein that interpersonal relationships progress through discrete, identifiable levels of intimacy. The specific entry and intensity variables and the labels for the levels may be debatable; they may change over time and across cultures and subcultures. Ju's (Chapter 12) conception of interpersonal relationships as cultural choice provides a theoretic framework from which to consider cultural change as a basis for changes in interpersonal relationship patterns. At the same time, the basic and general processes of relationship formation and growth seem to be established. From the work presented in this book, it can be confidently stated: Entry into interpersonal relationships is dependent on the communication of self-concept support on a set of crucial variables; likewise, the growth of interpersonal relationships is dependent on the communication of self-concept support on another set of crucial variables.

Proposition 4. The type and form of self-concept support is homogeneous by culture. From the studies presented in this book, Tables 7.1 (page 128) and 11.1 (page 190) show the homogeneous nature of crucial attributes within several cultures. Cushman and Kovacic (in press) also provide evidence to support this proposition. This proposition is so far secure. However, because of the limited number of cultures studied, testing in other cultures must continue to secure this proposition further.

Propositions 5–7. Chapters 7 and 11 provide indirect support for these propositions. All three require direct investigation to be firmly secured. Proposition 5—*conflict that threatens self-concept support on crucial relationship variables—the lack of it or attacks on it—is the most potentially dangerous type of conflict in interpersonal relationships*—is somewhat secure given the literature supporting it (Cushman, 1989; Cushman and Cahn, 1985; Cushman and Kovacic, in press; Genshaft, 1980; Levinger, 1980; Rands, Levinger, and Mellinger, 1981; Ritter, 1985; Ting-Toomey, 1983) and its deductive relationship to other propositions. Because 1–3 are secure, we can conclude that conflict that threatens self-concept support on the crucial variables threatens the very bases of the relationship's definition and development. Therefore, such conflict has tremendous potential to damage or destroy the relationship.

Proposition 6—negotiation of differences in perceptions of self-concept support on crucial relationship variables cements interpersonal relationships—is somewhat secure given the literature supporting it (Billingham and Sack, 1987; Birchler, Weiss, and Vincent, 1975; Cushman, 1989; Cushman and Cahn, 1985; Cushman and Kovacic, in press; Genshaft, 1980; Gottman, Markman, and Notarius, 1977; Noller, 1981; Rands, et al, 1981; Ting-Toomey, 1983) and its relationship to Proposition 5. The very basis of the relationship is threatened according to Proposition 5, but the pair is able to negotiate their differences and maintain or renew self-concept support on the crucial variables. In this way, the pair has developed the skill to proportionalize such problems (Cushman, 1989; Cushman and Kovacic, in press; see also chapters 7 and 11). When the pair has this ability to proportionalize, they are better able to negotiate other differences in their perceptions. With this foundation laid in the relationship, future differences are more likely to be perceived as negotiable and less threatening to the relationship. The relationship can be said to have been cemented.

Proposition 7—quality interpersonal relationships consist of intimacy, personal growth, and effective communication on the crucial relationship variables—is somewhat secure given its relationship to Proposition 5 and to the literature on relational quality (Aguirre and Kirwan, 1986; Crawford, 1977; Cushman, 1979; Cushman, 1989; Cushman and Cahn, 1985; Fincham and Bradbury, 1989; Gibbs, 1977; Hays, 1984; LaGaipa, 1977; Montgomery, 1981; Rettig and Bubolz, 1983; Spanier and Lewis, 1980). If conflict that threatens self-concept support on the crucial variables can destroy the relationship (Proposition 5), then effective communication of self-concept support on those variables must be crucial to relational quality. Such effectively communicated support leads to intimacy and personal growth on those variables, factors that have been linked to relational quality (Aguirre and Kirwan, 1986; Crawford, 1977; Cushman, 1979; Cushman, 1989; Cushman and Cahn, 1985; Fincham and Bradbury, 1989; Gibbs, 1977; Hays, 1984; LaGaipa, 1977; Montgomery, 1981; Rettig and Bubolz, 1983; Spanier and Lewis, 1980).

Persistent Questions

Although we can be secure in the proposition that self-concept support is the basis for interpersonal relationships, we do not yet understand the specific processes of communicating such support. In order to foster such understanding, investigations must use specific rigorous operationalizations of real and ideal self-concept, including identity, evaluative, and behavioral selves (see Chapter 1). These operationalizations must be tied to specific rigorous operationalizations of self-concept support, relationship type, relationship level, and communication. All these operationalizations must be dyadic and longitudinal.

In short, the conceptual foundation of the theory is strong, and preliminary tests have upheld the basic claims of attraction, attributes, and stages. The research in this volume supports the seven basic propositions, 1–4 directly and 5–7 indirectly. However, the particular and specific processes of self-concept support require further investigation, and direct tests of Propositions 5–7 must be conducted. These persistent questions necessarily lead us to a consideration of the future.

Where We Must Go: Future Directions

Development of this line of work is needed in both research and theory. The pressing questions currently unanswered must be researched. Simultaneously, however, a deeper analysis on the theoretic level can enrich that research. As such, recommendations for theoretic advancement are presented first, followed by recommendations for future research. These two sets of recommendations inform each other.

Recommendations for Theoretic Advancement

Theoretic advancements are recommended on two levels. First, the scope of explanation can be widened. Of course, these recommendations naturally lead to questions for research. Second, the underlying paradigmatic assumptions can be deepened. These recommendations lead to deeper explanations and more comprehensive methodologies for researching those explanations.

Expanding the scope. It is advocated here that specific expansions of the theory's scope be conducted inductively, based on the deductively derived general structure. The currently untested aspects of the basic theory are of immediate concern for research, which must be deductive by its very nature. Such research may lead to adjustments of details in the general theory and Propositions 5–7. Then, research based on recommendations for widening the scope can further develop the theory.

In its current state, the theory accounts for relationship formation and development in single-culture relationships. Although all the studies presented in this volume suggest that the tenets of the theory may be upheld in other cultures, the theory has not been widened to encompass truly intercultural relationships, where the partners are from different cultures. Such development is practically and theoretically warranted.

Bahk provides a strong basis for examination of same-sex and cross-sex friendships. More stringent investigations of the basic processes of relationship formation and development may be gained by expanding the theory of friendship to encompass different gender compositions. In the mate relationship, the theory has been limited to heterosexual relationships. Expanding the theory of mate relationship to encompass male and female homosexual relationships may provide a more rigorous test of the processes of mate relationship formation and development.

Finally, if the mechanism of self-concept support can account for the formation and development of relationships, it can also account for the maintenance and dissolution of those relationships. Following the secure propositions for relationship development, propositions for maintenance of the relationship at its highest level can be derived and tested—expanding on Propositions 5–7. Propositions for development can be reversed and tested for their ability to account for relationship dissolution. Chapters 7 and 11 discussed implications of Propositions 5–7 across their three categories of interpersonal communication. Empirical study of such implications may provide evidence for broadening the theory to better account for maintenance and dissolution.

Paradigmatic development. The theory is grounded in the rules perspective. (See Chapter 1 for a full explanation of the paradigmatic assumptions.) The rules perspective represents a neo-positivistic approach, rejecting the strict hypothetico-deductive objectivity of the positivists—opting instead for a deductive/inductive balance characterized by intersubjectivity. Giddens's (1979, 1984) theory of structuration is a notable recent development in neo-positivistic thinking. Structurational theory is explicated and applied in the field of communication by Poole and his associates (Poole and McPhee, 1983; Poole, McPhee, and Seibold, 1982; Poole, Seibold, and McPhee, 1985, 1986; Seibold and Meyers, 1986) in the specific area of small group processes. The theory represents a broad view of the structuring of society. Its basic tenets represent a body of paradigmatic assumptions that complement and enrich the rules perspective. Structuration theory attempts to reconcile two basic tensions: First, the tension between individual action and societal structures; second, the tension between social structures' stability and change (Poole, Seibold, and McPhee, 1985, 1986).

The paradigmatic assumptions underlying Cushman and his associates' general theory of relationship development can be advanced and deepened with the adoption of a structurational perspective. However, a full discussion of structurational theory is beyond the scope of this chapter and the purpose of this book. The following brief overview of the structurational perspective and how it can enrich the assumptions of the rules perspective is meant to highlight the extraordinary potential for paradigmatic development. In general, communication theory is in need of such paradigmatic work.

Social practices are the basic unit of analysis for structurational theory; formation and development of interpersonal relationships are common social practices. Structuration theory analyzes social practices by distinguishing *system* from *structure*. Systems are observable patterns of behavior; structures are unobservable rules and resources through which systems are generated. Structures are dual—both medium and outcome of action. Structures are thus continually produced and reproduced in interaction. *Structuration* is this process of continual production and reproduction, which occurs through the interaction of active, reflexive individuals (Poole, Seibold, and McPhee, 1986). Any given system can contain several elements of social structure because individuals appropriate structures into systems through interaction. Multiple structures interpenetrate, mediating and contradicting one another, thus affecting the ways in which they are appropriated into the system (Poole, Seibold, and McPhee, 1986).

The structurational view enriches the rules perspective in several ways. First, it recognizes that human interactions are suspended in a larger social environment. Second, it assumes that human capacity to control action is "bounded" by acknowledged and unacknowledged conditions and by intended and unintended consequences (Poole, Seibold, and McPhee, 1986). Compare this view to the practical syllogism espoused by Cushman, Valentinsen, and Dietrich, (1982):

A intends to bring about *C*;
A considers that to bring about *C* s/he must do *B*;
therefore, *A* sets her/himself to do *B*.

A structurational view recognizes the limits imposed by conditions, both acknowledged and unacknowledged. Further, the individual intends a particular set of consequences, but may bring about a different, unanticipated set of consequences.

Amidst these conditions and consequences, individuals rationalize, reflexively monitor, and motivate their actions. A richer view of goal-orientation is thus possible: "Human behavior is considered a constant flow in interaction, and goals are artificially segmented features of reflexive monitoring, defined with reference to an 'appropriate' time frame. . . . The idea of a preset motive governing action is an oversimplification, as is the argument that intention is purely retrospective" (Poole, Seibold, and McPhee, 1986, 248–49).

The duality of structure can also enrich the rules viewpoint. Structures (societal rules and resources) are the *medium* by which systems (in our case, interpersonal relationships) are created through interaction (Giddens, 1984). Rules for relationship formation and development are drawn upon to interact within and produce the social practices of interpersonal relationships. By their very existence, these social practices reproduce those structures, so that structures are the *outcome* of the interaction (Giddens, 1984). As outcomes, structures can be altered through social action (Giddens, 1984). Changes in societal patterns of relationships can thus be accounted for, without invalidating the general theory. Thus, Ju's (Chapter 12) notion of cultural choice can be upheld. With a structurational view, the general rules theory of relationship formation and development can account for alterations in its own rules; Nicotera's (Chapter 9) findings for her American samples may be the result of altered structures. In this way, the structurational viewpoint highlights the crucial nature of the interdependent relationship between theory and research. A structurational view of theory and research can enhance the theory beyond a descriptive form to show the operation of deeper societal structures.

Recommendations for Future Research

First, the seven propositions need to be thoroughly tested, 1–4 in other cultural settings, and 5–7 in general. Second, in all areas of the theory, dyadic longitudinal investigation is crucial. Bahk (Chapter 5) begins to achieve a dyadic picture with subjects' views of the accuracy of their perceptions of their best friends' self-concepts. Third, the role of communication in the relationship-formation and development process cannot take place without observations of actual interactions. This is true for the communication components of the propositions as well as the conversational penetration extension. Work in conversational penetration can enrich our understanding of indirect expressions of self-concept support. Finally, all suggestions for the expansion of the theory's scope are ripe for immediate research.

Paradigmatic development encompassing the structurational perspective brings with it a particular agenda for research. Structurational research cannot be conducted without a constant reliance on theory development. Such research is by its nature complex and pluralistic. A structurational research program must simultaneously decompose elements into meaningful units of analysis and synthesize findings into multilevel theories (Poole, Seibold, and McPhee, 1986). Such research must be simultaneously deductive in its verification of the observable (systems) and inductive in its derivation of the unobservable (structures); it must explicate microlevels of interaction and account for macrolevels of social institution (Poole, Seibold, and McPhee, 1986). Although daunting in its complexity, the structurational viewpoint—not done justice here—has much to offer to the theory of

Cushman and his associates paradigmatically and methodologically. Development in this vein is strongly advocated.

Conclusion

Interpersonal relationships are a driving force in our lives. Great attention has been focused on these relationships by scholars, therapists, talk-show hosts, and columnists. We all have interpersonal relationships, yet their formation, development, maintenance, and dissolution continue to perplex us. Though we would like to claim otherwise, scholars have had little success in developing a deep understanding of interpersonal relationships. The general theory of Cushman and his associates offers a unique view. The theory synthesizes the fragmented literature, provides a theoretic vehicle to explain relationships, grounds itself well in a set of paradigmatic assumptions, and offers the beginnings of a research program to validate and develop itself multiculturally. This volume has reviewed investigations that represent the beginnings of this exciting area of research. These investigations can be built upon to test the theory more rigorously and more comprehensively, to expand its scope, and to deepen its ground.

References

Aguirre, B., and P. Kirwan (1986). Marriage order and the quality and stability of marital relationships: A test of Lewis and Spanier's theory. *Journal of Comparative Family Studies* 17:247–76.

Altman, I., and D. Taylor (1973). *Social penetration: The development of interpersonal relationships*. New York: Holt, Rinehart and Winston.

Baxter, L. A., and C. Bullis (1986). Turning points in developing romantic relationships. *Human Communication Research* 12:469–93.

Billingham, R. E., and A. R. Sack (1987). Conflict tactics and the level of emotional commitment among unmarrieds. *Human Relations* 40:59–74.

Birchler, G. R., R. L. Weiss, and J. P. Vincent (1975). Multimethod analysis of social reinforcement exchange between maritally distressed and nondistressed spouse and stranger dyads. *Journal of Personality and Social Psychology* 31:349–60.

Chu, G. C. (1979). Communication and cultural change in China: A conceptual framework. In G. C. Chu and F. L. K. Hsu (eds.), *Moving a mountain: Cultural change in China* (2–24). Honolulu: The University Press of Hawaii.

Chu, G. C. (1985). The changing concept of self in contemporary China. In A. J. Marsella, G. DeVos, and F. L. K. Hsu (eds.), *Culture and self: Asian and Western perspectives* (252–77). New York: Tavistock Publications.

Chu, G. C., and Y. A. Ju (in press). *The Great Wall in ruins: Communication and cultural change in China*. Albany, NY: State University of New York Press.

Crawford, M. (1977). What is a friend? *New Society* 42:116–17.

Cushman, D. P. (1979). Communication in establishing, maintaining, and terminating interpersonal relationships. *Journal of Youth and Adolescence* 8:443–52.

Cushman, D. P. (1989). Communication in establishing, maintaining, and terminating interpersonal relationships: A study of mateship. In S. S. King (ed.), *Human communication as a field of study: Selected contemporary views* (87–104). Albany, NY: State University of New York Press.

Cushman, D. P., and D. D. Cahn (1985). *Communication in interpersonal relationships*. Albany, NY: State University of New York Press.

Cushman D. P., and B. Kovacic (in press). A rules perspective on communication theory. In F. L. Casmir (ed.), *Communication theory*. Albany, NY: State University of New York Press.

Cushman, D. P., B. Valentinsen, and D. Dietrich (1982). A rules theory of interpersonal relationships. In F. E. X. Dance (ed.), *Human communication theory* (90–119). New York: Harper and Row.

Duck, S. (1973). Similarity and perceived similarity of personal constructs as influencers of friendship choice. *British Journal of Social and Clinical Psychology* 12:1–6.

Fincham, F., and T. Bradbury (1989). Perceived responsibility for marital events: Egocentric or partner-centric bias? *Journal of Marriage and the Family* 51:27–35.

Genshaft, J. L. (1980). Perceptual and defensive style variables in marital discord. *Social Behavior and Personality* 8:81–84.

Gibbs, S. (1977). *A comparative analysis of friendship functions in six age groups of men and women*. Unpublished dissertation, Wayne State University, Detroit, MI.

Giddens, A. (1979). *Central problems in social theory: Action, structure, and contradiction in social analysis*. Berkeley: University of California Press.

Giddens, A. (1984). *The constitution of society: Outline of the theory of structuration*. Berkeley: University of California Press.

Gottman, J., H. Markman, and C. Notarius (1977). The topography of marital conflict: A sequential analysis of verbal and nonverbal behavior. *Journal of Marriage and the Family* 39:461–77.

Hays, R. B. (1984). The development and maintenance of friendship. *Journal of Social and Personal Relationships* 1:75–98.

Indvik, J., and M. A. Fitzpatrick (1986). Perceptions of inclusion, affiliation, and control in five interpersonal relationships. *Communication Quarterly* 34:1–13.

Knapp, M. (1978). *Social intercourse: From greeting to goodbye*. Boston: Allyn and Bacon.

LaGaipa, J. J. (1977). Testing a multidimensional approach to friendship. In S. Duck (ed.), *Theory and practice in interpersonal attraction* (249–70). London: Academic Press.

Levinger, G. (1980). Toward the analysis of close relationships. *Journal of Experimental Social Psychology* 16:510–44.

Montgomery, B. M. (1981). The form and function of quality communication in marriage. *Family Relations* 30:21–29.

Noller, P. (1981). Gender and marital adjustment level differences in decoding messages from spouses and strangers. *Journal of Personality and Social Psychology* 41:272–78.

Pam, A., R. Plutchik, and H. Conte (1973). Love: A psychometric approach. *Proceedings of the 81st Annual Convention of the APA*, 159–60.

Parks, M. R. (1977, December). *Communication correlates of perceived friendship development*. Paper presented at the annual conference of the Speech Communication Association, Washington, DC.

Poole, M. S., and R. D. McPhee (1983). A structurational analysis of organizational climate. In L. L. Putnam and M. E. Pacanowsky (eds.), *Communication and organizations: An interpretive approach* (195–219). Beverly Hills, CA: Sage.

Poole, M. S., R. D. McPhee, and D. R. Seibold (1982). A comparison of normative and interactional explanations of group decision-making: Social decision schemes versus valence distributions. *Communication Monographs* 49:1–19.

Poole, M. S., D. R. Seibold, and R. D. McPhee (1985). Group decision-making as a structurational process. *Quarterly Journal of Speech* 71:74–102.

Poole, M. S., D. R. Seibold, and R. D. McPhee (1986). A structurational approach to theory-building in group decision-making research. In R. Y. Hirokawa and M. S. Poole (eds.), *Communication and group decision-making* (237–64). Beverly Hills, CA: Sage.

Rands, M., G. Levinger, and G. D. Mellinger (1981). Patterns of conflict resolution and marital satisfaction. *Journal of Family Issues* 2:297–321.

Rettig, K., and M. Bubolz (1983). Interpersonal resource exchanges as indicators of quality marriages. *Journal of Marriage and the Family* 45:497–509.

Ritter, K. Y. (1985). The cognitive therapies. *Journal of Counseling and Development* 64:42–44.

Seibold, D. R. and R. A. Meyers (1986). Communication and influence in group decision-making. In R. Y. Hirokawa and M. S. Poole (eds.),

Communication and group decision-making (133–55). Beverly Hills, CA: Sage.
Spanier, G. B., and R. A. Lewis (1980). Marital quality: A review of the seventies. *Marriage and Family Living* 42:825–39.
Taylor, D., and I. Altman (1966). Intimacy-scaled stimuli for use in studies of interpersonal relations. *Psychological Reports* 19:729–30.
Ting-Toomey, S. (1983). An analysis of verbal communication patterns in high and low marital adjustment groups. *Human Communication Research* 9:306–19.
Udry, J. R. (1963). Complementarity in mate selection: A perceptual approach. *Marriage and Family Living* 25:281–89.
Woelfel J., and E. L. Fink (1980). *The measurement of communication processes: Galileo theory and method*. New York: Academic Press.
Wright, P. H. (1969). A model and a technique for studies of friendship. *Journal of Experimental Social Psychology* 5:295–308.
Wright, P. H. (1978). Toward a theory of friendship based on a conception of self. *Human Communication Research* 4:196–207.

About the Contributors

Changmo Bahk (MA, State University of New York, Albany) is a doctoral student at Michigan State University. He specializes in perception and communication in interpersonal and mediated contexts. His research interests include such topics as empathy, interpersonal relationships, and reality perception in mediated communication. He has presented papers on empathy at Eastern Communication Association and International Communication Association conferences.

Dudley D. Cahn (Ph.D., Wayne State University) is Professor of Communication at the State University of New York at New Paltz. In addition to co-authoring *Communication in Interpersonal Relationships* (Albany: SUNY Press, 1985) with Don Cushman, he has written *Letting Go: A Practical Theory of Relationship Disengagement and Reengagement* (Albany: SUNY Press, 1987). He has also edited *Intimates in Conflict: A Communication Perspective* (New York: Guilford, forthcoming). A Fulbright Scholar to Yugoslavia in 1987, he has received a distinguished service award from the World Communication Association.

Donald P. Cushman (Ph.D., University of Wisconsin) is Professor of Communication at the State University of New York at Albany. He is author of over 80 journal articles and book chapters. He is also author or co-author of five books, including *Message-Attitude-Behavior Relationships*, with R. McPhee (Academic Press, 1980); *Communication in Interpersonal Relationships*, with D. Cahn (Albany: SUNY Press, 1985); and *High Speed Management: Organizational Communication in the 1990's*, with S. King, forthcoming. In 1982 he received the Speech Communication Association's Charles Woolbert Award "for research of exceptional originality and influence which has stood the test of time."

Yanan Ju (Ph.D., University of Belgrade) is Associate Professor of Communication at Central Connecticut State University. He specializes in intercultural communication and organizational communication. His recent research interests include cultural change and its impact on organizational performance. He is an author or co-author of five books and dozens of book chapters and journal articles. Over the past ten years, he has won nine research fellowships from the East-West Center in Hawaii.

Charles Jude Korn (MA, State University of New York, Albany; work toward Ph.D. at Ohio University) is Assistant Professor of Speech Communication and Drama at Northern Virginia Community College, Manassas. He is committed to the research and teaching of interpersonal communication, including relational development and maintenance, intercultural communication, and speech communication theory and process. He has developed and taught courses ranging from critical thinking and writing to public speaking at seven colleges and universities. He has presented scholarly papers at regional conferences and been awarded for his excellence in teaching. He has served as a consultant to several individuals and companies as well as workshop presenter to several groups.

Andrew Azukaego Moemeka (Ph.D., State University of New York, Albany) is Visiting Professor at the Department of Communication, Central Connecticut State University, New Britain, and Associate Professor at the Department of Mass Communication, University of Lagos, Nigeria. His major area of research is development communication, with particular reference to use of mass media. Subsidiary areas of interest include intercultural communication, organizational communication, and interpersonal communication. He is a biographee in *Who's Who* for the United States, for Nigeria, and for the world. He has won academic and teaching awards in both Nigeria and the United States. He has written two books and several journal articles on development communication, rural development, radio broadcasting, journalism, culture, and social problems/change. He is at present editing a book, *Communicating and Development: A Multimedia Perspective*, for SUNY Press. He is a consultant to UNESCO, UNFPA, and the Nigerian government on Rural Development, Development Communication, Health Communication, and Education.

Anne Maydan Nicotera (Ph.D., Ohio University) is Assistant Professor of Human Communication Studies at Howard University. Her research emphases include interpersonal, organizational, and small group communication with particular emphasis on conflict. She is author or co-author of numerous journal articles, as well as papers at international, national, and regional conferences. She has won several awards for research and teaching.

Author Index

Subject Index